Reader's Guide
to
JOHN DONNE

Reader's Guide
to
JOHN DONNE

S. Dorsch

CENTRUM PRESS
NEW DELHI-110002 (INDIA)

CENTRUM PRESS
H.O.: 4360/4, Ansari Road, Daryaganj,
New Delhi-110 002 (India)
Ph.: 23278000, 23261597

B.O.: No. 1015, Ist Main Road, BSK IIIrd Stage
IIIrd Phase, IIIrd Block,
Bangalore - 560 085 (India)
Tel.: 080-41723429
Visit us at: www.centrumpress.com

Reader's Guide to John Donne

First Edition, 2009

ISBN 978-93-80106-60-1

PRINTED IN INDIA

Printed at Salasar Imaging Systems, Delhi-110035 (India)

Contents

Preface

John Donne (1572-1631) was the most outstanding of the English Metaphysical Poets and a churchman famous for his spellbinding sermons. Donne was born in London to a prominent Roman Catholic family but converted to Anglicanism during the 1590s. At the age of 11 he entered the University of Oxford, where he studied for three years.

According to some accounts, he spent the next three years at the University of Cambridge but took no degree at either university. He began the study of law at Lincoln's Inn, London, in 1592, and he seemed destined for a legal or diplomatic career. Donne was appointed private secretary to Sir Thomas Egerton, Keeper of the Great Seal, in 1598.

His secret marriage in 1601 to Egerton's niece, Anne More, resulted in his dismissal from this position and in a brief imprisonment. During the next few years Donne made a meager living as a lawyer. Obsessed with the idea of death, Donne preached what was called his own funeral sermon, "Death's Duel" just a few weeks before he died in London on March 31, 1631.

Author

Chapter 1

Introduction

John Donne was an English Jacobean poet, preacher and a major representative of the metaphysical poets of the period. His works are notable for their realistic and sensual style and include sonnets, love poetry, religious poems, Latin translations, epigrams, elegies, songs, satires and sermons. His poetry is noted for its vibrancy of language and inventiveness of metaphor, especially as compared to those of his contemporaries.

As Donne came from a Roman Catholic family he experienced some persecution until his conversion to the Anglican Church. Despite his great education and poetic talents he lived in poverty for several years, relying heavily on wealthy friends. In 1615 he became an Anglican priest and, in 1621, was appointed the Dean of St Paul's Cathedral in London. Some scholars believe that Donne's literary works reflect these trends, with love poetry and satires from his youth and religious sermons during his later years. Other scholars, such as Helen Gardner, question the validity of this dating since most of his poems were published posthumously (1633). The exception to these is his *Anniversaries* which were published in 1612 and *Devotions upon Emergent Occasions* published in 1623. His sermons are also dated, sometimes quite specifically by date and year.

EARLY LIFE

A portrait of Donne as a young man, c. 1595. Artist unknown. In the collection of the National Portrait Gallery, London. John Donne was born in London, England, sometime near the end of 1571 or between January and 19 June in 1572, the third of six children. His father, of Welsh descent, also called John Donne, was a warden of the Ironmongers Company in the City of London and a respected Roman Catholic who avoided unwelcome government attention, out of fear of being persecuted for his Catholicism.

John Donne Sr. died in 1576, leaving his wife, Elizabeth Heywood, the responsibility of raising their children. Elizabeth Heywood, also from a noted Catholic family, was the daughter of John Heywood, the playwright, and sister of Jasper Heywood, the translator and Jesuit. She was a great-niece of the Catholic martyr Thomas More. This tradition of martyrdom would continue among Donne's closer relatives, many of whom were executed or exiled for religious reasons.

Despite the obvious dangers, Donne's family arranged for his education by the Jesuits, which gave him a deep knowledge of his religion that equipped him for the ideological religious conflicts of his time.

Elizabeth Donne nee Heywood married Dr John Syminges, a wealthy widower with three children, a few months after John Donne Sr's death. The next year, 1577, John Donne's sister Elizabeth died, followed by two more of his sisters, Mary and Katherine, in 1581. Before the future poet was ten years old he had thus experienced the deaths of four of his immediate family. Part of the house where John Donne lived in Pyrford.

Donne was a student at Hart Hall, now Hertford College, Oxford, from the age of 11. After three years at Oxford he was admitted to the University of Cambridge, where he studied for another three years. He was unable to obtain a degree from either institution because he refused to take the Oath of Supremacy required of graduates.

In 1591 he was accepted as a student at the Thavies Inn legal school, one of the Inns of Court in London. In 1592 he was admitted to Lincoln's Inn, another of the Inns of Court legal schools. His brother Henry was also a university student prior to his arrest in 1593 for harbouring a Catholic priest. Henry Donne died in prison of bubonic plague, leading John

Donne to begin questioning his Catholic faith. During and after his education, Donne spent much of his considerable inheritance on women, literature, pastimes and travel.

Although there is no record detailing precisely where he travelled, it is known that he visited the Continent and later fought with the Earl of Essex and Sir Walter Raleigh against the Spanish at Cádiz (1596) and the Azores (1597) and witnessed the loss of the Spanish flagship, the *San Felipe,* and her crew. According to Izaak Walton, who wrote a biography of Donne in 1640:

".. he returned not back into England till he had stayed some years, first in Italy, and then in Spain, where he made many useful observations of those countries, their laws and manner of government, and returned perfect in their languages. "

By the age of 25 he was well prepared for the diplomatic career he appeared to be seeking. He was appointed chief secretary to the Lord Keeper of the Great Seal, Sir Thomas Egerton, and was established at Egerton's London home, York House, Strand close to the Palace of Whitehall, then the most influential social centre in England. During the next four years he fell in love with Egerton's niece Anne More, a girl of 17 (some say 16 or 14), and they were secretly married in 1601 against the wishes of both Egerton and her father, George More, Lieutenant of the Tower.

This ruined his career and earned him a short stay in Fleet Prison along with the priest who married them and the man who acted as a witness to the wedding. Donne was released when the marriage was proved valid, and soon secured the release of the other two. Walton tells us that when he wrote to his wife to tell her about losing his post, he wrote after his name: *John Donne, Anne Donne, Un-done.* It was not until 1609 that Donne was reconciled with his father-in-law and received his wife's dowry.

Following his release, Donne had to accept a retired country life in Pyrford, Surrey. Over the next few years he scraped a meagre living as a lawyer, depending on his wife's cousin Sir Francis Wolly to house him, his wife, and their children. Since Anne Donne had a baby almost every year, this was a very generous gesture. Though he practiced law and worked as an assistant pamphleteer to Thomas Morton, he was in a state of constant financial insecurity, with a growing family to provide for. Before her death, Anne bore him eleven children (including still births).

The nine living were named Constance, John, George, Francis, Lucy (after Donne's patroness Lucy, Countess of Bedford, her godmother), Bridget, Mary, Nicholas and Margaret. Francis and Mary died before they were ten. In a state of despair, Donne noted that the death of a child would mean one less mouth to feed, but he could not afford the burial expenses. During this time Donne wrote, but did not publish, *Biathanatos,* his daring defense of suicide.

EARLY POETRY

Donne's earliest poems showed a brilliant knowledge of English society coupled with sharp criticism of its problems. His satires dealt with common Elizabethan topics, such as corruption in the legal system, mediocre poets, and pompous courtiers, yet stand out due to their intellectual sophistication and striking imagery.

His images of sickness, vomit, manure, and plague assisted in the creation of a strongly satiric world populated by all the fools and knaves of England. His third satire, however, deals with the problem of true religion, a matter of great importance to Donne. Donne argued that it was better carefully to examine one's religious convictions than blindly to follow any established tradition, for none would be saved at the Final Judgment by claiming "A Harry, or a Martin taught [them] this."

Donne's early career was also notable for his erotic poetry, especially his elegies, in which he employed unconventional metaphors, such as a flea biting two lovers being compared to sex. In Elegy XIX, "To His Mistress Going to Bed," he poetically undressed his mistress and compared the act of fondling to the exploration of America.

In Elegy XVIII he compared the gap between his lover's

breasts to the Hellespont. Donne did not publish these poems, although he did allow them to circulate widely in manuscript form. Because love-poetry was very fashionable at that time, there are different opinions about whether the passionate love poems Donne wrote are addressed to his wife Anne, but it seems likely.

She spent most of her married life either pregnant or nursing, so they evidently had a strong physical relationship. On 15 August 1617 his wife died five days after giving birth to a still-born baby, their twelfth child in sixteen years of marriage. Donne mourned her deeply, including writing the 17th Holy Sonnet. He never remarried; this was quite unusual for the time, especially as he had a large family to bring up.

CAREER AND LATER LIFE

Donne was elected as Member of Parliament for the constituency of Brackley in 1602, but this was not a paid position and Donne struggled to provide for his family, relying heavily upon rich friends. The fashion for coterie poetry of the period gave him a means to seek patronage and many of his poems were written for wealthy friends or patrons, especially Sir Robert Drury, who came to be Donne's chief patron in 1610.

It was for Sir Robert that Donne wrote the two *Anniversaries, An Anatomy of the World* (1611) and *Of the Progress of the Soul,* (1612). While historians are not certain as to the precise reasons for which Donne left the Catholic Church, he was certainly in communication with the King, James I of England, and in 1610 and 1611 he wrote two anti-Catholic polemics: *Pseudo-Martyr* and *Ignatius his Conclave*.

Although James was pleased with Donne's work, he refused to reinstate him at court and instead urged him to take holy orders. Although Donne was at first reluctant due to feeling unworthy of a clerical career, Donne finally acceded to the King's wishes and was ordained into the Church of England in 1615.

A few months before his death, Donne commissioned this portrait of himself as he expected to appear when he rose from the grave at the Apocalypse. He hung the portrait on his wall as a reminder of the transience of life. Donne became a Royal Chaplain in late 1615, Reader of Divinity at Lincoln's Inn in 1616, and received a Doctor of Divinity degree from Cambridge in 1618.

Later in 1618 Donne became the chaplain for the Viscount Doncaster, who was on an embassy to the princes of Germany. Donne did not return to England until 1620. In 1621 Donne was made Dean of St Paul's, a leading (and well-paid) position in the Church of England and one he held until his death in 1631.

During his period as Dean his daughter Lucy died, aged eighteen. It was in late November and early December of 1623 that he suffered a nearly fatal illness, thought to be either typhus or a combination of a cold followed by the seven-day relapsing fever. During his convalescence he wrote a series of meditations and prayers on health, pain, and sickness that were published as a book in 1624 under the title of *Devotions upon Emergent Occasions*. Meditation XVII later became well known for its phrase "for whom the bell tolls" and the statement that "no man is an island".

In 1624 he became vicar of St Dunstan-in-the-West, and 1625 a Royal Chaplain to Charles I. He earned a reputation as an impressive, eloquent preacher and 160 of his sermons have survived, including the famous Death's Duel sermon delivered at the Palace of Whitehall before King Charles I in February 1631.

It is thought that his final illness was stomach cancer. He died on March 31, 1631 having never published a poem in his lifetime but having left a body of work fiercely engaged with the emotional and intellectual conflicts of his age. John Donne is buried in St Paul's, where a memorial statue of him was erected (carved from a drawing of him in his shroud), with a Latin epigraph probably composed by himself.

LATER POETRY

"Each man's death diminishes me, for I am involved in mankind. Therefore, send not to know for whom the bell tolls, it tolls for thee." — *John Donne*

His numerous illnesses, financial strain, and the deaths of his friends all contributed to the development of a more somber and pious tone in his later poems. The change can be clearly seen in "An Anatomy of the World" (1611), a poem that Donne wrote in memory of Elizabeth Drury, daughter of his patron, Sir Robert Drury. This poem treats Elizabeth's demise with extreme gloominess, using it as a symbol for the Fall of Man and the destruction of the universe.

The poem 'A Nocturnal upon S. Lucy's Day', being the shortest day concerns the poet's despair at the death of a loved one. In it Donne expresses a feeling of utter negation and hopelessness, saying that "I am every dead thing...re-begot / Of absence, darkness, death".

This famous work was probably written in 1627 when both Donne's friend Lucy, Countess of Bedford and his daughter Lucy Donne died. It is interesting to note that three years later in 1630 Donne wrote his will on Saint Lucy's day (December 13th), the date the poem describes as "Both the year's, and the day's deep midnight."

The increasing gloominess of Donne's tone may also be observed in the religious works that he began writing during the same period. His early belief in the value of skepticism now gave way to a firm faith in the traditional teachings of the Bible.

Having converted to the Anglican Church, Donne focused his literary career on religious literature. He quickly became noted for his deeply moving sermons and religious poems. The passionate lines of these sermons would come to influence future works of English literature, such as Hemingway's *For Whom the Bell Tolls,* which took its title from a passage in Meditation XVII, and Thomas Merton's *No Man is an Island,* which took its title from the same source.

Towards the end of his life Donne wrote works that challenged death, and the fear that it inspired in many men, on the grounds of his belief that those who die are sent to Heaven to live eternally. One example of this challenge is his Holy Sonnet X, from which come the famous lines "Death, be not proud, though some have called thee / Mighty and dreadful, for thou art not so." Even as he lay dying during Lent in 1631, he rose from his sickbed and delivered the Death's Duel sermon, which was later described as his own funeral sermon. Death's Duel portrays life as a steady descent to suffering and death, yet sees hope in salvation and immortality through an embrace of God, Christ and the Resurrection.

LEGACY

John Donne is commemorated as a priest in the calendar of the Church of England and in the Calendar of Saints of the Evangelical Lutheran Church in America on March 31. The memorial to John Donne, modeled after the engraving pictured above, was one of the few such memorials to survive the Great Fire of London in 1666 and now appears in St Paul's Cathedral south of the choir.

STYLE

John Donne is considered a master of the metaphysical conceit, an extended metaphor that combines two vastly different ideas into a single idea, often using imagery. An example of this is his equation of lovers with saints in "The Canonization."

Unlike the conceits found in other Elizabethan poetry, most notably Petrarchan conceits, which formed clichéd comparisons between more closely related objects (such as a rose and love), metaphysical conceits go to a greater depth in comparing two completely unlike objects, although sometimes in the mode of Shakespeare's radical paradoxes and imploded contraries. One of the most famous of Donne's conceits is found in "A Valediction: Forbidding Mourning" where he compares two lovers who are separated to the two legs of a compass.

Donne's works are also witty, employing paradoxes, puns, and subtle yet remarkable analogies. His pieces are often ironic and cynical, especially regarding love and human motives. Common subjects of Donne's poems are love (especially in his early life), death (especially after his wife's death), and religion. John Donne's poetry represented a shift from classical forms to more personal poetry. Donne is noted for his poetic metre, which was structured with changing and jagged rhythms that closely resemble casual speech (it was for this that the more classically-minded Ben Jonson commented that "Donne, for not keeping of accent, deserved hanging").

John Donne was famous for his metaphysical poetry in the 17th century. His work suggests a healthy appetite for life and its pleasures, while also expressing deep emotion. He did this through the use of conceits, wit and intellect — as seen in the poems "The Sunne Rising" and "Batter My Heart". His work has received much criticism over the years, with very judgmental responses about his metaphysical form.

Donne's immediate successors in poetry tended to regard his works with ambivalence, while the Neoclassical poets regarded his conceits as abuse of the metaphor. He was revived by Romantic poets such as Coleridge and Browning, though his more recent revival in the early twentieth century by poets such as T. S. Eliot tended to portray him as an anti-Romantic.

Chapter 2

Colon and Semi-Colon in Donne's Prose Letters

We cannot know now, and may never know, how Donne punctuated any but one of his English poems. This awkward situation makes it impossible to maintain the twentieth-century editor's drive toward the stability of a fixed and authorial text in the case of Donne's poetry.

Perhaps this is not altogether a bad thing: seventeenth-century coterie poetry belonged to manuscript culture, and so was exempt from the requirements of stability introduced by print; we may distort the object of study by making it appear more stable than it in fact was. But modern editorial principles require a standard of judgement in Donne editions. On what grounds can we say that one editor's punctuation is superior to another's?

Application of the punctuation principles of the seventeenth century would seem to be a good idea under these circumstances. Punctuation chosen from scribal manuscripts would be at least authentic, if not authorial. Or perhaps Donne's own habits could be applied to the scribal copies.

Consideration of the punctuation of selected holograph prose letters reveals, as I mean to show, that we can derive editorial choices for both prose and poetry from the punctuation principles evident in Donne's practice in the prose letters. Understanding of Donne's punctuation style may help us edit scribal copies of his poems and can certainly help us understand those works which survive in his hand.

Two significant obstacles stand in the way, the first of

which is the belief that seventeenth-century punctuation was haphazard. A few scholars have argued against this view, largely in vain, since the early twentieth century. Percy Simpson appears to have originated the belief that Elizabethan punctuation was concerned with breath pauses for the voice and showed regularly applied dramatic principles. Although Simpson's analysis is overdependent on syntactic concepts, his corrective argument has been regularly maintained and augmented to the present day by Raymond Alden, A. C.

Partridge (*Orthography*), Mindele Triep, and most recently by Anthony Graham-White. If we maintain with these scholars that seventeenth-century prose punctuation was "rhetorical," concerned with breathing and vocal delivery, we not only lose the difference between dialogue and prose, which is apparent even today in our plays and other fiction; we also get, in the name of breath pauses, rhythms which serve neither prose nor poetry.

A.C. Baugh, Charles C. Fries, and Walter J. Ong have argued against the "rhetorical" theory, although Baugh does see rhythm as inherent when syntax and logic coincide. Baugh, Fries, and Ong are united in their belief that early modern English punctuation had something to do with sentence structure, although no one has pursued the point beyond the strictures of post-nineteenth century syntactic rules.

The rhetorical, or breath-pause, argument cannot apply to Donne. His prose and poetry have no occasion to show the chief features of dramatic punctuation in the early seventeenth century. Donne's dramatic voice is a voice for the mind and the eye, directed always toward a reader, not a listener. The mind does not pause for breath, although the eye is helped by visual signals as to the arrangement and relative importance of ideas.

The second obstacle to understanding Donne's punctuation is lack of attention to the punctuation evidence we do have in Donne autograph manuscripts. Although his verse punctuation is known only through one poem, his prose letters survive in relative abundance, and comparison of the two reveals that his prose and verse punctuation principles are virtually identical. Donne's punctuation style in the sample studied here is consistent over time and changing circumstances and is congruent with seventeenth-century handbook descriptions, although the handbooks do not completely explain Donne's practice. He seems to have developed a highly individual style in punctuation, as in much else.

More than two hundred of Donne's letters survive in his own hand. The eleven letters studied here comprise a homogenous sample which recommends itself in more than one way to stylistic analysis. Nine of the eleven letters are from the Loseley papers. Of these, eight were written to Sir George More or to Sir Thomas Egerton in 1601/2 on the subject of Donne's marriage.

Their content is of interest in itself. The ninth is a brief business letter written to More in 1629. The remaining two are dedicatory letters which accompanied presentation copies of manuscripts of *Pseudomartyr* in 1610 and were written to Henry, Prince of Wales (Portland papers) and Sir Thomas Egerton (Bridgewater MS) respectively.

The eleven letters comprise a sample of 3700 words (exclusive of salutations, closings, and endorsements), a length generally considered sufficient for significant results in stylistic studies of frequently-occurring features. The letters contain relatively abundant examples of period, colon, and semicolon. The microfilms and photocopies consulted seemed quite clear as to the long stops, although the commas, not considered here, were often faint enough to require independent confirmation.

The 1601/2 letters as a group further recommend themselves for analysis by being written on the same subject to the same two recipients over a short period of time. Furthermore, the letters to More and Egerton were conditioned by similar social relationships: both More and Egerton were older, more powerful men whom Donne had offended.

The dedicatory letter to Sir Thomas Egerton and the business letter to More were included in order to analyze Donne's style in writing to those men at a later date when their passions might be supposed to have cooled; I wished to see whether Donne's punctuation style in 1601/2 might be the product of haste or of the emotional turmoil he might be supposed to have felt in the early months of his marriage. This proved not to be the case.

The dedicatory letter to Prince Henry was included in order to compare Donne's style on a very formal occasion to that which he employed in writing to social familiars. The more formal letter shows a predominance of periodic sentences and an absence of long stops within them.

The average sentence length of the sample is similar to that in the holograph Carey verse letter; so are the longest and shortest sentences of the sample. As in the Carey verse letter, loose rather than periodic sentences predominate in the sample, although the *Pseudomartyr* dedicatory letters do contain periodic sentences. Verbal and thematic stylistic similarities between the poetry and the prose letters in general have been remarked on by others.

In the sample studied, four kinds of sentences can be discerned: the periodic, and three types of loose sentences, which I will call the delayed-point, the argumentative, and the cumulative. Each has its own distinctive punctuation, and although the usages at times overlap, it is still possible to discern them.

Application of the punctuation principles described below, which are both historically appropriate and characteristic of Donne's style, should make it possible to edit Donne's scribal manuscripts on a more empirical basis, even though editorial unanimity will probably never be achieved.

How much consistency in punctuation can we expect from Donne? Surprisingly, certain of his purely conventional punctuation practices are very consistent, even by our standards. His abbreviations of "Lord" and "Lordship(s)" are identical in thirty-seven out of forty-four instances. Only three sentences appear to have missing final punctuation. In each of the three cases, an upper-case letter follows the place where the period should appear.

And, during a time when capitalization of the first words of sentences may not have been required for good style, only eleven of ninety-six sentences in the sample begin with a lower-case letter. The Carey verse letter contains many sentences which begin at the beginning of a line with lower case letters; not all these letters are those which Donne formed alike in the upper and lower case. But both the Carey poem and the prose letters in this sample are quite clear about initial capitals, with few exceptions.

Printed editions from the first half of the seventeenth century are, on the other hand, very consistent in capitalizing the first words of sentences. Standardization of initial capitalization may have been an innovation of print culture. Beginning a sentence in the lower case is by no means characteristic only of the letters in the sample which were written under stress, but is more frequent there, perhaps because these letters are much longer than the others.

Considering that Donne was his own scribe in these letters, and no doubt made the same errors and oversights as any copyist, if he did indeed recopy, these letters show a high degree of scribal consistency for his or any age. They contain few obvious errors, most of them corrected, and only a handful of strikeovers followed by second thoughts. Some of the letters under consideration show signs of having been proofread, as when a word is inserted above the line in smaller characters.

In some places, however, strikeouts within the line are immediately followed by correction, showing that perfect fair copy was not thought necessary, or perhaps that this was not the copy actually sent to the recipient. Manuscript culture may have encouraged the sending of imperfect copies as evidence of spontaneity.

None of the letters shows punctuation corrections, although of course punctuation may have been deliberately or absentmindedly changed, or purposefully or accidentally omitted, at any point in the writing or copying. Punctuation is particularly easy to alter in a finished manuscript, as in adding a mark or changing one mark to another, although removal of marks would probably leave some trace which would not show in the photocopy which I am using.

One presumes that the poet, if he reread his copy, would

change anything that was clearly counter to his intentions. Such tokens of care as appear here in matters of convention suggest that the letters of 1601/2 were not the effusions of a desperate man (which he may have been), but rather the controlled performances of a disciplined stylist (which we know he was).

Edmund Gosse's punctuation of the "incoherent note" sent by Donne to Egerton upon his release from prison (107) is an example of the confusion that an editor may unwittingly create in trying to "correct" Donne's punctuation:

Only in that coin, wherein they that delight to do benefits and good turns for the work's sake love to be paid, am I rich, which is thankfulness, which I humbly and abundantly present to your Lordship, beseeching you to give such way and entertainment to this virtue of mercy, which is always in you, and always awake, that it may so soften you, that as it hath wrought for me the best of blessings, which is this way to health, so it may give my mind her chief comfort, which is your pardon for my bold and presumptuous offence (To Egerton 13 Feb 1601/2; Gosse's transcription).

Gosse's transcription, which modernizes spelling and capitalization as well as punctuation, shows no colons or semicolons, but Donne punctuated the letter this way:

Onely in that Coyne, wherin they that Delight to do benefitts, and good turnes for the works sake Loue to be payd, ame I riche, wch ys Thankfullnes; wch I humbly and abundantly p^{r}sent to yor Lp.

Beseeching yo^{w}, to giue such way and Entertainmt to this vertu of Mercy, wch ys allways in yo^{w}, and allwayes awake, that yt may so soften yo^{w}, that as yt hath wrought for me, the best of bodily blessings, wch ys, this way to Health, So yt may gaine my Mind her Cheife Comfort, wch ys yor pardon for ^{my} or bold and p^{r}sumtuous offence. All-mighty god be allwayes so wth yo^{w} in this world as yo^{w} may be sure to be wth him in the next (To Egerton 13 Feb. 1601/2).

The period after "Lp" in l. 8 is almost certainly a full stop; Donne never indicated that abbreviation with a period anywhere else in the 1601/2 letters. Gosse omits this stop and spells out the abbreviation. This mends the sentence fragment, but erases the clear separation Donne made between the thanks and his subsequent petition. And Donne's semicolon at the end of line 6 indicates that the sentence, and its sense, is not complete without the presentation of thanks. If Donne had placed a colon instead of the semicolon here, more stress would go to the presentation, and less to the thanks themselves.

All this is lost in Gosse's transcription, which does indeed give the impression of incoherence. It is quite possible that this impression fitted Gosse's larger purpose all too well; in addition to his general and well-known carelessness, in his biography of Donne in which the extract quoted above appeared, Gosse's intention was to construct a psychological portrait of the poet with particular attention to sexual relationships.

This example illustrates the truth of John T. Shawcross's remark that criticism should stress the artefact itself rather than what it seems to reveal about the author ("Poetry, Personal and Impersonal: The Case of Donne" 66). In fact, there is nothing in the punctuation of any of the letters in the sample to suggest anything about the state of mind of the man who wrote them.

It is not, then, unrealistic to look further into the letters' punctuation style for evidence of Donne's punctuation principles. We may define a principle as a belief which guides practice but may not determine it inflexibly: even though frequent departures will call into question whether the principle exists except in name, one may sometimes lapse, or find reason to suspend a principle.

Because principles may be intuitively held but not articulated, consistent practice may be the only evidence of their existence. This may be particularly true of Donne's punctuation, since the language we use to discuss syntax did not exist during his lifetime. But English syntax has not changed so much since then that we cannot recognize practices that are clearly related to the integrity of the phrase and to syntactic completion.

The sample of letters studied here demonstrates a

principled use of colon and semicolon, unaltered by the peculiar demands of metrical punctuation in verse.

Metrical punctuation seems not to have been a dominant feature of Donne's poetry; his caesural marking and end-line marking in the Carey letter coincide with the stylistic and organizational practices in these prose letters. Apostrophe use in the Carey letter appears to be metrical; significantly, only one prose letter in the sample uses any apostrophes at all.

There are two apostrophes in the letter to Prince Henry, both inserted instead of "e" before final "d" in preterites. One such apostrophe appears in the Carey letter; all three apostrophes are unusual for Donne. They may appear as formal acknowledgements that the "e" is colloquial usage; both the Carey letter and the Prince Henry letter are very formal in tone and other stylistic features.

As noted above, the Prince Henry letter contains most of the periodic sentences in the sample. Donne's use of the colon in these prose letters is sparse, and congruent with the practice described in the handbooks of Mulcaster, Jonson, Butler, and Daines. Butler and Jonson say that completed sense precedes a colon, but that the sentence itself is completed by what follows.

Daines and Mulcaster simply say that a colon divides a sentence or "followeth some full branch." Donne's practice shows exactly this: all the colons in the sample follow what we would call independent clauses, which could stand on their own, but which do not entirely comprise the main idea of the sentence.

Each colon introduces a change of topic to the sentence in which it appears. No periodic sentence in the sample contains a colon, although both Daines and Mulcaster seem to describe such usage; in the sample, periodic sentences are marked by distinctive syntax, but not by punctuation other than commas. Usually the member that follows the colon is a dependent clause or phrase, although independent clauses do appear in that position.

No sentence in the sample has more than one colon. In the sample, a loose sentence punctuated by a colon after the first independent clause changes its topic and often delays its main point, which is then stated in the portion of the sentence following the colon; sometimes this second portion is parallel in wording or in conceit, if not in syntax, with the first:

... So long since, as at her being at yorkhouse, this had foundacon: and so much then of promise and Contract built vpon yt, as w[th]owt violence to Conscience might not be shaken (To More 2 Feb.1601/2).

Notice the parallel conceit of "foundacon"/"built" and "shaken," and the parallel introductory phrases "So long since" and "so much then." Even though the second member is not syntactically independent, it is emphasized by the change of topic from the "foundacon" to the "Contract" which eventuated. Donne's main point here is not the elapsed time of his courtship, but rather the solemn obligations of the mutual attachment. Mutuality is stressed again in the next sentence:

... At her Lyeng in town this Last parliam[t], I found meanes to see her twice or thrice: we both knew the obligacons that Lay vpon us, and wee adventurd equally, and about three weeks before Christmas we married.

Perhaps Donne anticipated accusations of having betrayed Ann's innocence, a valid concern given her youth. He changed the topic here from his own devices for gaining access to his lady to the venture they undertook together. The sentence just quoted is one of several cases in the sample in which a syntactically complete member follows a colon. If the four independent clauses there had been punctuated with semicolons then, according to my analysis, an entirely different effect would have been achieved, that of stressing the narrative sequence of events:

... At her Lyeng in town this Last parliam[t], I found meanes to see her twice or thrice; we both knew the obligacons that Lay vpon us; and wee adventurd equally; and about three weeks before Christmas we married. [Punctuation adjusted]

This punctuation is also Donnean; Donne made frequent use of the semicolon to co-ordinate short parallel clauses. But when he did so, he was presenting reasoned argument. In his own punctuation and in his own hand, we see another meaning: as the sentence came from his hand, it changes its topic from the efforts Donne made to see his love to the mutuality of their risky attachment. Donne's sentence is completed by his threefold assertion of their equal commitment. Sometimes what follows the colon may offer explanation necessary to support the assertion that precedes the colon:

... I humbly besee^c^he yo^w^, to take of these waytes, and to put my favlt into the balance alone, as yt was donne, wthowt the addicon of these yll reports: And though then yt wyll be to heauy for me, yett then yt wyll Less greive yo^w^ to pardon yt (To More 11 Feb. 1601/2).

Again a syntactically complete member follows the colon. Here again the second member changes the topic, this time from the fault to the hoped-for pardon, and it gives a reason for More to consider the known fault and not any other accusations: it will then be easier to pardon the fault. This whole letter is an entreaty for forgiveness, culminating in the final sentence, which ends in a plea for clemency:

... I can p^r^sent nothing to yor thoughts wch yo^w^ knew not before, but my submission, my repentance, and my harty desire, to do any thing satisfactory to yor iust displeasure: Of wch I beseech yow to make a charitable vse and Construction (To More 11 Feb. 1601/2).

The l. 50 colon marks a change of topic from Donne's abject repentance to his petition. Such a petition could not be part of the utter surrender of the first member, but it is the main idea of both the sentence and the letter with which this sentence closes. Donne's semicolons in the sample are more numerous than his colons, but still relatively infrequent, even though some sentences contain several.

His semicolons, in fact, often appear in clusters. When a semicolon is the first long stop of the sentence, it appears after what we would call an independent clause unless the sentence itself is a fragment. What follows the semicolon may or may not be syntactically complete, but if several members in a row are co-ordinated by semicolons, they are always parallel in thought and often parallel, or nearly so, in syntax. Their content then is stressed in three ways: by syntax, parallelism, and punctuation.

Donne has two distinct uses for the semicolon. One usage, the argumentative, occurs when he is making an appeal to reason, usually setting out a brief list in one sentence. A cluster of such semicolons may follow a colon, but never precedes a colon in this sample.

Daines seems to describe this argumentative usage when he writes of semicolons used "to make some short deliberation of little sentences". The principle of making "a short deliberation" seems to govern those sentences composed only of members divided by semicolons.

But whether clustered semicolons appear in a sentence alone or in the second branch of a sentence divided by a colon, they alert the attentive reader to the fact that a series is presented. The argumentative usage is frequent in some letters and absent in others. It appears twice in Donne's first letter to Sir George More after his marriage. The first occurrence reads:

The reasons, why I did not foreacquaint yo^{w} wth it, (to deale wth the same plainnes that I have usd) were these. I knew my p^{r}sent estate Lesse then fitt for her; I knew, (yet I knew not why) that I stoód not right in yor opinion; I knew that to have giuen any intimacon of yt, had been to impossibilitate the whole matt^{r} (To More 2 Feb. 1601/2).

A colon after the first sentence here would be consistent with modern usage and with other usage in the sample. But a colon would connect the secrecy of the marriage with the reasons for secrecy. Donne seems to have chosen to separate the two ideas as firmly as possible, with a period. The three-branched second sentence, with a reason in each branch, stands on its own as an argument composed of three reasons which are not subordinated at all to the sentence before.

Donne's tone here is independent, verging on the impertinent, and stands in strong contrast to the vigorous self-abasement to which he resorts later in his correspondence with More. The changing tone of the 1601/2 letters is of equal interest with their content, and should be the subject of further study.

Donne all but abandons argumentative semicolon usage and the strategy of reason in subsequent letters to More, relying instead on appeals to mercy and compassion, but he continues to use the argumentative sentence, with its semicolon-marked and often syntactically parallel branches, in letters to Egerton, culminating in a notable occurrence of this usage in the letter in which he makes his case for restoration to his position:

I was carefully and honestly bred; enioyd an indifferent fortune; I had, (and I had vnderstandinge inough to valew yt) the Sweetnes and Security of a freedome, and indepency; wthowt markinge owt to my hopes, any place of profitt, I had a desire to be yor Lps servant; by the favor wch yor good Sonns love to me, obteind (To Egerton March 1 1601/2).

This five-part sentence contains three independent clauses. It may be that the syntactic incompleteness of "enioyed an indifferent fortune;" and "by the favor which your good Sonns love to me, obtained" are oversights, but rigid syntactic regularity does not seem to have been a requirement for seventeenth-century loose sentences. Even the formal dedicatory letter to Egerton contains a fragment, as does the Carey verse letter.

The sample shows no evidence whatever that the semicolon must co-ordinate syntactically equal members as it does for us. But Donne has clearly linked here his lack of self-interest in desiring to serve Egerton and has separated that from the favour he gained with Egerton through his son. Here, near the beginning of the letter, Donne reviews his early career for Egerton before going on to make his case. Observe the difference another punctuation might make:

I was carefully and honestly bred; enioyd an indifferent fortune; I had, (and I had vnderstandinge inough to valew yt) the Sweetnes and Security of a freedome, and indepency, wthowt markinge owt to my hopes, any place of profitt; I had a desire to be yor Lps servant, by the favor wch yor good Sonns love to me, obteind. (To Egerton March 1 1601/2; punctuation adjusted)

This adjusted punctuation replaces the semicolons in ll. 20 and 22 with colons which correct the syntax of the two incomplete members by attaching them to the clauses which precede them. But this arrangement of clauses connects Donne's "indepency" [sic] with his desire to serve Egerton, implying that he was disinterested because he could afford to be. The adjusted punctuation also implies that Donne desired to be recommended to Egerton through his son.

Donne's punctuation carefully avoids both of these tactless blunders. The whole organization of this letter as Donne wrote it is businesslike, almost lawyerly, and does credit to his diplomatic training. No later letters in this sample give occasion for the use of what we might call the "argumentative semicolon."

The second kind of semicolon usage occurs in sentences whose full meaning is cumulative rather than presented in series or delayed until after a colon. These sentences most resemble the usage described in Butler and Jonson who say that the semicolon comes after incomplete sense.

Sentences with cumulative branches marked by semicolons occur frequently in letters to both More and Egerton, especially in passages in which he appeals to mercy or compassion. Although the sentiments expressed in these sentences may not be to our taste, their construction is clearly differentiated from that of other sentences containing colons or "argumentative" semicolons. Whether or not this differentiation was deliberate will probably never be known, but its consistency makes it eligible as a stylistic principle.

... My Conscience and such Affection as in my Conscience becomes an honest Man, emboldneth me to make one request more, wch ys that by some kind and Comfortable Message yo^{w} would be pleasd to giue some ease of the afflictions wch I know yor Daughter in her Mind suffers; and that (if it be not against yor other purposes) I may wth yor Leave wright to her; for wthowt yor Leave I wyll neuer attempt any thing concerning her (To More 13 Feb. 1601/2).

The sentence builds to Donne's belated promise to approach Ann only through her father. He comes to this point by way of a plea for mercy for her, and then a request that he might write to his wife. By reminding More that his daughter's happiness is at stake here, he strengthens his case. In the next sentence of this letter, Donne addresses Egerton in another plea for mercy: All these Irons are knocd of; yett I perish in as heavy fetters, as ever, whilst I Languish vnder yor Lps Anger. (To Egerton 1 March 1601/2)

The first semicolon acknowledges Donne's release from prison; the rest of the sentence portrays his life as still a form of imprisonment, where he "languishes" in "fetters" because of Egerton's continued displeasure. It is the continuity between past imprisonment and continuing unhappiness that comes across here. The branch after the semicolon continues the theme of prison, while the semicolon itself signals the incompleteness of the thought in the first member.

The following sentence from the first letter to More contains all three usages of colon, cumulative semicolon, and argumentative semicolon. The delayed main point is the argumentative series, which is clearly directed to More's intellect; it is hardly well calculated to assuage his anger.

... I know this Letter shall find yo^{w} fvll of passion: but I know no passion can alter yor reason and wisdome; to wch I aduenture to comend these perticvlers; That yt ys irremediably donne; That if yo^{w} incense my L, yow Destroy her and me; That yt is easye to giue vs happines; And that my Endeuors and industrie, if it please yo^{w} to prosper them, may soone make me somewhat worthyer of her (To More 2 Feb. 1601/2).

The colon in l. 50 signals a change of topic: More's anger is treated dismissively, while his reason is emphasized, both by the colon and by the parallel sense and syntax of the branches which follow. The first two semicolons here point forward to sense completion: More's reason is to be addressed by "particulars," which are marked by argumentative semicolons. These last three semicolons present Donne's arguments in a parallel series which is the main point promised by the colon.

Donne is very consistent in distinguishing the four types of sentence by punctuation. Periodic sentences are punctuated only by commas; a delayed-point sentence may contain one colon; an argumentative or a cumulative sentence often contains several semicolons; in an argumentative sentence, the branches usually show parallel, or almost parallel syntax. Either an argumentative series or a cumulative series, or both, may comprise the second branch of a delayed-point sentence. Donne uses colons to emphasize the importance of what follows them, and semicolons to co-ordinate lists and to build to a climax.

By these rules, some colons in the sample might have been semicolons (or vice versa), had Donne so chosen, and some sentences do not use colon or semicolon everywhere they might. But imagining how Donne might have punctuated differently involves thought about what he meant to say. Any editorial choice of punctuation for prose or poetry from the available manuscript and early edition variants must depend upon how we read Donne's organization of his sentences.

If punctuation must be seen as an act of interpretation, then scribal manuscript punctuation (including Donne's own) is also interpretation, and the various scribal readings may be evaluated for their closeness to Donne's actual practice by empirical means. But while we may get closer to Donne's style, we will never restore it.

And, in any case, the poet himself might have punctuated different copies of the same text differently. Why should punctuation choices which could easily be different, and which Donne himself may not have consciously calculated, be the object of so much effort? Only because if we neglect punctuation, we may lose differences in style, tone, and attitude, and even mistake Donne's meaning.

Consider the difference an alternative approach to punctuation might make in the last stanza of "A nocturnall upon St. Lucies day:"

But I am None; nor will my Sunne renew.
You lovers, for whose sake, the lesser Sunne
At this time to the Goat is runne
To fetch new lust, and give it you,
Enjoy your summer all;
Since shee enjoyes her long nights festivall
Let mee prepare towards her, and let mee call

This houre her Vigill, and her Eve, since this
Both the yeares, and the days deep midnight is (ll. 37-45).

How should this stanza be punctuated? Shawcross reminds us that the editor is obliged to make sense of the text—to interpret it. He has done so here. His interpretation, read in seventeenth-century terms, is consistent with Donne's practice in the letters of the sample, and suggests by means of the semicolon at the end of l. 41 (which originates in Grierson's 1912 edition) that "midnight" is the essential completing idea of the sentence and the poem. And Shawcross's edition makes a sharp break by means of a period between the nothingness of l. 37 and the lovers of ll. 38-41.

Donne's seventeenth-century copyists were also interpreting the text, sometimes by emending verbals, very often by applying punctuation. Let us treat their varying punctuations as interpretations and try to discern which may be closest to Donne's practice.

There are eight scribal manuscripts of this poem in addition to the 1633 first edition. Each copyist punctuates this stanza differently. The 1633 punctuation may be ruled out at once, because it places a semicolon at the caesura in l. 37 and then a colon at the line's end; Donne never placed a semicolon before a colon in the sample studied here.

But I am None; nor will my Sunne renew:
You lovers, for whose sake, the lesser Sunne
At this time to the Goat is runne
To fetch new lust, and give it you,
Enjoy your summer all,
Since shee enjoyes her long nights festivall,
Let mee prepare towards her, and let mee call
This houre her Vigill, and her eve, since this
Both the yeares, and the dayes deep midnight is (1633 Edition ll. 37-45).

Five of the scribal manuscripts also fail to show Donnean style because they use few or no colons or semicolons. In a loose sentence of this length, Donne characteristically used at least one, and usually more than one, heavy stop. Only two manuscripts show a style like that of the sample; they are

Trinity College Cambridge and Trinity College Dublin (referred to here as CT1 and DT1 respectively):

But I am none; nor will my Sun renewe
You Lovers, for whose sake the lesser Sunne
At this tyme to the Goate is runne
To fetch new Lust, and give it you
Enioy your summer all.
Since shee enioyes her long nights festivall
Lett mee prepare towards her, & lett mee call
This houre her vigill, & her Eve, since this
Both the yeares, & the dayes deepe midnight is (Puckering MS).

The long stops of CT1 and DT1 are identical, which is noteworthy in itself. A scribe often punctuated different copies of the same text differently; this scribe did not. CT1 and DT1 are also distinguished by being derived from the same archetype.

If we accept the CT1/DT1 punctuation of this stanza then, much as some commentators might like to stress the implied optimism of "her Vigill, and her Eve", the earliest consistent scribal testimony turns abruptly from the enjoyment of "you lovers" to a new sentence beginning with "her long night's festival" and building from there to completion in the despair of "midnight," an interpretation very close to that given in Shawcross's edition of the poem.

Is the CT1/DT1 punctuation Donne's? Almost certainly not. The scribes showed great independence in applying punctuation which made sense to them. But we may be justified, I think, in privileging a seventeenth-century interpretation which does not violate Donne's style, which appears early in the scribal tradition, and which preserves the more difficult reading of ll. 37-38 over any later interpretations, even very good ones, that have been created by punctuation.

Not punctuating the end of l. 37 at all allows the poem to say both "my sun will not renew" and "my sun will not renew you lovers," a syntactic ambiguity characteristic of Donne's poetry.

Further study may fill out the picture of Donne's

punctuation practice. It is not yet clear that the style just described is uniquely Donnean. Ernest Sullivan has said that the longer prose works such as *Biathanatos* and *Pseudomartyr* resemble the poetry much less than the prose letters do; those longer works may be amenable to study, since *Biathanatos,* at least, bears some traces of the author's hand.

Commas in Donne holographs have been little analyzed, and may perhaps be shown to be more systematic in their usage than they are now commonly believed to be. And the emergence of competing readings for various poems on the basis of an understanding of Donne's consistent application of punctuation conventions available to him may enrich our understanding of the poems.

Donne editors may yet come closer to that happy state of affairs in punctuation described by Francis Clement in 1587, in which "the breath is relieved, the meaning conceived, the eye directed, the ear delited, and all the senses satisfied."

Chapter 3

John Donne's Use of Space

Donne's writing shows he was fascinated by new discoveries. He took up the modern idiom of maps and discovery with delight. But he was also deeply attached to the past, and his assumptions about space belonged to an old tradition: a cosmographic rather than cartographic way of imagining space.

This paper is about Donne's spatial imagination: its cosmographic assumptions, and its many contradictions — between old and new ways of imagining the cosmos, between cosmographic and cartographic ways of imagining the world, and between his spatial imagination itself and his narrative voice.

We are almost always aware of where Donne's speakers are, but he creates that sense of place with startling economy: with prepositions rather than descriptions. His characters inhabit peculiarly simplified locations and spatial arrangements: a town under siege; a "little roome"; a "pretty roome"; a room encircled by the outside world, by spies, by pilgrims, by cosmic spheres or the sun; centres and circles.

It was not the appearance but the shape of space that interested Donne, and he used the same shapes over and over again in his poetry and prose, as if they formed a kind of language for thinking about relationships; as if he had a spatial apprehension of a thought (rather than the "sensuous apprehension of a thought" for which Eliot praised him), and imagined a relationship's intangible configurations of power, passivity, privacy and fusion in spatial terms, as shapes.

We can see that Donne's writing is full of circles:

symbolic, loving, social and spiritual. We can argue that he phrased ideas to himself in spatial terms. However, our distance from his assumptions about space makes it difficult for us to understand why. His spatial language took forms and meaning from a traditional conception of space, which seems very odd to us today. We generally think of space as a characterless abstraction.

We think of it without picturing circles, or considering forces. We think of space without imagining the cosmos. But space was a different story for Donne. It was material, forceful, meaningful, full, and arranged into concentric circles. This was the concept of space the new philosophy called into doubt, while cartography offered an alternative way to picture it, in two rather than three dimensions, and all these contradictory ways of imagining space play against each other in the foreground of Donne's poetry.

However, the traditional interpretation of space formed the background to his spatial imagination. He expected space to mean something; to take certain shapes, which indicated forces.

The tradition came out of the belief that the cosmos was a finite sphere, with nothing outside it. Plato laid out cosmic space in spheres in the *Timaeus*. Aristotle adapted and developed this arrangement in his lectures *On the Heavens* and in *Physics* by making it part of his explanation of why things moved as they did. Plato described "space" as the "receptacle" or fundamental and characterless substance in which changing qualities enacted themselves.

Aristotle identified Plato's space (kh"ra) with his own prime matter. Like Plato, he rejected the opinion of the atomists. Space was not a three-dimensional void in which particles moved. It was the outcome of material dimension, hence his denial that "space" as we might imagine it — as a void or three-dimensional abstraction — existed at all.

Augustine built the idea that space was a set of concentric spheres into Christian philosophy when he interpreted the Book of Genesis in accordance with it in *The City of God*. It became an assumption necessary to understanding how and why things moved, with Aquinas' interpretation of Aristotle's *Physics,* and quasi-doctrinal once Aquinas based certain of his proofs that God existed upon Aristotelian premises, and concluded his *Commentary* upon Aristotle's *Physics* on the triumphant note:

> And thus the Philosopher ends his general discussion of natural things with the first principle of the whole of nature, who is over all things, God, blessed forever, Amen.

Of course, there were very many variations upon this cosmic scheme, many of them highly creative, but almost all of them were variations upon the common theme of cosmic "cohaerence... just supply and... Relation," operating across the concentric spheres of space the symbolic value of the traditional scheme explained why the "new Philosophy" called "all in doubt." Variations were fitted onto the following basic model. The cosmos was centred upon earth and arranged in concentric spheres. The sphere enclosed by the orbit of the moon was called the sublunary sphere and the sphere above it, the celestial sphere.

In the sublunary sphere everything was always becoming something else, living and dying, but the celestial sphere was made from better, purer, simpler stuff than the sublunary sphere, and the heavenly bodies lasted for all time, and moved for all time in a regular pattern. The pattern could be understood numerically as a set of ratios.

Their purity was associated with their supposedly circular motion, and contrasted with the rectilinear motion of sublunary things, which moved up and down and came together and fell apart because they were composite. They were made from the four elements of earth, water, air and fire, each of which naturally belonged to a different sphere of the sublunary realm, and sought its natural place, so pulling natural bodies up and down and apart.

Perhaps this description has led us to picture the cosmos as a set of concentric spheres, set up like an armillary sphere. But we have to be careful not to imagine an abstract arrangement in three dimensions. Space was material, and the shapes of space had force and meaning. In the *Almagest*

Ptolemy wrote that "almost every particular attribute of material nature becomes apparent from the peculiarities of its motion from place to place. [Thus we can distinguish] the corruptible from the incorruptible, by [whether it undergoes] motion in a straight line or in a circle... and passive from active, by [whether it moves] towards the centre or away from the centre." Like Plato, Aristotle and his Christian followers made "the contrast between circular and rectilinear motion a symbol of the contrast between the eternal and the transient, hence also between the psychical and the physical, even the divine and the mortal."

These metaphysical attributes of space allowed Donne to imagine metaphysical relationships in spatial terms; in terms of the sphere, circle, centre, circumference and set of concentric circles that gave shape to space in the closed cosmos, where space took shape and meaning from the forms that filled it. But the new philosophy of the seventeenth century challenged this idea of the cosmos, so calling "all in doubt," a doubt caught up by an odd moment in Donne's 1609 satire, *Ignatius His Conclave.*

Copernicus is in hell, arguing he deserves a leadership role there because he threw the world into confusion with his new cosmology, and doing well until Ignatius argues that Greeks such as "Heraclides, Ecphantus, & Aristarchus" said the earth moved long before he did and, besides, he "may be right" in what he said.

And even Satan could not be certain. The new philosophy brought uncertainty with it, and while Bacon pictured a ship sailing past the old bounds of knowledge in the frontispiece to his New Atlantis, Donne referred to it as a sign of the frailty and decay rather than the progress of human knowledge in "The first Anniversary," as if the old certainties were not wrong, but "lost."

Donne's poetry plays upon the uncertainties of the time. He co-opts them to his own uncertainties: his radical changes of perspective; his radical juxtapositions of different perspectives; his balancing of possibilities. He uses different ways of imagining space to illustrate different attitudes, sometimes referring to the new philosophy, and sometimes writing as if he'd never heard of it. He chooses the philosophy that illustrates what he wants to say. In a letter to a friend he writes, "methinks the new philosophy is thus appliable well, that we which are a little earth should rather move toward God, than that He... should move toward us."

But in "The Sunne Rising" he fits the old philosophy onto that same image of a circle and its centre, for the lovers' position at the centre of the cosmos indicates the central importance and centrifocal tendency of their love. He chooses the philosophy that illustrates what he wants to say. However, he fits both philosophies and both relationships onto that one image of a circle and its centre, and the arrangement of relations that it represents in spatial terms.

That image takes its shape and meaning from the shape and meaning of space in the "closed cosmos," where space is arranged in concentric circles. Donne describes the cosmic arrangement as "natures nest of boxes: the heavens contain the earth; the earth, cities; cities, men. And all these are concentric..." and contained by "all the vaults and circles of the severall spheres of heaven" (S. 4. 5.150). This image of concentric circles appears over and over again in his writing, working like a master-image upon which he maps many, various, and sometimes contradictory ideas.

For instance, he uses this image of concentric circles to illustrate his sense of the proper relationship between social ranks. He writes, as in the heavens there are but a few circles that go about the whole world, but many epicycles, and other lesser circles, but yet circles; so of those men which are raised and put into circles, few of them move from place to place, and pass through many and beneficial places, but fall into little circles, and, within a step of two, are at their end, and not so well as they were in the centre, from which they are raised...

Here he maps a social hierarchy onto the architecture of concentric circles in the heavens, so we picture the spatial arrangement and movement of people, with that mix of abstraction and visualisation that is so curious in his imagery.

Donne maps the relationship between friends onto the same model. In a letter to Goodyer of 1609 he writes, The first sphere only which is resisted by nothing, absolves its course every day; and so doth true friendship well placed often iterate in act or purposes the same offices.

But as the lower spheres, subject to the violence of that, and yet naturally encouraged to a reluctation against it, have therefore many distractions and eccentricities, and some trepidations, and so return but lamely and lately to the same place and office; so that friendship which is not moved primarily by the proper intelligence, discretion, and about the natural centre, virtue, doth perchance sometimes, some things, somewhat like true friendship; but hath many deviations...

What an extraordinary way to compare friendships! His image comes from Plato's *Timaeus,* source of the idea that a first sphere moved without resistance around inner spheres facing resistance. The model has the advantage of letting him map many different human relationships onto one master-image, so he can compare friendships, and not just friends.

And it sets those human relationships within the vast and impersonal terms of the universe. It exposes those human relationships to the immense and impersonal terms of the cosmos, as the lover in "A Lecture upon the Shadow" exposes his own relationship to cosmic immensity. Another writer might use the contrast to diminish the relationship. Donne uses it to clarify the value of the relationship, for its very vulnerability becomes the measure of its intensity.

Donne organises "Goodfriday, 1613. Riding Westward" around the same image, of intelligences moving spheres:

Let mans Soule be a Spheare, and then, in this,
The intelligence that moves, devotion is,
And as the other Spheares, by being growne
Subject to forreigne motions, lose their owne,
And being by others hurried every day,
Scarce in a yeare their naturall forme obey:

Here the image of the enclosing sphere of the sun, and the sun, contains the physical movement of the speaker "Riding Westward." Once again Donne contrasts the purity of the higher sphere and intelligence with the "distractions and eccentricities" of the speaker moving in a lesser sphere, to provide a spatial image of the speaker's complaint about distractions of "Pleasure or businesse."

This poem concerns the death of Christ. Since Christ's incarnation contracted "That All, which always is All everywhere" into the "little roome" of humanity, it seems fitting that the speaker breaks the logic of the cosmic arrangement, as he does with the paradox,

Could I behold those hands which span the Poles,
And turne all spheares at once, peirc'd with those holes?

But he also breaks the logic of the cosmic arrangement with the introduction of cartographic imagery — the East and the West of the poem. The contradiction between cosmographic and cartographic imagery expresses divine grace in spatial terms, for the sun reaches both East and West and overarches all the world.

This adds to the irony of the last clause, "I'll turne my face" — an irony that plays upon the religious ironies of prevenient grace, for the sun moves to shine in the face of those who ride westward. And all the movements traced in the poem — the path of the rider, westwards, and the arc of the sun overhead, and the turning of his back and the turning of his face — help to illustrate the to-and-fro movement of the rider's consciousness.

Different and sometimes contradictory perspectives can play together on Donne's imaginative sites. This is part of the peculiar power of the rooms in Donne's poetry, I think: they counter-balance love against the awareness of an outside world unkind to love. Lovers in Donne's *Elegies* often retreat to rooms "ambush'd round with houshold spies": a "husbands towring eyes," a jealous husband, an "Hydroptique father... with glazed eyes," "spies and rivals... [and a] fathers wrath." Their rooms are images of a love staked against the outside world, measuring its value by its dangerousness.

The lovers in Donne's *Songs and Sonets* do not only stake their rooms of love against the outside world. They take over the outside world. Their contraction of the world, thus, finds an image and equivalent in the "contraction" of the Elegy-form into the stanzas, or "little rooms," of the *Songs and Sonets* (Donne plays on the pun in "The Canonization"). In the *Elegies* the lovers "themselves exile" in rooms "close and secret, as... [their] soules."

In many of the *Songs and Sonets,* they answer exile as defiantly as Coriolanus, with "I banish you." Many of Donne's *Songs and Sonets* gather excitement as the lovers transform withdrawal: they are shut out from the world; they shut out the world; they are the world. We see the dynamic shift in "His parting from her."

First the lover says, "come Night,/ Environ me with darkness." But soon he claims he could give darkness to the night, "and say,/ Out of my self, There should be no more Day." He makes himself the active centre of the darkness. The lover in "A nocturnall upon S. Lucies day" also makes himself the negative centre of the poem. Nature mocks him — "Yet all these seem to laugh / Compar'd with me..." — as it mocks the lover in "Twicknam Garden" who looks upon happiness from outside: the trees laugh. But both lovers work from the margins, to create a world that centres upon them: "Hither with christall vyals, lovers come"; "Study me then, you who will lovers be..."

We see the same dynamic in "The Canonization." Here society rather than nature mocks the lover with its ongoingness: "Alas, alas, who's injured by my love?" But the lover defies the world's definitions: "Call us what you will, wee are made such by love." In the following stanzas he builds a room for love, and a world around it. This impulse for living and loving, despite the world, sends a quickening pulse through these stanzas. We feel the same sudden creative power in "The Sunne Rising," when the lover stops trying to shut out the sun and starts demanding it centre upon the room of his love.

The lovers do not simply stake out a room against the world, but find a whole world in their room. They become their own "mirrors and... spies," taking over from the "houshold spies" of the *Elegies*: "wee in us finde th'Eagle and the Dove"; "She'is all States, and all Princes, I, / Nothing else is." We feel a sudden corresponding expansiveness in the poem.

When the lovers transform their withdrawal, they demand we fit our imagining of "That All, which always is All everywhere" into their "little roome." It is no longer only a matter of pitting different perspectives against each other. It is a matter of fitting them together. These rooms demand a startling imaginative juxtaposition equivalent to the startling visual juxtaposition of "A bracelet of bright haire about the bone," or the startling temporal juxtaposition of "his first minute, after noone, is night."

"'Tis greatest now, and to destruction / Nearest," he writes in "The Progresse of the Soule." Such opposites are never simply opposites, in Donne, but formed upon each other; the lover in "A Lecture upon the Shadow" sees, "We doe those shadowes tread." The closeness of opposites in Donne's vision gives the dramatic "cleernesse" of contrast to every emotion; it is this awareness of shadows that makes the "cleernesse" "brave."

Our pleasure in the imaginative power of the lover is undercut by our knowledge of the sun's unstoppable passage in "The Sunne Rising," as our confidence in "The Canonization" is undercut by knowing the power is imaginative.

When we read "A Valediction: Forbidding Mourning," we know mourning may be postponed, but morning cannot be. The lover stakes a place for love in a world we know he does not control, for his own images remind us of its range and its variousness. The lover's confidence is a kind of courage. Against the knowledge that "paine is true" he sets the reality of pleasure.

His celebration of "one little roome" as "everywhere" plays tricks of scale — "the world's contracted thus."[38] But he also plays different perspectives off against each other by switching from cosmographic to cartographic imagery. Each way of imagining puts the poet in a different imaginative position. A cosmographic sense of space put the poet imaginatively at the centre of a three-dimensional universe, whilst a geographic sense of space puts the poet imaginatively above and apart from a two-dimensional representation of the world. Their juxtaposition creates the imaginative equivalent of irony: an irony, or split-vision, the reader experiences for, since Donne's imagery is spatial, his settings are images, not simply to see, but to inhabit.

In "The Good-morrow" he says,

Let sea-discovereres to new worlds have gone,
Let Maps to other, worlds on worlds have showne,
Let us possesse one world, each hath one, and is one.

Here the difference between a cartographic and cosmographic imagination is caught in the contrast between the verbs, "showne" and "possesse." We picture the maps piled on top of each other. This is one outcome of sea-discovery, for the people at home: a vision of the surface of the world. But then he seeks to "possesse" a world, and this is the world one has and one is: the cosmos, or macrocosm of the human microcosm.

This is the system that puts people at its centre. And from this point, the lover imagines himself and his beloved as the two halves of the earth: "Where can we finde two better hemispheares...." They are the world other people looked upon in the map. The reader sees them from both perspectives, picturing both the world in Maps and the hemisphere in each lover's eye.

Such imaginative irony is remarkable because it does not play the present off against the future or the past (though that kind of irony is also found in Donne's poetry). It plays spatial perspectives off against each other. It is an irony caught in the very present moment of the speaker's experience, making dividedness part and parcel of the full creative consciousness of the speaker.

This can give Donne's poetry a poignancy clear of nostalgia and cynicism, for the speaker's awareness of a world elsewhere, that will not wait for lovers, makes his here and now seem both more precious and more precarious.

The contradictions within Donne's spatial imagination create a perspectival irony. But Donne does not only play different spatial perspectives off against each other. He also plays his spatial vision off against his narrative voice. So many of his love poems are set at the edge of some delight, and written in resistance to the inevitable; poems forbidding the sun, or the morning, or the break of day.

But when his speakers assert power over time, they actually imagine power over space: the power of gold, beaten "to aery thinnesse," to reach across space; the power of a compass to organise sequence into a coherent spatial image; the power of lovers to reach beyond time into the celestial sphere. They try to fit time into the atemporal patterns of space.

The image of concentric circles is beautifully expressed in "Loves Growth" where he turns time itself into an expanding set of concentric circles:

... as in water stirred more circles be
Produced by one, love such additions take,
Those like so many spheres, but one heaven make...

He transforms a passage of years into a pattern of circles, using spatial imagery against time, denying its ability to change the lovers' relationship, just as the lover in "A Valediction; Forbidding Mourning" uses the image of compass-drawn circles to deny time will keep the lovers apart. Donne's speakers often wield the image of a circle against time in this bitter-sweet, teasing way. Here his wit offers a way to live in the valedictory moment.

There is, of course, a long tradition associating eternity with circles. It was built into the old cosmology and its associated physics. However, a circle can defeat time in two ways. It can defeat time by turning into itself, over and over again, making every ending a beginning. This is how God makes a Christian life into a circle. Donne says "God is a circle himselfe, and he will make thee one" (VI. viii. 175). Such immortality is a kind of timelessness.

However, he says immortality is qualitatively different from eternity. He imagines a different kind of timelessness for God. God's eternity is "not a Circle where two points meet, but a Circle made at once; This life is a Circle, made with a Compasse, that passes from point to point; That life is a Circle stamped with a print, an endlesse and perfect Circle, as soone as it begins... (S. 2. 9.200). God's eternity is without sequence, and Donne imagines it as a space, describing God as "millions upon millions of unimaginable spaces in heaven."

The lover in "A Valediction; Forbidding Mourning" echoes a biblical phrase when he says his love, like the logic of a circle "makes me end, where I begun." Donne gives the source of the phrase in a Sermon: "When I begin, says God to Eli, I will make an end; not onely that all Gods purposes will have their certain end, but that even then, when he begins, he makes an end... as a Circle is printed all at once, so his beginning and his ending is all one" (S. 4.3.96).

But the difference I mentioned, between God's printed circle and a human being's drawn circle, comes into play here. The lover is trying to get beyond the human condition of time by treating it as a space. The image of time as a circle rests upon the belief that there is a world apart from time, and his logic is the illogical logic of faith and love.

He ignores the time intervening between his ending and beginning, and the fact that a lover can return where but not when nor as he began. His circle cannot be printed; it must be drawn out. This fallacy runs like a crack through his argument and makes us feel nervous, and that nervousness is an essential part of the brilliance of the poem. It is Donne's fencing partner. It's why the argument feels courageous.

Donne's poetry presents the conflict between love and time in the conflict between his spatial imagery and his narrative style. A scenario is non-discursive. But Donne's poems are emphatically discursive. Though his speakers claim to be safe from time, the evolution of their argument reminds us time is passing as they speak. His lovers must find their place in a world of time, and they must defend their space against that world of time; a world that threatens to break into their spatial enclaves and break up their perfect moments.

We feel the conflict between space and time as a premonition of failure or decline. The confidence of Donne's lovers is edged by our fear and we feel the brave, defiant brilliance of their arguments with the inevitable.

Chapter 4

Feminist Performance and the Silence of Isabella

In a chapter entitled "When Is a Character Not a Character?" Alan Sinfield presents the argument that the female figures in Shakespeare's plays are not really "characters" at all, since they do not possess continuous and psychologically consistent interior lives. Although such roles as that of Desdemona, Olivia, and Lady Macbeth are written so as to suggest the presence of uninterrupted interior consciousness, this impression collapses under the pressure of the plot's movement toward closure, which reveals the figures to represent nothing more than a "disjointed sequence of positions that women are conventionally supposed to occupy".

In order to preserve a textual organization that sustains a particular gender hierarchy, female characters abruptly shift from one stereotypical version of femininity to another without coherent linkages between them.

For instance, despite their volubility throughout the early acts, at the conclusions of the plays, as Sinfield notes, Shakespeare's women often "fall silent at moments when their speech could only undermine the play's attempt at ideological coherence". Thus, "the point at which the text falls silent is the point at which its ideological project is disclosed". One of the most prominent of such silences appears at the end of *Measure for Measure,* where Isabella, "the bold woman silenced most spectacularly when marriage is proposed", fails to react verbally to the Duke's two offers of wedlock.

According to Sinfield, this lack of response occurs because Isabella is suspended between two conventional female roles, and the disjunction between them makes manifest the agenda of the text's gender politics.

The question for feminist performance criticism then becomes, what attitude towards the text's ideological project should a contemporary feminist performance take? Two options are suggested by Sinfield's account of the way in which literary critics tend to respond to the interpretive problems created by such puzzling silences:

Some commentators will then seek to help the text into coherence...[by] supplying characters with feasible thoughts and motives to smooth over the difficulty. This has been the virtual raison d'être of traditional criticism. Other commentators may take the opportunity to address the ideological scope of the text—how its closures provoke collusion or questioning.

When producing such a play, theatrical personnel may also choose either to gloss over or to expose the ideological agenda of the text as revealed by the silence of the female character. As an example of the first strategy, consider the moment in the final scene of *Measure for Measure*, immediately after Claudio ha been unmuffled, when the duke says to Isabella,

If he be like your brother, for his sake
Is he pardon'd; and for your lovely sake
Give me your hand and say you will be mine.
He is my brother too: but fitter time for that.
(5.1.488-491)

Although the Duke asks the young novice to "say" she will be his, the text allots Isabella no verbal reply to this proposal. To provide a plausible reason for her silence, modern stagings, such as director Michael Langham's 1992 production at Stratford, Ontario, have commonly interpolated a mimed reconciliation between Isabella and her brother that distracts her attention away from Vincentio's request. As C. E. McGee remembers,

The Duke's schemes achieved a happy ending in the

joyous reunion of Isabella and Claudio, whose embrace took place downstage centre when the Duke, with typically bad timing, made his first proposal of marriage to Isabella. The line "But fitter time for that"...expressed his recognition that she was too delighted to see her brother alive again to hear a word of the Duke's offer.

Although such an enactment does offer "feasible thoughts and motives" to account for Isabella's lack of response, the impulse to justify her silence in a practical way detracts from a production's ability to explore the ideological significance of that silence and to employ it in the production's overall treatment of gender dynamics.

On the other hand, many revivals over the last twenty-five years have exploited Isabella's silence to make a political statement validating female resistance to the type of treatment Isabella receives from the play's male characters. This countertrend began with John Barton's landmark 1970 Royal Shakespeare Company production, in which "Isabella quite firmly did not agree to marry the Duke" ("Directing" 65). Reviewer D.A.N. Jones refers to Barton's version as "a feminist production" which concluded with "Isabella glaring at the audience, silent rage written all over her high forehead and stubborn chins".

As much as I might agree with the modern feminist politics which prompt such a performance choice, I simultaneously recoil from the choice itself because, instead of illuminating the text's ideology of female speech, it imposes upon the play an interpretation of Isabella's behaviour that contradicts everything that the text tells us about the silence of women up to that point.

As I hope to demonstrate, the first four acts of the play code Isabella's silence as obedience and submission while her formidable resistance is always embodied by speech. It is true, as Marilyn L. Williamson points out, that "we have other examples in Iago and Hieronimo, where silence after eloquence may signify not acquiescence, but defiance of an urgent authority".

However, both of those characters are male, while the

resistant female character in Othello, Iago's wife Emilia, expresses her refusal to be governed with impassioned words. At the end of the play, in response to her husband's command, "hold your peace!" Emilia cries,

I peace?
No, I will speak as liberal as the north.
Let heaven and men and devils, let them all,
All, all, cry shame against me, yet I'll speak.
(5.2.226-29)

A production of *Measure for Measure* certainly may, as critic Barbara J. Baines argues, elect to assume that Isabella "is not silenced but, instead, chooses silence as a form of resistance to the patriarchal authority"; but the text provides no basis for resolving the ambiguity of the moment in that particular fashion. Like Isabella herself pondering the privileges of the votarists of Saint Clare, I find myself "wishing a more strict restraint" upon theatrical license to import a feminist ideology into performance instead of responding, in a feminist way, to the ideology of female speech that the text itself presents.

At the beginning of the play, Isabella occupies the position of a novice poised to enter the sisterhood of Saint Clare, a religious order which severely restricts the speech of its members. As the nun Francisca tells Isabella,

When you have vow'd, you must not speak with men
But in the presence of the prioress;
Then, if you speak, you must not show your face;
Or if you show your face, you must not speak.

Because these limitations apply only when a sister speaks with men, we may assume that they are designed to prevent the arousal of male sexual desire, which presumably occurs when women speak and display their beauty at the same time. As Baines observes, "The law of the convent thus anticipates the danger to chastity inherent in man's gaze and in women's speech that will become apparent when Isabella and Angelo meet". Indeed, Angelo's first soliloquy after meeting Isabella plainly demonstrates that his sudden passion is excited by the combination of her voice and radiance:

What, do I love her,
That I desire to hear her speak again?
And feast upon her eyes? (2.2.177-79).

However, as Angelo's first aside during his confrontation with Isabella also makes clear, her speech alone is a powerful incitement: "She speaks, and 'tis such sense / That my sense breeds with it" (2.2.142-43). In fact, when Claudio asks Lucio to send his sister to plead with Angelo, he characterizes Isabella's beauty itself as a form of speech:

For in her youth
There is a prone and speechless dialect
Such as move men; beside, she hath prosperous art
When she will play with reason and discourse,
And well she can persuade. (1.2.172-76)

According to Claudio, Isabella possesses the ability to "move men" with her "prone and speechless dialect," a submissive silence that metaphorically speaks as eloquently as her verbal skill to "play with reason and discourse." The difference between the two is that Isabella's rhetorical "art" is persuasive: she can lead men to believe what she wants them to believe.

The effect of her "prone and speechless dialect," however, is out of her control; it moves men to passion based solely on their reading of her silent and passive figure. Thus, from a male point of view, the "speech" of female beauty alone is manageable because it is submissive and subject to interpretation.

However, if a woman speaks aloud, her voice can be disturbing to men because it commands the power to arouse male desire and yet frustrate its fulfillment. For example, once Isabella's manner of speaking incites Angelo's lust, he attempts to gain the object of his desire by blackmailing her into trading her virginity for her brother's life, but Isabella refuses him with a vehement speech:

I will proclaim thee, Angelo, look for't.
Sign me a present pardon for my brother,
Or with an outstretched throat I'll tell the world aloud
What man thou art. (2.4.150-53)

Not only does Isabella's resistance take the form of a vocal reply, but her speech itself also contains a threat to use her most effective weapon against men, her "outstretched throat," to damage Angelo's reputation. Later, after Angelo thinks he has slept with Isabella, he betrays a residual anxiety over the danger to his honour posed by Isabella's voice when he exclaims,

But that her tender shame
Will not proclaim against her maiden loss,
How might she tongue me! (4.4.21-23)

From the moment of Isabella's refusal of Angelo's demand, the text casts her into the new subject position of a shrew, a woman who scolds and vocally intimidates the men around her. This aspect of her portrayal reaches its apex in her exchange with Claudio in prison, where she harshly condemns his desire to live at the expense of her chastity:

Take my defiance,
Die, perish! Might but my bending down
Reprieve thee from thy fate, it should proceed.
I'll pray a thousand prayers for thy death;
No word to save thee. (3.1.142-46)

Again, as she did with Angelo, Isabella verbally denies a man's attempt to barter away her virginity and threatens to use her own words to launch a counterattack against him. At this midpoint in the play, Isabella has metamorphosed from a novice longing for the convent's strict restraints on speech to the unbridled scolding of a shrew; in order to achieve closure, the text strives to reverse this process and bring the voice of the woman back under authoritative control. At this moment, the text brings forward the disguised Duke to take charge of Isabella's speech through his plan to remedy her situation with a bed-trick. He advises her,

Go you to Angelo; answer his requiring with a plausible obedience; agree with his demands to the point. Only refer yourself to this advantage: first, that your stay with him may not be long; that the place may have all shadow and silence in it; and the time answer to convenience. (3.1.243-49)

Under the Duke's guidance, Isabella must adopt an

obedient voice and agree to comply with Angelo's demands under the cover of silence. Of course, the Duke intends Mariana to take Isabella's place in Angelo's bed, but the success of the plot depends upon Isabella's willingness to give up her vituperative speech and say whatever the Duke directs her to say. When the bed-trick fails to save Claudio, however, the Duke must make further use of Isabella's voice by having her accuse Angelo publicly of violating her virtue.

"To speak so indirectly I am loth," Isabella tells Mariana (4.6.1), but she makes the accusation nonetheless. As Marcia Riefer points out, "Whatever autonomy Isabella possessed in the beginning of the play...disintegrates once she agrees to serve in the Duke's plan. As soon as this 'friar' takes over, Isabella becomes an actress whose words are no longer her own". The Duke's revised scheme also involves Mariana, who appears masked in the final scene to make her own accusation against Angelo. When she first steps forward, the following dialogue ensues:

Duke. First, let her show her face, and after, speak.
Mariana. Pardon, my lord; I will not show my face
Until my husband bid me. (5.1.170-72)

Mariana's refusal to show her face and then speak evokes the law of the convent in the context of marriage, with the husband substituting for the prioress as the authority who allows exceptions to the general rules governing conversation between the sexes.

This exchange is crucial because it establishes marriage as an institution, like the nunnery, that limits female speech, but places the ultimate control of that speech in male hands. Therefore, when the Duke asks Isabella to marry him, he offers her a lifestyle with the same type of "strict restraint" on conversation as the cloistered existence she wished to adopt.

Her silence in response, isolated from the rest of the play, could conceivably indicate a refusal, but elsewhere in the text, Isabella's resistance is always characterized by virulent speech; likewise, her silence is associated with that "prone and speechless dialect" that implies obedience and submission to the will of a man.

I believe the text does not allow Isabella a verbal reaction, even though the Duke asks for one, because her silence in and of itself embodies her acceptance of the proposal and the constraints on female speech that marriage requires. The play concludes with the Duke's reiteration of his marriage offer, which makes clear that Isabella is expected merely to listen passively to his proposition:

Dear Isabel,
I have a motion much imports your good;
Whereto if you'll a willing ear incline,
What's mine is yours, and what is yours is mine.
(5.1.531-34)

No longer encouraged to "say" she will be his, Isabella is now simply expected to "incline" her "willing ear," which allows the Duke, and the audience, to impose upon her silent figure the affirmative answer he desires.

In Sinfield's terms, Isabella's silence reveals the text's ideological project, which is to bring the unruly voice of the main female character under masculine control within the context of marriage. However, I find that I must disagree with Sinfield's contention that this silence is required to render unobtrusive a sudden, implausible shift from one conventional female role to another.

In this case, Isabella's silence serves as the psychological bridge between her original position as a strictly restrained novice and her new, but commensurate social status as an obedient wife. Although one way to make a feminist statement with the play in the theater is to use stage business to refashion her acquiescence into a refusal to bow to male control, this strategy runs counter to the complete text's presentation of the issue of female speech.

Instead, I would advocate that a feminist production should attempt to portray the text's ideology of female speech as clearly as possible while at the same time avoiding the validation of its assumptions, among them that it is "right" or "natural" that a woman's voice be governed by a man. Albeit this approach may preclude the achievement of traditional comic closure, few productions over the last fifty years have suggested that the marriages which conclude *Measure for Measure* happily resolve all the conflicts that the play dramatizes. As an alternative, a feminist production might explore the possibility of subverting the appeal of the text's ideology of gender relations in order to imply that other, more progressive conceptions of female speech are in fact preferable.

To conclude, I will provide a description of a projected staging of the finale of *Measure for Measure* designed to clarify the ideological significance of Isabella's silence while simultaneously encouraging an audience to react negatively to the values implied in her decision to turn control of her voice over to her future spouse.

The key to this enactment lies in the text's association of the limitations on female speech with facial coverings: the wimple worn by nuns to shield their countenances from men with whom they might converse, and the mask which Mariana refuses to remove before speaking to the Duke unless her husband bids her. These veils mark the point at which the female roles of religious votary and wife intersect, and they may therefore operate symbolically on the stage to elucidate Isabella's passage between these two social positions at the conclusion.

Although Isabella is "yet unsworn" at the beginning of the play and consequently not bound by the convent's speech restrictions, in this performance, her costume, the white habit of a novice, would include a wimple, whose application in the presence of men would be demonstrated to her by the nun Francisca when the law of the convent is first introduced in 1.3. During the rest of the play, while Isabella speaks to men, she would continue to wear the wimple open so that its reemployment to shield her face at the end of the play could easily be connected to its original purpose.

In addition, Mariana's facial covering for her final appearance would possess an identical design, in a colour other than white, to draw attention to the parallel yet distinct symbolic functions of both veils. Isabella's wimple would contribute to the staging of the final scene most prominently after the Duke interrupts Isabella and Claudio's reunion with his startling offer of marriage: "Give me your hand and say you will be mine. / He is my brother too."

Isabella's silence in response stems partly from her surprise at the unexpected nature of the proposal; not only has the Friar turned out to be her sovereign in disguise, but he has also asked her to forego, in favor of matrimony, the restrictive religious life to which she has intended to dedicate herself. Unable to react to this momentous request on such short notice, she turns away from the Duke and crosses downstage, prompting Vincentio's remark "but fitter time for that."

During the ensuing forty lines, while the Duke turns his attention to the pardoning of Angelo, Lucio, and the rest, the actress playing Isabella must pursue the interior work of weighing the Duke's proposal and coming to the realization that the limitations of married life for women match the strict restraints of the convent and are therefore acceptable to her. When the Duke finally approaches Isabella and makes his second proposal—"if you'll a willing ear incline, / What's mine is yours, and what is yours is mine"—she turns to him and, with deliberation, veils herself with the wimple, but does not speak.

For a moment, an audience may interpret her gesture as an indication that Isabella intends to return to the nunnery, but when she dutifully extends her hand to the Duke and drops to her knees, bowing her head in a posture of submission, viewers would be forced to re-read her initial veiling as part and parcel of her acceptance of the Duke's proposal. This compulsory reinterpretation of the symbolism of the veil would, I believe, associate Isabella's silence simultaneously with the restrictiveness of both marriage and the convent, thereby revealing the overlapping limitations on female speech imposed by both institutions.

Since no stage direction for a processional exit exists in the Folio, the play may conclude, after the Duke's final couplet, with a tableau dominated by the veiled and kneeling Isabella holding the hand of the upright Duke, which fades into a blackout.

Although, in this enactment, Isabella accepts the Duke's offer of marriage, this staging differs from similar past productions in that Isabella's decision is not emotionally validated by the performance.

Isabella's dutiful submissiveness, as well as her lack of obvious pleasure in acceptance, would, in my estimation, lead a modern audience to respond negatively to the ideology of the text, embodied in the implied assumption that marriage demands the resignation of a woman's freedom of speech to her husband's will.

In this way, the play can make a feminist statement in the theater, not by reshaping the text to fit a feminist ideology, but by portraying the ideology of the text, however distasteful to modern sensibilities, from a feminist perspective.

Chapter 5

Measure for Measure and Othello

It has been said that all Shakespeare's plays taken together form one long play. Something of the kind can be said of the collected work of any real artist. Not the smallest fascination of Ibsen is the unity of his work, the profound meaning in the relation of play to play. To write both *Brand* and *Peer Gynt* is not just twice the job of writing one of the two; it is to force the reader to read the plays as thesis and antithesis in an artist's effort at synthesis.

As Bentley moves here from Shakespeare to Ibsen, I wish to move from his conclusion back to Shakespeare. Studies of *Measure for Measure* over the past fifteen years have called attention to its kinship with numerous plays in the Shakespearean corpus. A quick citation survey of scholarship indicates attention is most frequently drawn to comparisons with the other so-called problem plays, *All's Well That Ends Well* and *Troilus and Cressida* and next with the two great tragedies, *King Lear* and *Hamlet*.

Five articles over this period link *Measure for Measure* in incidental ways with *Othello*, but somewhat surprisingly overlooked has been the fundamental thesis-antithesis bond between these two plays that makes their kinship an especially strong one. Much more than just sharing a trait or a source, the two constitute a consciously conceived paired study of the humanly generated processes of redemption and damnation.

Recognizing how *Measure for Measure* counterbalances *Othello* not only elucidates each through the intertextual discourse generated, but also raises a cautionary flag to much current opinion that, in emphasizing the dark vision of *Measure for Measure,* denies to the play an integrated and overall comic vision. Recognizing how it systematically counterpoints *Othello* provides one means for accentuating its comic conception in the broadest sense of an optimistic overall vision.

First, external circumstances of source and date invite us to think of *Measure for Measure* and *Othello* together. These are the only Shakespearean plays whose stories derive from Giraldi Cinthio's collection of novellae, *Hecatommithi* (1565). *Othello* is the first novel of the third day and *Measure for Measure*'s source, "Promos and Cassandra," is the fifth novel of the tenth day.

They are also the two plays Shakespeare wrote in 1604. The first mention of *Othello* is in a remnant manuscript of the revels records that indicate its performance on All Saints Day, November 1, 1604. The first mention of *Measure for Measure* is from the same remnant, citing its production eight weeks later on Saint Stephen's Day, December 26, 1604. Andrew Gurr notes of Shakespeare that, "he wrote one serious play and one light play a year, more or less, throughout his active writing career". Evidently, a dialectical, measure-for-measure way of thinking influences Shakespeare's compositional sequence of plays.

Looking at the texts themselves, consider some of the paralleling or contrasting circumstances and characteristics that would incline one to interpret the one play in light of the other. First instance: the issue of being passed over. In the opening scene of *Measure for Measure* Escalus is passed over for the position of deputy in a most explicit fashion. The Duke praises Escalus as peerless in his knowledge of government and then declares without explanation that he is taking leave of his duties and appointing Angelo as his deputy.

Escalus, in response to the Duke's request for his opinion on the choice, expresses approval—as he more or less must under the circumstances—but also shows at no subsequent time any hurt pride at not being chosen.

In the first scene of *Othello* Iago declares to Roderigo, to whom he seldom tells the truth, that he has no desire to further Othello's interests as in the case of this sudden elopement because, having been passed over by Othello for position of lieutenant, he feels bitter and desires to avenge his wounded pride. The shallowness of Iago's speciously proclaimed motive—did "great ones" of the city really petition Iago's candidacy to Othello?—is heightened by contrast with Escalus' benign acceptance when actually passed over. Second instance: interceding women. In *Measure for Measure* Isabella pleads with Angelo to rescind his sentence of death on Claudio. In *Othello* Desdemona pleads with Othello to rescind his sentence of demotion on Cassio.

The former action begins the destabilizing of Angelo, a step necessary for the restoration of order in Vienna. The latter commences the destabilizing of Othello and the ensuing tragedy. Third instance: reading one's nature in one's face. Pompey, drawing transparently upon his street-wise bag of tricks to free his client, Froth, from the charge of fornication, bids Escalus to look into Froth's face (2.1.147-156) and condemn him if he sees any harm in it.

While Pompey literally may be pointing out the lack of any signs of syphilis on Froth's face, this comic play upon the notion that one's guilt or innocence is written upon one's face is contrasted by the frightening scene in *Othello* where, desperate in his suspicions, Othello terrifies Desdemona by staring into her face to find some confirmation for his maddening doubts of her fidelity (4.2.25-26).

Fourth instance: actual and supposed procuress. Where Isabella quite literally serves as a procuress in the assignation of Angelo with Mariana (the supposed Isabella), Emilia is wrongly accused by Othello of being the same for Desdemona with Cassio.

Fifth instance: procuring called a mystery. When the executioner, Abhorson, complains that his mystery (that is, his profession) will be tainted by a bawd's being made his assistant, Pompey with disarming wit defends his former work as a legitimate profession by explaining how it too is a mystery (painting being part of the prostitute's trade).

The word *mystery* in this sense of profession occurs in *Othello* when Othello tells Emilia to practice her mystery, as bawd, and guard the door while, like a client to his whore, he has secret conference with Desdemona. Again a broadly humorous play of thought in *Measure for Measure* appears in *Othello* as a terrifying expression of a feverish, tormented mind, plagued with hellish imaginings. Both passages, it happens, occur around line 30 of the second scene of the fourth act of their respective plays.

These assorted specific echoes occur between plays whose overriding archetypal symbols are of redemption and damnation respectively. *Measure for Measure* culminates in a vision of heavenly judgment. The single scene of Act Five commences with trumpets sounding the return of the Duke, who at the gate of the City, with Friar Peter present, holds court where all have been summoned to present their petitions and hear his judgments.

By contrast to this vision of the heavenly city, Act 5 in *Othello* begins with the maimed Cassio and Roderigo howling into the darkness, heard but unassisted by passers-by in the night, first Othello and then Lodovico and Gratiano. Into this Bosch-like scene comes the light-bearer, Iago with a torch, to complete the stage emblem of hell.

It is easy to see *Othello* as a play in which Shakespeare is depicting the process of demonic possession where the envious, alienated soul infects his victims with lies and the habit of lying such that all bonds of trust, truth, and understanding are severed and everyone devolves to an Iago-like state of hellish isolation.

Reinforcing the scenic archetypes are the names. In *Measure for Measure* Angelo, Peter, Thomas, and others, as Roy Battenhouse has shown (1035-1036), signal a scriptural and providential ethos, with the comic devil Lucio exposed, and his power, residing in his self-promoted reputation of one who knows, defused. Lucio's lineage stems from the comic devils of the earlier providential Christian drama.

In *Othello*, Iago, by contrast, embodies the frightening power of the malicious Arch-Deceiver and his chief victims, Othello and Desdemona, have embedded within their names a foreshadowing of their dire fates.

These archetypes signal where matters rest at the ends of their plays. At the beginning of *Measure for Measure,* Vienna is a world in which "there is scarce truth enough alive to make societies secure" (3.2.239). By contrast the state of Venice in *Othello* is envisioned as civilization's finest expression of an ordered society. The visions proclaim, alternatively, that no society is so depraved that it might not be redeemed, and no society so refined that it might not be subverted.

The chief irony with which these two plays confront us is that at the root of the processes of both redemption and damnation is deception. Lying is a dominant motif in both plays, and distinguishing the motives and methods behind the lying in each play defines the subtle line between the restoration and disintegration of civil order.

Deception is chiefly associated with the Duke and Iago, though lying is a behaviour in which most of the main characters in both plays indulge. The archetypal models for deception are, for Iago, Satan, and, for the Duke, God. Jonas Barish notes that disguise lies at the very heart of the Christian solution to the fall and damnation:

There were *two* archetypal disguises, that of Satan as the serpent and that of God made flesh...and the latter, no less than the former, contained a significant element of deception. The second disguise, doubtless, was necessitated by the first. The incarnation came to reverse or mitigate the ill effect of the serpent.

Nevertheless, by turning disguise to holy purposes, it sanctified it; it accorded it the highest possible authorization, and this fact was reflected both in the mediaeval drama, with its representation of scriptural history as a contest of guile between Christ and Satan, and in such Renaissance motifs as the character of Duke Vincentio in *Measure for Measure,* using craft against craft for holy ends.

In observing that "the second disguise...was necessitated by the first," Barish rightly draws a key distinction that separates the two. Deception rooted in demonic disguise initiates falsehood to mislead and destroy innocence and truth; deception rooted in *imitatio dei* counterbalances existing deception with deception. Fallen humanity can no more look truth in the eye without being blinded than King Lear can listen and learn from the direct teachings of Cordelia and Kent in the opening of *King Lear*.

Good counsel must disguise itself in an antic persona, as Kent does, in order to function efficaciously in a fallen world. So too, the Duke, in choosing education over enforcement as the route to reforming Vienna, must assume a disguise, the fool's garb of a disenfranchised friar, as the means through which he can take the pulse of the state, speak freely with others, test, and discover.

Like Kent, but for different reasons, he cannot function truly in his own person. The deception to which the Duke's disguising action is a counter is the disabling lie that the Duke is a fornicator. If we assume that Lucio's easy slandering of the Duke as a fornicator has become commonplace gossip in Vienna, then the Duke, in his own person, has been deprived by this lie of moral authority and forced into other means of guidance.

Slander having made him appears morally less than he is, the Duke assumes a disguise as chaste Friar whereby the superficial deception restores a moral image consonant with the moral reality. As M. M. Mahood has neatly observed, "When the seeming truth of things is found to be a fiction, fiction may be the only way to the truth".

This "lie that is not a lie" constitutes the fundamental contrast with Iago who truly is not what he seems. Iago's outward appearance is no disguise of his literal self—Iago is Iago—but it belies completely the image of his soul. Honest Iago is not so. His deception is, thus, the exact inverse of the Duke's.

Finally, substitution lies at the centre of both the Duke's and Iago's method, though in the former case its end is liberating and spiritually bonding, while in the latter it is possessive and spiritually isolating. The Duke frees the mind of those whose lives he directly influences by casting them in different roles. The route to social reform rests in the education of the sensibilities, in the capacity to go outside of oneself and to see and experience life through the eyes of another, to acquire a measure of sympathy and selflessness that will discourage complacent judgment of another and will foster a recognition of those same faults in oneself for which one is prepared to judge another, thus coupling a generosity toward others with a willingness to amend one's own behaviour.

A person so balanced in nature will inspire admiration and imitation. To Jacque's invitation to sit and chide the world, Orlando replies, "I will chide no breather in the world, except myself against whom I know most faults" *(As You Like It*: 3.2.280-81).

It is to this state of mind that Duke Vincentio will lead the best models of the state, Angelo and Isabella, by the end of the play. Angelo, who initially is angry that the "law hath slept," suddenly finds himself substituting for the Duke and looking at the world through the eyes of one empowered to govern it.

As human nature collides with power, he learns what it is like to see the world from the perspective of an abuser of power; a fornicator, a liar, a coward, and a criminal facing the death penalty. Isabella, seizing willingly upon the Friar's bed-trick subterfuge, allows Mariana to substitute for her in Angelo's bed, and she in turn substitutes for Mariana in declaring publicly her shame at the hands of Angelo.

In the course of events, Isabella sees the world through the eyes of a procuress, a publicly avowed fornicatress, a conspirator against the state, a condemner, avenger, and forgiver. Substitution becomes the dominant motif in *Measure for Measure,* as Alexander Leggatt has elaborately delineated. Through it, Angelo and Isabella escape their self-imposed isolation and are schooled in humility and tolerance by finding themselves looking at the world through the roles of those they had most condemned.

In contrast to the Duke's scenarios, which lead the participants to expanded visions, Iago constructs repeatedly a carnal reading of all witnessed events, seeding the minds, in turn, of Brabantio, Roderigo, Cassio, and finally Othello. He offers not multiple points of view for each character but only one point of view for all characters, and that point of view is his own. As each believes himself to enjoy a special confidentiality with Iago, Iago, playing upon their trust, substitutes his way of thinking for theirs. Defining the motivation for all actions as selfish and beastly, Iago wrests from the minds of his victims belief in the spiritual upon which all civil order ultimately rests.

He, thus, comes between his victims and the ones with whom the victims had formerly been bound. With Othello he enacts a literal substitution by becoming *de facto* both Othello's lieutenant in place of Cassio and his bride in place of Desdemona (3.3.460-480).

In sum, the most singular distinction between the dynamics of reformative deception and degenerative deception lies in the factor of disguise. In Shakespeare, it is always only the good people who disguise. A play, in that it is a fiction, is a grand disguising, just as an actor in character is disguising, and literal disguising by characters within the fiction is a mirror of dramatic activity.

Such "deception" is at its root self-absenting. Imaginative play so conceived becomes a mutual exercise of discovery between the playwright, the actors, and the audience. The process is educational in the literal sense of persons being drawn out by mutual engagement in a fiction. The process is transactional, free will is not compromised, and disguise is the mediational factor at its centre.

Where deception is not self-absenting, but imposing, then it is a closed system, bent upon a predetermined objective and upon orchestrating the world to fit one's own will rather than attuning one's will to the rhythms of the world. Iago is a creature of self-projection, not imagination.

Disguise cannot be a tool in such a deceiver's chest, because the only eyes through which he can see the world are his own. The only fiction of which he is capable is feigning concern for others, a lie in service to self, conceived not to initiate a forum of mutual discovery but only to wrest into his own power by fraud persons more trusting and less depraved than he is.

Andrew Leggatt complains that *Measure for Measure* provides no picture of redemption at the end: "The defiance of Pompey and the final distribution of pardons make law enforcement look futile; there is no certainty that the city will ever be cleaned up".

However, if the Duke's reputation has been cleared by his unveiling by Lucio, and if the would-be saints, Angelo and Isabella, have been chastened, purified, and made more sympathetic by the fires of humiliation, then arguably the leadership for reformation in the state is now in full view for emulation, and the state's best examples of moral intent are clear.

This clarity of moral leadership, according to Erasmian humanist principles, is the way that society must ultimately be reformed. If example, not punitive enforcement, is the route to reform, then redemption lies in refinements of those most capable of moral leadership, like Spenser's Red Cross Knight. This change does occur in *Measure for Measure,* and it makes all the difference.

Chapter 6

Narcissism and Metadrama in Richard II

Over the last thirty years, Shakespeare criticism has demonstrated a growing awareness of the self-reflexive or metadramatic elements in his works. Lionel Abel's 1963 study, *Metatheatre: A New View of Dramatic Form,* provided perhaps the first significant analysis of the ways in which Shakespeare thematizes theatricality, in the broadest sense of the term, in his tragedies, comedies, and histories.

In his discussion of *Hamlet,* he makes the observation—perhaps a bit commonplace and obvious to us thirty years later—that the famous "play within a play" is only the most blatant example of self-conscious technique found throughout the tragedy: once we begin to look closely, we notice that nearly "every important character acts at some moment like a playwright, employing a playwright's consciousness of drama to impose a certain posture or attitude on another".

Elsewhere in his book, Abel argues implicitly that Shakespeare, though he often used metadramatic techniques more in the interest of developing character than creating "an event," the way later playwrights do, nevertheless composed plays which "are theatre pieces about life seen as already theatricalized". In making such statements, Abel laid the groundwork for a number of subsequent studies, from Thomas F. Van Laan's *Role-Playing in Shakespeare,* which appeared in 1978, to Judd D. Hubert's more recent *Metatheatre: The Example of Shakespeare.*

Critics following Abel's lead have been especially

interested in Shakespeare's second tetralogy. James L. Calderwood, for instance, reads the Henriad as Shakespeare's reflection not only on a period of British history during which political authority, political "truth," gave way to corruption and falseness, but also on the potentially disturbing artificiality of his own work.

Calderwood identifies the "fall of speech" as the main metadramatic theme in the Henriad, and outlines a progression in which words and their meanings are severed by political corruption and then gradually reunited.

Bolingbroke, by usurping Richard's throne, in effect replaces a unified sacramental language, one in which "words have an inalienable right to their meanings," with "a utilitarian one in which the relation between words and things is arbitrary, unsure, ephemeral".

Henry's son, Hal, eventually achieves "an earned kingship," thus restoring language for his people. Equally important, perhaps, is the process Shakespeare himself goes through, for in making "political affairs...metaphors for art," he ultimately establishes the legitimacy of his own dramatic medium.

Calderwood's reading of the *Henriad* as an allegory of Shakespeare's own development as a self-conscious artificer is intriguing, but of more interest to me here is his point that these plays dramatize a world in which signifiers and their signifieds are separated from one another. At the centre of this world stands Richard II, perhaps the most flamboyantly theatrical, the most self-consciously lyrical, of all of Shakespeare's characters prior to Hamlet.

Richard personifies the disjunction between signs and meanings about which Calderwood writes; he is a man who, in losing his kingly name (signifier), subsequently loses the most basic vestiges of his identity (signified). Yet though he recognizes the disjunction, the "fall of language," he continually tries to use discourse—and not just any discourse, but discourse at its most creative, its most metaphorical—to maintain an identity, a sense of self.

Maintaining that sense is of paramount importance to

Richard, whom more than one critic has called narcissistic because of self-absorption, his fanciful interiority. Marvin Glasser, for instance, has commented that "much of what Richard says sounds like a soliloquy because of his failure to relate to otherness," to the exterior world.

His "vision, while consciously self-dramatic, conflates within and without, self and other". It is Richard's narcissism with which I am primarily concerned in this essay, for it, especially when considered in light of some of Jacques Lacan's theories, helps to illuminate the effect of Shakespeare's metadrama in this play.

Like the narcissistic Lacanian subject, Richard paradoxically needs others, even as he shuns them in favor of his own interior reality; he depends upon others to provide him a "mirror" in which to see his own complete image perpetually.

In theatrical terms, he must have an "audience" at all times for his "role" to mean anything. And like Lacan's subject, he is forever deluded; he is spoken by a discourse which he mistakenly believes he controls; he is just another signifier in a chain of signifiers for which there are no corresponding signifieds. Though Richard apparently recognizes his situation in the end, he nonetheless attempts to use language to deny his own lack of identity.

Starting in Act 1, Shakespeare sets Richard up as an actor who loves to put on a show. Yet the king's penchant for theatricality may be overlooked in the first scene, in which Richard hears the accusations of Bolingbroke and Mowbray against one another, because the ceremonial nature of that scene makes actors of *all* the characters. As Leonard F. Dean astutely observes, although Shakespeare deviates from his sources in much of *Richard II*, he evidently makes a "practical decision" to follow Edward Hall's account of the Bolingbroke-Mowbray incident, and to open this play and the entire Henriad with it.

Beginning with this scene, in which "the real feelings of Richard, Bolingbroke, Mowbray, and even Gaunt are necessarily masked to a large extent by the calculated neutrality of the ceremony," allows Shakespeare to introduce immediately the "theatricalism of politics" and the extended analogy of "state" and "stage". Thus metadrama is used to meditate on the general nature of political affairs. But in 1.3, when Richard dramatically interrupts Bolingbroke and Mowbray's joust by "throw[ing] his warder down" and proclaiming, "Let them lay by their helmets and their spears", Shakepeare begins to focus on Richard's own individual theatricality.

As most critics have noticed, the soon-to-be-deposed ruler's narcissism, which results in his flair for drama, becomes more pronounced with his return from Ireland. Upon learning that he no longer has any forces with which to fight, Richard gives several extended speeches which, as Glasser remarks, sound more like soliloquies than dialogues with those around him. He seems to want to "wallow" in his misery:

No matter where, of comfort no man speak;
Let's talk of graves, of worms and epitaphs,
Make dust our paper and with rainy eyes
Write sorrow on the bosom of the earth.
(3.2.144-147)

The writing metaphor is significant here, because it suggests Richard's reluctance to give up his verbal powers as king even as he recognizes that they are diminishing. Even more important is the way in which Richard uses others to stage what is essentially a private performance directed at himself and by himself.

"Let's talk," he says, and then ruminates until Carlisle protests, "My lord, wise men ne'er sit and wail their woes, / But presently prevent the ways to wail" (3.2.178-79). It is as if Richard uses his subjects as looking glasses in which he can see himself perform.

This, essentially, is the role Richard's subject play throughout. Although the king complains that "He does me double wrong / That wounds me with the flatteries of his tongue" (3.2.215-16), Shakespeare makes it clear that he has survived previously on such flattery. Even earlier in the crucial second scene of Act 3, Richard needs Carlisle to tell him "That power that made you King / Hath power to keep you King in spite of all", and the leader follows with a monologue whose self-assurance inspires in us both anger and pity toward him:

Not all the water in the rough rude sea
Can wash the balm off from an anointed king.
The breath of worldly men cannot depose
The deputy elected by the Lord.
For every man shrewd steel against our golden crown,
God for His Richard hath in heavenly pay
A glorious angel. Then, if angels fight,
Weak men must fall, for Heaven still guards the right.
(3.2.55-62)

Richard's performance here is only as good as his audience's reaction, however, and though there are no lines from Carlisle, Aumerle, or any of the soldiers present, in production, some directors have these characters express their agreement through physical gestures. What we come to realize about Richard is that his royal power, and even his imagination, ultimately stem from sources external to him.

The external nature of Richard's character, of his psychology, marks him as an excellent example of Lacan's conception of the narcissist. For in Lacanian thought, the notion that any person has a distinctive psychic substance, a complete, internally-determined meaning, is pure illusion. We are defined by other people and their discourses; our unconscious resides not within us, but outside of us.

This is partly what Lacan means when he makes the famous statement, "the unconscious is the discourse of the Other". The narcissist is decidedly ambivalent toward others, but he nevertheless needs others for any conception of himself. This process of rejection and identification begins in the so-called "mirror stage," when a child first recognizes itself in the reflection of a mirror or, perhaps more often, in the image of another person.

Throughout our lives, we feel bound to and alienated from ourselves and others. The relationship which the mirror stage sets up is one of signification, as Terry Eagleton lucidly explains:

We can think of a small child contemplating itself before the mirror as a kind of 'signifier'—something capable of bestowing meaning—and of the image it sees in the mirror as a kind of 'signified.' The image the child sees is somehow the 'meaning' of itself.

Though this process is modified as we grow older and are introduced into language, it basically defines how we deal with reality, according to Lacan; he notes in the opening chapter of *Ecrits* that this "mirror stage" introduces "the dialectic that will henceforth link the I to socially elaborated situations". And for the narcissist, the search for "meaning" is undertaken with an even greater sense of desperation than what the "average" person exhibits.

Richard II is, of course, precisely a narcissist in this mold. He puts on very theatrical performances, in which language is an integral prop, to give himself a definite position in reality, to perceive himself (through others) as a Gestalt. Why would a king, we might wonder, need to do so? If anyone is secure about his identity, it ought to be a ruler.

Yet Richard's world is an increasingly ambiguous one, as Shakespeare (and astute critics such as Calderwood) goes to great pains to show: with the passing of medieval absolutism and the divine right of kings, appearances and realities, signifiers and their signifieds, do not harmonize.

Despite Richard's several speeches confirming his faith in the old, unified order, he seems to know, at some level, the harsh reality of his world. This might explain why he "take[s] his correction" from Bolingbroke so "mildly," as the queen puts it.

Even if Richard has some understanding of his situation, his conscious recognition of it still comes only gradually. He begins to see that he is simply an empty signifier, dependent on other empty signifiers for any sense of identity at all, as early as the scene in Wales. Yet perhaps it is in 4.1, the deposition scene, that Richard becomes most fully aware of his plight. There, he performs with all of his earlier fervor but receives an entirely different response, and he acknowledges the changed situation when he says, "God save the King!

Will no man say amen? / Am I both priest and clerk? Well then, amen". The struggle which Shakespeare presents in this scene is an intense one, as Richard summons all of his lyrical and dramatic powers to stave off loss of identity. He tries to turn his deposition, his very loss of self, into theatre, and thus, into a role.

"Now mark me how I will undo myself," he says to Bolingbroke and his former subjects. But there is more than theatre in the question he asks after he has ceremonially "undone" his kingship: "What more remains?"

The audience recognizes, with Shakespeare, and with Richard himself to some degree, that all along this king has been, to use Thomas F. Van Laan's words,

> A series of gestures; either those belonging to his social office or, as now, those arising from his own dramatization of losing that office. And he has also been a series of responses by others, who—*like mirrors*—have let him see reflected by them the success of his performance. (123; emphasis mine)

This realization is heightened when Richard asks Bolingbroke for a mirror. When it is brought to him, he says, "Give me the glass, and therein will I read", then proceeds to break it into "a hundred shivers". Paradoxically, the act of shattering the mirror makes clear the "truth" about Richard's subjectivity: that he has never been an autonomous individual, a self-determining *Gestalt*.

His sense of self has been dependent on others; his little dramas have only been meaningful insofar as others have witnessed them. Within a Lacanian paradigm, Bolingbroke's typically terse response to Richard's histrionics here—he plays upon the former king's lament that "sorrow hath destroyed my face" by commenting that "The shadow of your sorrow hath destroyed / The shadow of your face" (4.1.291-94)—becomes intriguingly suggestive.

The "shadow" of Richard's sorrow in this scene, or, in a more precise modern translation, the *reflection* of it, is Henry himself: he is the mirror, the other, who defines Richard from an external position, who dismantles from the outside Richard's identity as king (metaphorically represented in the broken "shadow" of his face, the image in the shattered looking glass), despite the narcissist's subsequent statement that "my grief lies all within" (4.11.295). Again, it is Richard's audience, not himself, which bestows upon him an identity—an identity that can be taken away.

The newly deposed king's subsequent stay in solitude in Pomfret castle confirms this for him. Although his former groom arrives in 5.5 to offer a last bit of flattery, to call up in Richard's mind one more time his image as king by saying that he had relished the opportunity "to look upon my sometimes royal master's face", existence in solitude is disquieting for him.

Prior to his conversation with the groom and his own death at the hands of Exton, Richard tries to perform once again, and though he knows that in his cell there "is not a creature by myself," he resolves to "hammer...out" a play. Yet in the end, he knows he needs another for his own narcissism to be satisfying. In this production, he plays "in one person many people," but is "contented" with none of them (5.5.31-32).

One wonders if Shakespeare, who also, in a sense, played "in one person many people," was satisfied with his drama. He should have been. *Richard II* remains an important play in the Bard's canon because it illuminates the complex relationship between the individual and social institutions, between the private and the public, between self and other. Viewed from a Lacanian perspective, Richard's situation is our situation.

As a king, he believes he is a stable signifier pregnant with meaning, when he is merely a variable sign with no ultimate substance of his own; he thinks he speaks the discourse of governmental, religious, and social authority when he is actually spoken by that discourse. Similarly, we conceive of ourselves "as free, unified, autonomous, self-generating individuals," though we are, according to Louis Althusser's reading of Lacan—once again summarized and clarified by Eagleton—merely "the 'decentered' function of several social determinants" (172-73).

If one follows such reasoning, one begins to see oneself as an actor, much like Richard (though he perhaps achieves, in the end, a modicum of awareness about his situation which Lacan would probably not afford to most).

The goal is to establish a role, an identity, in the presence of others, in the presence of *the* Other, the entire set of institutions which make up our culture.

This goal is probably not the effect Shakespeare intended when he wrote his metadramatic history. But if *Richard II* conveys ideas which can be considered relevant some four hundred years later, he probably would not have minded.

Chapter 7

Eternal Form and Timely Variations

Arguing that Renaissance poetics are heavily grounded in Plato's *Timaeus*, S. K. Heninger contends that the essence of a poem lies in its structure. The very arrangement of the parts constitutes the "form" (taken in the Platonic sense) or the "idea" (in the Greek sense) of the work.

The parts taken in isolation may be viewed as a particular manifestation of that form, only once-removed from the ultimate reality. And the narrative of the poem recounts the temporal events of our existence, always contained within the ever-present, although perhaps unapparent, dimension of pure and eternal forms.

The analogy between poetic form and perceived and ideal realities is pertinent in that it also informs the idea of poem as microcosm. Many poems of this period, it is widely believed, exhibit this twofold conception of structure as "form" and narrative as the extension of that form because they were intended to provide a miniature representation of universal or cosmological organization.

The reading I am proposing here, both relies upon and challenges this understanding of poetic form. While it is true that form can and does represent the static, atemporal existence of a poem, I argue that form can also be interpreted temporally, as narrative.

More specifically, in Renaissance poetry that exhibits stanzaic variation, the reader is challenged to consider the development of each stanza and compare it to the stanzas that precede and succeed it. Stanzaic variation poses the questions, where does a given form come from and where is it going? It is with this line of inquiry that I will attempt to explain some of the perplexing variations in Edmund Spenser's *Epithalamion*.

On the subject of *Epithalamion*, all current structural studies must begin with A. K. Hieatt's *Short Time's Endless Monument*, a testament to the significance of form in Spenser's poetics. Hieatt's recognition of the poem's construction of 365 long lines, corresponding to the days of the year; 68 short lines, representing a sum of the 52 weeks, 12 months, and 4 seasons of the annual cycle; and 24 stanzas, corresponding to the diurnal and sidereal hours, is about as close to an undebatable argument as one could hope to make in the discipline of literary criticism.

But the conjunction of the formal demands that Hieatt identifies, namely the 365 long lines and 24 stanzas, presents an insurmountable problem: 365 lines will not divide equally into 24 stanzas. The poet must vary the stanza patterns in order to fulfill his calendrical scheme. Yet the needs dictated by this structural consideration alone fail to account for the degree of variation that we find in *Epithalamion* since Spenser could have achieved this line count with fewer interruptions of standard form.

In no way do I presume to offer a comprehensive solution to this difficulty. Some of the variations are perplexing. Nonetheless, I intend to show that by dividing the poem into two groups of stanzas, one representing static and the other dynamic uses of form (that is to say, one group of atemporal and one of temporal stanzas), we can go further than previous attempts in explaining the stanzaic arrangement of *Epithalamion*.

It will be best to begin by considering the 19-line stanza which I take as the standard form of *Epithalamion* simply because it is the most frequently used structure, appearing 12 times in the poem, and because Spenser distributed this verse form relatively evenly about the poem. The form of that stanza is A B A B C c D E D E e F G G F H h R R (upper case letters refer to long lines, lower case to short lines, and "R" designates the refrain). If we attend to the long line distribution of the poem (and I'm using Hieatt's distinction here of pentameter as constituting a long line), there is a further sense of regularity. Exclusive of the refrain the long lines are symmetrically arranged, weighing the first grouping evenly with the third in a 5-4-5 organization. This is a balance that Spenser does not maintain throughout.

Having considered the regularity with which this stanza appears in the poem and the internal balance that it exhibits, I am led to consider this 19-line stanza as constituting a form in its traditional unchanging sense. These 12 stanzas offer a fixed presence in the poem, while the remaining 12 stanzas do not exhibit this regularity.

The first of the variant patterns to appear in the poem, and which occurs 5 times in the first 6 stanzas, is an 18-line pattern which closely approximates the standard stanza. That stanza form and its relation to the standard stanza can be expressed as follows:

Standard: A B A B C c D E D E e F G G F H h R R
1st 18-line: A B A B C c D C D E e F G G F *f* R R

In this organization, the absence of one line from the standard stanza is apparent in the third gathering of long lines, thus yielding a 5-4-4 pattern and effectively foregoing the symmetrical balance evident in the 19-line counterpart. All things considered, however, it is hard to imagine a less conspicuous way to adjust the rhyme scheme to accommodate for the omission of one line.

Not only has Spenser maintained the envelope rhyme in lines 12-15 of the stanza, but he manages to keep the subsequent couplet as well. In effect, the F rhyme in the 15th line serves double duty in order to make the necessary adjustment in stanza length as inconspicuous as possible.

In fact, when we consider the overall structure of line totals that the poet was working toward and the logistical problems that the poem's overall agenda poses, we can recognize this development as constituting one of the slightest variations conceivable. If the poem consisted of these two stanza patterns exclusively—something that Spenser could have done with only an intermittent substitution of a long for a short line and still arrived at his intended totals—we could explain all the stanzaic deviations in terms of the scheme that Hieatt identifies.

In the tenth stanza, however, the modulations become inexplicable according to Hieatt's scheme. At this point, Spenser introduces a revised 18-line pattern which compensates for its shortage of a line in a different way.

Standard: A B A B C c D E D E e F G G F H h R R
2nd 18-line: A B A B C c D C D *d* E F F E G g R R

This pattern is repeated in stanzas 16 and 21. In effect, the original 18-line pattern, which last appears in stanza 6, is replaced with this new arrangement. Spenser has again made the one-line shortening as inconspicuous as possible. Here as before, one rhyme in the 18-line pattern fulfills the role of two rhymes in the standard stanza arrangement, but now this compensation takes place in the 10th rather than the 15th position.

Before moving on to subsequent patterns, it is perhaps worthwhile to take inventory. The three stanza patterns discussed thus far, the standard 19-line pattern and the two 18-line variations, constitute the only repeated verse forms in the poem and account for 20 of the 24 stanzas. The remaining four are all unique and as such would seem to draw particular attention to themselves.

Stanza 11 is a 19-line variation which deviates from the standard form because of a minute difference in rhyme scheme. This stanza alone interrupts the narrative development of form by offering a variation on the standard stanza that does not resemble the second 18-line variation that occupies this section of the poem, and, further, it is the only variation not necessitated by a change in line count. The only change is a substitution of an interweaving rhyme pattern for an envelope pattern in lines 12-15 of the 19-line stanza.

Standard: A B A B C c D E D E e F G G F H h R R
Stanza 11: A B A B C c D E D E e F G F G H h R R

What this change facilitates is a symmetrical structure (exclusive of the two final couplets) in which lines 7-9 (D E D) are imbedded within two couplets (C c and E e) and two interweaving quatrains (A B A B and F G F G). Significantly, the content of these imbedded lines reinforce this arrangement because they elaborate on the bride's "inward beauty":

There dwells sweet loue and constant chastity,
Vispoted fayth and comely womanhed,
Regard of honour and mild modesty... (191-3)

The importance of the bride's virtuous character is clear with a poet like Spenser who devoted an entire book of *The Faerie Queene* to chastity. But within the epithalamic tradition, Spenser is unable to give this subject the central position in the poem, because the arrival at the altar and nuptial ceremony must occupy the middle of this construction (Fowler 104).

In lieu of placing a catalogue in the elevated locus and in the process disrupting convention, the poet creates a central position in the 11t^{h} stanza and effectively enthrones her chastity in a central dwelling of its own. Unlike stanza 11, the second unique stanza, stanza 15, returns us to the pattern found in the second 18-line variation, despite its being a 17-line form. In order to see this correspondence, we need only compare stanza 15 to both the standard form and the second 18-line variation.

Standard: A B A B C c D E D E e F G G F H h R R
2nd 18-line:A B A B C c D C D *d* E F F E G g R R
Stanza 15: A B A B C c D C D *E* F F E G g R R

That the shortage has been adjusted for in the 10th line certainly aligns the 15th stanza with the 10th, 16th, and 21st, thus maintaining a kind of consistency through correlative developments. The unexpected brevity of this stanza can be partly explained by its content which expresses the eager groom's yearning for darkness to descend; here, the poet anxiously cuts short the verse, seeing that the 24 stanzas correspond to the hours of the day, in hopes of speeding along the progress toward nightfall.

No new stanza patterns appear until the 23rd stanza. Here we find an 18-line stanza which has only two short lines and which employs an unprecedented rhyme in the 16th position, thus inviting comparison with the first 18-line variation.

Standard: A B A B C c D E D E e F G G F H h R R
1st 18-line: A B A B C c D C D E e F G G F *f* R R
Stanza 23: A B A B C c D C D E e F G G F *E* R R

It appears that this stanza represents a near return to the 18-line stanza that opened the poem. For the first time since the 6th stanza, there is a gesture toward the long-line distribution of the first 18-line stanzas in the exhibition of a 5-4 grouping (the second 18-line variation having a 5-3-5 arrangement). In order for the return to be complete, however, the 16th line would have to be short, thus completing the 5-4-4 arrangement.

Not only is the 16th line of this pattern pentameter, but the rhyme differs from that of the original 18-line pattern as well (the original pattern repeating the F term in that position). Yet it is significant that in adapting the 19-line standard form to the 18-line variant that opens the poem, Spenser uses this, the 16th line, to account for the necessary change in pattern.

So if we consider Spenser's stanza patterns in terms of where they deviate from the predominant form (and it is this feature that allows us to see the affinity between stanza 15 and the second 18-line variation), the final full stanza of the poem belongs to the same category as the first 18-line stanza.

Further, it would seem that Spenser draws particular attention to the 16th line of this stanza because it constitutes an anomaly within the poem on other counts as well. First of all, it ends in a near rhyme—"this" following "possesse" and "happiness" —and acoustic relationships of this nature are rare in *Epithalamion*.

But this term is even more conspicuous in that its position makes the rhyme a spatial, as well as aural, stretch because it extends the rhyme over four intervening lines. Such an arrangement is both unprecedented in this poem and uncharacteristic of Spenser's poetics in general. The cumulative effect of this variance is to draw attention to the 16th line and in doing so to emphasize the relationship between stanza 23 and the first 18-line verse form.

This incomplete gesture to a return to the beginning of the poem corroborates with the views of several critics, Alastair

Fowler among them, who argue for a cyclical organization in *Epithalamion*. And it is fitting that the structure of the poem should begin to make its return to its own formalistic origin in the 23rd stanza, the stanza in which the poet offers his prayer for healthy progeny.

Stanza 23, therefore, represents regeneration in both structure and content. The suggestion in this passage is that the children will perpetuate this cycle as they move from morning to a peak at midday to the creation of their own progeny during the decline of their day. The calendrical cycles repeat for a new generation as Spenser employs a verse form that suggests a new beginning of an endless cycle near the end of his poem.

The final unique stanza is the 24th, the *tornata* or closing *envoy*. Consisting as it does of only seven lines (employing an A B A B a C C rhyme scheme), it has a number of distinct characteristics, but the one most worthy of notice in the context of piecing together a narrative of formal development is a formal similarity that links this stanza to the previous stanza. As noted, the verse form of stanza 23 represents a move toward the opening 18-line stanza pattern. The only line which inhibits this correlation is the 16th line, which conflicts with the pattern of the first stanza in both rhyme and meter.

Stanza 24 offers an apparent corrective to this incongruence in that its antepenultimate line (corresponding to line 16 of the 18-line stanzas) is not only a short line but a tetrameter line, and the only other tetrameter verse in *Epithalamion* is the 16th line of the first stanza (the other short lines being trimeter).

Therefore, not only does the final stanza offer a formal completion of the return to the 18-line stanza that begins the poem, but in terms of the antepenultimate line, stanzas 24 and 1 bear a stronger metrical resemblance to each other than they do to any other stanza in the poem. Perhaps we could even view the first and last stanzas as providing a smooth transition between the antepenultimate lines of stanza 23 (a pentameter line) and stanza 2 (a trimeter line).

This possibility finds further support in the content of the corresponding line in the final stanza which reads "But promist both to recompense". Such being the case, the variant stanzas have come full circle and begin the same progression of development again.

The close relationship between the first and last stanzas has been well documented by Max Wickert who finds the segments to be the poem's "most obvious match". Among other observations, he supports his claim with the acoustic similarities present in the rhymes of "ornaments / accidents / recompense" and "ornament / moniment" in the last stanza and "lament / dreriment" in the first stanza. Such echoes effectively draw the end of the poem back to the beginning, thus acoustically reinforcing the cyclical form of Spenser's poem.

Thus far, then, we have separated Spenser's *Epithalamion* into two groups of stanzas, each accounting for 12 of the poem's 24 stanzas. Those groups are, first, the unchanging forms that we have become accustomed to in Renaissance poetry, and, second, what we might call the mutable stanzas which fluctuate through the course of the poem. These latter stanzas begin with one form, then deviate from that form, and finally gesture toward a return to the original form.

Having treated each of the verse forms in some detail, we should briefly turn our attention to the arrangement of these stanzas in the context of the whole poem. At least one other study has already suggested a symmetrical organization in the stanzas of Spenser's poem. Germaine Warkentin pursues this division of stanzas to some degree but merely categorizes the stanzas by line count, with no attention to variant patterns.

What she proposes, with some difficulty, is a symmetry similar to Wicker's in that she centers her proposed arrangement upon stanzas 12 and 13. If, however, we pay closer attention to actual verse form and distinguish between constant and variable forms, a different and less anomalous symmetry appears in *Epithalamion*:

Stanza:	1	2	3	4	5	6	7	8	9	10	11	
Form:	V_1	V_1	S	V_1	V_1	V_1	S	S	S	V_2	V_3	
Stanza:	12	13	24	23	22	21	20	19	18	17	16	15	14
Form:	S	S	V_6	V_5	S	V_2	S	S	S	S	V_2	S	V_4

S = ABABCcDEDEeFGGFHhRR
V_4 = ABABCcDCDEFFEGgRR
V_1 = ABABCcDCDEeFGGFfRR
V_5 = ABABCcDCDEdFGGFERR
V_2 = ABABCcDCDdEFFEGgRR
V_6 = ABABaCC
V_3 = ABABCcDEDEeFGFGHhRR

This arrangement still does not account for every stanza. If, however, Spenser intended (as it would appear by this symmetry) to centralize the 13th stanza, then he would have had either to exclude one of the stanzas at the perimeter of the construction or interrupt the symmetry within the organization as is the case in the above scheme.

If this arrangement is intended, then we must ask, why centralize stanza 13? Although it is true that most accounts of the poem's organization designate both stanzas 12 and 13 as the centre (and the 24-stanza structure clearly supports this view), stanza 12 merely focuses on the bride's approach to the altar and the actual marriage does not take place until the 13th, at which point the poet asks, "Why blush ye to give me your hand, / The pledge of all our band?"

Further, Spenser's arrangement of the standard verses corroborates this designation of the poem's centre. Of the 12 standard stanzas, it is the 6th that occupies this central position.

One implication of this position is that the ratio of part to whole among the standard stanzas as defined by the centre in this symmetrical arrangement is 12:6 or 2:1. As Heninger points out, in the Pythagorean tuning system, this ratio defines the diapason, a relationship of the universal harmony. That Spenser would employ musical ratios in a poem preoccupied with singing and that he would position his marriage at a point that suggests harmony are not surprising.

If, indeed, Spenser enacts an equal division of stanzas among those that are constant and those which vary, and if he intended a symmetrical arrangement around the 13th stanza with the constant stanzas occupying the centre (for obvious reasons), then all of the unmatched stanzas (5, 6 and 20) are unavoidable. As long as the 6th standard stanza occupies the central position, then one standard stanza must remain unmatched somewhere in the second half of the poem.

In effect, Spenser perpetuates the symmetrical arrangement through a pattern of correspondent interruption. Such an arrangement is corroborated by the rhymes found in stanzas 5 and 6 and those found in 20. Stanza 5's rhyme of "bed / hed" (75, 77) is echoed in the later stanza's "bed / spread"; there is a further reverberation in lines that end with the words "playes" and "play".

Similarly, stanza 6's "delight / dight / Night" (96, 97, 99) have their counterpart in "delight / night" (362, 363). As a result, even though the stanza patterns themselves do not correspond, there are poetic associations which connect these sections of the poem and perpetuate the symmetry through an acoustic association.

Overall, the significance of this symmetrical scheme is that it captures the mutable use of form within a larger static or eternal scheme. While we can recognize an organizational pattern by considering the variant stanza patterns in a chronological or temporal context, that diachronic use of form is effectively contained within a larger static order that reaffirms the presence of an eternal dimension. Temporality is formally present but ultimately reinscribed in a more comprehensive, atemporal form.

However, the fact that the variant stanzas ultimately contribute to a static scheme should not obscure a key point that informs this reading: form in Renaissance poetry may constitute a temporal and dynamic aspect of a poem. Hieatt and others have used *Epithalamion* to demonstrate how form *represents* time, but this poem also shows how form can *participate* in temporality.

While the symmetrical arrangement of standard and variant stanzas may be perceived synchronically, the 12 variant stanzas, through a cyclical pattern of differentiation and reassimilation, are involved in a scheme of tension and resolution that can only be recognized diachronically.

As a result, it appears that one routinely accepted notion in the study of Renaissance poetics, that of an unproblematic distinction between eternal form and temporal narrative, may be in some cases an oversimplification, and that those Renaissance poems which appear to be irregular in form demand closer scrutiny.

Such closer scrutiny might begin by questioning the ways in which critics have thus far handled such variations. In the discussion surrounding *Epithalamion*, it has been customary for critics to treat the perplexing shifts in form in one of two ways. One is by referring to the influence of the *canzone* form, as Germaine Warkentin and H. S. V. Jones have done; in fact, the poem has made it into at least one dictionary of literary terms as an English representative of this Italian verse form.

Yet this explanation is problematic because the stanza pattern of the *canzone* traditionally varies among individual poems and not within the same poem. The other way critics have approached these apparent anomalies is to see them as moments of poetic freedom and to assert the inexplicability of such modifications; even Hieatt uncomfortably states that Spenser varied his stanza forms "without apparent reason".

This approach is also unsatisfactory because the assertion of poetic freedom and irrational choice, while certainly an element of poetics, potentially threatens to dismiss the significance of variation and to foreclose further critical discussion. Such approaches are not limited to accounts of Spenser's use of form. They have also been used either to explain or to dismiss perplexing variations in the works of other Renaissance poets. For example, critics have viewed the work of William Drummond as demonstrating the influence of the *canzone* verse form as well as exhibiting rhyme schemes that are only explicable in terms of being the "most convenient at the moment".

Such accounts of poetic variation should invite our careful reconsideration of a poet's design. In such cases, we should attempt to rethink poetic form in a way that admits the potential for participation in temporality. Only then would we allow ourselves to see apparent irregularities as actually constituting deliberate modifications that contribute to the design of a poem on a temporal level.

Chapter 8

The Ironies of Britomart's Quest

Although Britomart appears in only two cantos of Book V of Spenser's *Fairie Queene*, she dominates these cantos. Quickly shifting into action, forcefully wielding weapons, she engages in a second quest for Artegall. Having discovered her true love in IV.vi—completing the quest begun in III.i—she must reappear in the middle of Artegall's book to save both him and the hierarchical norms of the culture.

Throughout the poem, Britomart has ingeniously used her disguise as a male knight to achieve various ends. Her disguise makes her a rich and complex figure; she achieves an "extraordinary amplitude, containing the full range of human experience, from masculine striving to maternal generation" (Paglia 51).

Britomart has usually been regarded as thoroughly female at her core, although her androgynous quality makes her akin to Queen Elizabeth. While Britomart is not named as a mirror to Elizabeth, she clearly does resemble the sovereign in many ways. Book V involves her explicit movement into the political sphere, where she enjoys a brief but perfect reign as princess. Throughout her adventures, the usually masked Britomart has the heart and stomach not just of a king, but of a warrior.

Britomart's manly mask is mirrored and inverted by Artegall's forced assumption of an "unmanly maske"—women's clothes—by the evil Amazon queen, Radigund. Artegall's capitulation to Radigund, in a scene echoing his first sight of Britomart, is one of the great shocks in Book V. It proves to be the motive behind Britomart's return. She once again dons concealing armor, once again assumes her manly mask, so that she may free Artegall and correct Radigund's inverted society. Of course, the landscape of Book V is less imaginary than that in earlier books, with the allegory now closely paralleling real political figures and events. This world is an ironic one, filled with all kinds of role reversals and inverted political systems.

Britomart's previous adventures had been characterized by comedy—mistaken identity and various other comic effects. But her role is far more sober in Book V. The comedy, now principally revolving around Artegall and Radigund, assumes a darker tone.

"The male cultural response to the doubled erotic and political power of a female may legitimately include laughter" (Quilligan 163), and this laughter is nervous and grim. Britomart's actions attain an even greater irony—she is a woman dressed as a man who saves a man dressed as woman; she achieves political power and promptly hands it over.

The actions by and around Britomart in Book V are all subtle, mystifying and disturbing. Her main actions fall into three broad scenes—the adventures at Dolon's castle, the dream in the Temple of Isis, and the battle with Radigund. But first let us consider the prompt for Britomart's actions: Artegall's fall before a woman and his eventual treatment as a woman.

One of Artegall's greatest obstacles in his quest for Justice is the Amazon queen, Radigund, whom he mistakenly chooses to fight in single combat. The climactic moment clearly echoes his second fight with Britomart in Book IV:

[He] her sunshinie helmet soone unlaced,
Thinking at once both head and helmet to have raced.
But when as he discovered had her face,
He saw his senses straunge astonishment,
A miracle of Natures goodly grace,
In her faire visage voide of ornament…
At sight thereof his cruell minded hart
Empierced was with pittiful regard
That his sharpe sword he threw from him apart (*V.v.11-13*)

The revelation of Radigund's face halts Artegall and ultimately leads to his submission; it also strongly recalls his first sight of the undisguised Britomart in Book IV. His identical reaction proves to be a flaw: "we...recognize that any woman's beauty will elicit the same response" (Bean 248). Artegall voluntarily submits to Radigund.

She then makes him her thrall, strips him of "all the ornaments of knightly name," and forces him to put on "womans weeds, that is to manhood shame" (v. 20). He now appears more feminine than Britomart has at almost any time in the poem. From the narrator's viewpoint, Artegall has been thoroughly degraded and humiliated.

Britomart reappears in canto vi when Talus arrives to tell her that Artegall is "in harlots bondage tide". She is driven to anger, knowing that Artegall "was not forst, nor overcome in fight", and one might well read sexual rivalry in her reaction. In any event, Britomart does not moan very long; she soon resumes her armor, and thus her disguise, and rides off with Talus.

On the first night, they lodge with a seemingly benign old man, Dolon. She refuses to reveal her female identity, and later she is nearly trapped in her bower by the suddenly wrathful Dolon. The whole scene is quite mysterious until the narrator reveals that Dolon's eldest son was slain by Artegall, and that Dolon believes he is exacting revenge: "For sure he weend that his present guest/Was Artegall, by many tokens plaine".

This time Britomart is mistaken for her own lover, and so her disguise becomes still more fascinating and problematic. It may even be argued that Britomart has in a sense become Artegall, since Artegall himself has been deprived of his "moral essence" through his "feminization by Radigund" (Paglia 55-56). In another sense, Britomart very much does resemble the Artegall of Book V. Throughout this Book, Artegall and Talus mete out justice in a decidedly violent fashion.

Although Britomart is strong and martial, she has never yet been depicted as brutal. But at the end of canto vi, she does Artegall one better by killing Dolon's remaining sons, impaling one upon her spear and pitching the other into the water to drown. This violence sets us up for the battle against Radigund, but first Britomart visits the Temple of Isis, where she has a dream that prophesies her progeny and suggests the sexual terms between men and women. Camille Paglia regards the dream as a foretelling of Britomart's "procreative fate," completing the "progression from solitary knightly quester to obedient wife and mother".

However, Pamela Benson observes an inherent tension in the dream, reading it as more political than sexual. In her view, Britomart is a definite mirror of Elizabeth—both women "represent virtue in this fallen world where force is necessary; they need to have relations with the savage crocodile, but, under feminine control, male aggression and sexual energy are productive of peace".

Interestingly, the dream contains another variation on disguise. After the dream, one of the priests says to Britomart,

Magnificke virgin, that in queint disguise
Of British armes doest maske thy royall blood,
So to pursue a perillous emprize,
How couldst thou weene, through that disguised hood,
To hide thy state from being understood? (V.vii.21)

The term "British armes" indicates that she still maintains an outward male appearance, but the emphasis is not on her gender disguise; rather, the priest sees through her disguise to discover her "royall blood" and estate. He also notes the prophetic content of the dream, interpreting the crocodile as "The righteous Knight, that is thy faithfull lover".

Britomart and Artegall will "joyne in equall portion of thy realme", yet this political balance of sexes will not last since "the lion of great might" in the dream represents their son and a resumption of the male royal line. The return to the natural hierarchy is crucial, as Britomart later appears to be an agent of patriarchy when she kills Radigund.

One of the key passages about women in *The Faerie Queene* is found in Book V.v, soon after Radigund imprisons and humiliates Artegall:

But vertuous women wisely understand,

That they were borne to base humilitie,
Unlesse the heavens them lift to lawfull soveraintie. (v. 25)

On the surface, at least, we see an illustration of this patriarchal attitude in Book V.vii. We have two types of rulers—Radigund, whose uncontrolled power and intent to invert or subvert "normal" society make her utterly destructive; and Britomart, whose power is more subtle and appears to defer to the male power structure.

Yet there are undeniable similarities between these two female antagonists. Louis Montrose notes that "Radigund is Britomart's double, split off from her as an allegorical personification of everything in Artegall's beloved that threatens him" ("Dream" 78).

But if Britomart is Radigund's double, she functions more like a negative image—white against black—or a grossly distorted mirror image of the Amazon. While Britomart demonstrates again a high degree of violence and ruthlessness, she does so expressly against Radigund. After several stanzas of hacking and slashing, Britomart "with one stroke both head and helmet cleft". She decapitates Radigund, the leader of this subversive female society.

Surprisingly, Britomart drops her disguise for this battle. Up to now, she has rigorously maintained her disguise; the rare moments of revelation have been accidental. Yet now that she is clearly revealed as a woman, Britomart ironically appears to be fighting for male authority. She is much admired by all for killing Radigund and restoring natural order:

During which space she there as princes rained,
And changing all that forme of common weale,
The liberty of women did repeale,
Which they had long usurpt; and them restoring
To mens subjection, did true justice deale:
That all they, as a goddesse her adoring,
Her wisdome did admire, and hearkned to her loring. (vii.42)

Benson notes that "Britomart uses her sovereignty to divest herself of power, and her action shows that proven excellence in women—even her own—does not justify reversing the natural hierarchy of the sexes...". However, she does, for the moment, reign as princess. Indeed, this passage is filled with praise of Britomart and, we assume, of Elizabeth: she deals true justice, is admired for her wisdom, and is adored as a goddess.

Yet if she is really restoring all women, especially herself, to men's subjection, then Britomart's mirror of Elizabeth turns opaque. No reading of this episode is complete without considering the irony of the situation: by "reinstating masculine rule over Radigund's Amazon empire, Britomart reinstitutes a governing structure that obtains everywhere but in England under Elizabeth" (Quilligan 170).

In her time, Elizabeth was regarded as the exceptional woman ruler, who gained the throne by unusual circumstances. Yet she was circumscribed in her role: "Only insomuch as Elizabeth has fit and continues to fit the pattern of the virtuous woman who is raised to authority but does not seek it, is she and will she be worthy of praise" (Benson 293). While Elizabeth would be praised as the legitimate ruler, she need not be admired.

It may be more accurate to say that she is tolerated, for the "image of a woman in power carried strong associations with anarchy in sixteenth-century England..." (Marcus 147). Because Britomart apparently marries and apparently defers her power, she is less obviously akin to Elizabeth than Belphoebe, whom Spenser explicitly names as a mirror to the queen and who never relinquishes power to male authority.

However, Montrose argues that the "queen herself was too politic, and too ladylike, to wish to pursue the Amazonian image very far. Instead, she transformed it to suit her purposes, representing herself as an androgynous martial maiden, like Spenser's Britomart" ("*Dream*" 79). Yet Spenser's text is clearly very tentative in making this connection.

The poem undeniably contains subtle touches of criticism alongside the praise of the queen. Montrose argues that the attitude of the "male/poet/subject" is "necessarily ambivalent—alternately or simultaneously adoring and contestatory..." ("*Subject*" 330). Mary Bowman sees the text as somewhat critical of the queen, precisely because her power is so great. Her interpretation of the dream at the Temple of Isis has little to do with Artegall and everything to do with the upcoming Britomart/Radigund confrontation, which itself is closely tied to the Elizabethan court and recent political history; for her, Britomart's victory represents "the death of Mary Stuart, the paradoxical reinforcement of patriarchal structures," and Elizabeth's "fictional deferral to male power".

The queen's deferral of power to her male courtiers is indeed fictional—yet another type of disguise. In reality, Elizabeth "uses her power to control" and tame "the men in a Petrarchan game".

By the end of canto vii of Book V, we have seen Britomart for the last time. With the male hierarchy restored and Britomart apparently ready to assume a traditional female role, Spenser seems to reach closure with an anti-feminist attitude that would dishearten most modern readers.

Yet, looking more closely, we cannot be certain that Britomart's identity is settled or resolved. She is betrothed but not yet married, and she looks more than ever like Queen Elizabeth. But because she is not named as a mirror of the queen, she is disguised in yet another way.

In contrast, Artegall's identity is much more settled. His mask is forced upon him, and it is clearly temporary. His adoption of woman's weeds produces a broad comic effect upon the reader; indeed, this adoption is refreshing in the generally disturbing Book V. But Britomart does not find the scene at all amusing:

...when she saw that loathly uncouth sight,
Of men disguiz'd in womanishe attire,
Her heart gan grudge, for very deepe despight
Of so unmanly maske, in misery misdight. (vii.37)

The irony runs very deep. Britomart grudges this "maske" which simply reverses the mask she dons for most of the poem. The issue is best explored in the context of gender roles. It may be more shameful for a knight to be even apparently unmanned than for the country to be run by a female sovereign. Yet *The Faerie Queene* continually poses questions on the rights of each gender to knighthood and sovereignty.

Spenser's view of sovereignty, as expressed in Book V, can only be regarded as ironic—or, more properly, ambiguous. Bowman argues that Britomart does represent Queen Elizabeth's tremendous authority and thus her final victory proves to be only a straw victory for men.

The tension between female power and the male power system still remains, and this tension forces Spenser to remove this "mirror" who was never named as such (Bowman 526-27). Spenser must surely be aware that he is treading dangerous waters in writing about the queen. In the poem, the bad poet Malfont writes "rayling rymes" that blaspheme the queen, and his punishment is to have his tongue "nayld to a post". Should Spenser offer anything that could be taken as criticism, much less as blasphemy, he might indeed risk a fate like Malfont's.

Despite her internal or symbolic tension, Britomart remains exceptionally strong and heroic; she may not be ready to be disclaimed. With substantial appearances in three books, a record that no other character can claim, we might expect to see Britomart yet again in *The Fairie Queene*. We can only speculate on Spenser's unwritten books, just as we can only speculate on the poem's degree of political tension. Paglia argues that when Britomart's "radiance dims in marriage, her hermaphroditic power will pass into the British royal dynasty".

But Britomart's marriage remains a potential rather than an absolute certainty, even as she retains her power. Although no longer disguised at the end of Book V, she remains paradoxical, perhaps unreadable; we cannot determine whether she is a mirror or a non-mirror of Elizabeth. At some level, Britomart remains masked, and her final appearance leaves the ambiguity with which Spenser treats his character, his queen, and his culture.

Chapter 9

Evidence of a Performative Aesthetic

"Witchcraft by a Picture" is a short poem, its seeming simplicity making it an ideal test case for evidence of dramatic implication. If dramatic influence is evident here, in what seems a minor work, then this perspective is all the more compelling as a general interpretation of Donne's greater works. Do dramatic elements emerge from our interpretations that corroborate the general belief in Donne's dramatic artistry?

"Witchcraft by a Picture" contains elements which suggest that this line of interpretation has merit; moreover, the poem is characteristic of his tendency frequently to intimate his attitude toward his own art. In small, it reveals Donne's aesthetic principles.

To what extent is it valid to think of Donne as a dramatic poet, and what does that mean in regard to the poetry? It is difficult for the veteran Donne scholar to avoid imagining Donne in the theatre. Since he was in London at the time that Marlowe and Shakespeare were producing dramas, it is enticing to believe Donne to have been in the first-night audiences for *Dr. Faustus* and *The Taming of the Shrew*.

We revel in "what-if," wondering how such powerful experiences would have influenced Donne. From such whimsy, we have advanced sweeping generalities about Donne's dramatic tendencies—suggesting Donne's poetry to be drama reduced in size—but often neglecting the poetry that corroborates this bias.

Of the *Songs and Sonets*, "Witchcraft by a Picture" is one of the few that may be construed as being a sonnet. It seems typical of Donne's work, there is little doubt of its authorship, and it provides editors few problems with variants or other gremlins of the trade.

Our tendency is to ignore it because it is brief and seemingly straightforward. I contend, however, that the poem contains indications of Donne's belief about his art which, if heeded, would alter our current lines of inquiry and lead us toward a relatively sure definition of Donne's aesthetic which is largely performative.

The most obvious reason for scrutinizing the poem is that it reveals the habitual tendency of Donne to upset generic and traditional principles. Donne plays with the form by forcing the poem into two stanzas of seven lines each, structuring the stanzas with alternatingly rhymed quatrains followed by singly-rhymed tercets. This form frustrates our expectation of generic octave and sestet, deriving from Italian models, but etymologically classifies the poem as "sonnet" or "little song."

Furthermore, each stanza comprises two main independent clauses, marked by semi-colons at the ends of the quatrains. Both stanzas subdivide their quatrains into similar independent clauses, though they function in apposition more so than to further the thought.

Such deployment scoffs at the English or Shakespearean form and strains the usual parameters of less rigid Italian patterns, all of which usually treat the quatrain as a single, unbroken unit. In upsetting this expectation, the poem draws our attention to its own unusual artistry and does so emphatically.

Although I suggest no direct relationship, this warping of tradition is consistent with the tendency for the English stage of that day to be controversial, non-conformist, and iconoclastic; if we consider how seldom the plays of this period maintain the Aristotelian unities, we have an obvious analogue to Donne's methods.

In the poem, the rather melodramatic burning in the eyes and drowning in the tears is parodied by the oxymoronic conflation of burning water. It worked for Milton, but not in the context of compliment. These were, of course, Petrarchan conceits, and Donne is having fun at his persona's expense, perhaps showing the exaggerated artificiality of the lover, who is ironically a lover attempting to get away from his mistress rather than trying to attain her.

We can infer this desire to escape from her by the concluding comment that the picture will be "free" from her "malice," the same ill-intentions that would supposedly have her murdering the persona by drowning and burning him. The parody of the reversed intention, a radical departure from the generic sonnet, is further evidence of an emphasis on the poem's artificial construction, its performative context. The parody is a further indication of Donne's literariness.

What the formal and contextual iconoclasms produce is an awareness that the poet is drawing attention to the poem's unusual nature. This implies that the articulation of poetic statement is a salient characteristic of the poem's meaning.

If form follows function, then here the function must be, in part, to raise doubt concerning the conceptual mode that the sonnet represents. This tension is enhanced by a reference within the poem to art, overtly the art by which the mistress might do harm to the picture of the persona, and thus to him.

A poem that contains reference to the concept of art comments in some way on the art of the poem. As an image, "art" is reflexive when incorporated into a work of art, as this poem emphatically is and does. As stated, the formal play that structures this poem encourages this metapoetic or metafictive view, but that is not the only element that suggests this. It is crucial to the poem's strategy that the mistress is also an artist and that the persona is in effect disagreeing with the kind of "art" she produces.

Metafiction is reflexive imaginative discourse or "fiction that includes within itself a commentary on its own narrative and/or linguistic identity" (Hutcheon 1). In his comprehensive survey of Donne's imagery, Rugoff found eighty-seven references to the arts in the body of Donne's poetic works. These include references to poetry, painting, and music, and a little over two dozen such references to theatrical terms: "masks" (masques), "scenes," "acts," "actors," "theatre," the "stage," and "playes." Rugoff does not grant any of the art images special attention; instead, he merely cautions that Donne's poetry treats the arts variously and with unequal development.

He does not attribute any special function to these art terms, nor does he recognize that they tend to insinuate a metapoetic frame of reference. By my count, including terms that are ambiguous and widening the net to include references to speech acts, Donne's poetry contains well over 400 metacommunicative or reflexive references. This particular type of referentiality, this "matrix of imagery," contributes to a metafictive context for the poetry.

Although Rugoff seems unaware, can we credit that Donne would ignore the ironic tensions these terms generate? He is much more likely to embrace and emphasize this heightened gesture of literariness.

Taken together, these images constitute an identifiable portion of the poetry's commentary on its own linguistic identity or literariness. If they do not provide a full commentary on the narrative situation or linguistic context of the poetry in which Donne has placed them, they are at least suggestive of such a perspective.

They are a symbolic and imagistic invitation to read the poetry as possessing a literary identity. A synthesis of these images and a consideration of what we might infer from Donne's use of them complete this unfinished commentary and go far to contradict Hughes' assertion that we know nothing about Donne's aesthetics.

The mistress of "Witchcraft by a Picture" is a would-be artist or one who would like to control more powerful artistry, for the persona leaves it in a conditional clause that she lacks the "wicked skill / By pictures made and mard, to kill" (5-6), though according to the persona she has the will to do so. Her skill, her artistry, aims to become "wicked" witchcraft, involving the burning of his picture in her eye, and the drowning of his picture in her tear:

I fixe mine eye on thine, and there
Pitty my picture burning in thine eye,
My picture drown'd in a transparent teare,
When I look lower I espie... (1-4)

Since her art is an issue between the persona and mistress, it is important to scrutinize it. She practices her art with pictures. In his poetry, Donne's two dozen references to pictures fall into two groups: pictures that are crafted as visual images painted on canvas and bound to a frame, that is, pictures or paintings which are *objets d'art*; and pictures that are images or possibly reflections from mirrors, tears, eyes, or glass-like objects.

Suffice it to say that there are many Donne poems that rely on the picture-as-image construct. There is considerable overlap of connotation, but it is clear that the other group denotes pictures that have physical form, a painting, and that these paintings are markedly different from the less tangible images.

Poems using the *objet d'art* sense of picture as reflexive image include: "Elegie: Going to Bed," "Elegie: His Picture," "The Legacie," "Sonnet: The Token," "Phryne," "To Mr. T. W.: At once, from hence," the epistle introducing the "Metempsychosis," the "Somerset Epithalamion," "Elegie on the L. C.," and of course "Witchcraft by a Picture."

One of the most simple and clear examples of physical pictures or paintings are the persona's reference to the picture as a gift or exchanged item in "Sonnet: The Token." Here the speaker asks that the mistress not send various items that bespeak a love relationship in preference to her swearing her love.

In the succession of items he considers and discards, pictures are "most desir'd, because best like the best", and they are just below verse in that persona's hierarchy of tokens. A similar idea inheres in Donne's verse-letter, "To Mr. R. W.: If, as mine is, thy life a slumber be," where an analogy is made between the letter and the "Patient" lover sending "His Picture to his absent Love". These pictures, used as gifts, are valuable as expressions of affection, and this is the presumed context for the picture in "Witchcraft by a Picture"—it was given as a gift. But ultimately, gift pictures are not sufficient to enforce affection, since they are only approximations of the persona's presence.

In the famous poem, "Elegie: Going to Bed," the persona offers a simile between women's use of gems for adornment and pictures, even if on book covers: "Like pictures or like books gay coverings made / For lay-men, are all women thus array'd".

This comparison is initiated by a mythological reference to Atalànta's balls (the golden apples that Venus gave to her challenger) which were dropped in front of Atalanta to distract and delay her from the goal. The surrounding lines imply that it is not the distracting pictures themselves that are the goal of the lover, but instead the contents or things the pictures represent.

Furthermore, it is the special right or duty of the inclusive "wee" in the next line to be shown the true nature of women; mere lay-men are apparently easily duped by the outward covering (calling to mind the injunction that they can't judge a book by its covers).

This resonates with "Witchcraft by a Picture" in that both poems suggest a delusory or compulsory effect deriving from picture usages. That is, the mistress in "Witchcraft by a Picture" works with tangible pictures to coerce the persona. On the other hand, the persona employs the image-picture as well as the gift painting.

As in other of his poems, Donne uses both senses of picture-as-art-object and the image or presence of picture in "Witchcraft by a Picture," and he gains interpretative tension from the interplay between meanings. The term "picture" is repeated five times and distributed fairly evenly within the poem's fourteen lines, this repetition emphasizing the importance of the shifting image. The initial picture is the image of the persona as lover found reflected in the eyes and through the tears of the mistress. In this case she is possibly a reluctant lover or cruel mistress, or at least that is the role the persona envisions for her.

Another possibility might connect her tears with the departure he later reveals as his intention, suggesting that she is crying at the thought of their separation, a context Donne seems to favor as reason for writing (similar to the valediction poems). These tears of sorrow, however, are unwelcome, for they are drowning his picture, thus eliciting the persona's pity for his own image.

This impression is encouraged by the sonnet's turn, which is made ambiguous by the division into seven-line units rather than the eight of the traditional octave. The eighth and ninth lines thus emphasize the finality of the persona's position; having experienced her tears, he is ready to move on, "But now I'have drunke thy sweet salt tears, / And though thou poure more I'll depart" (8-9).

The image use is initially consistent, of picture-as-image, but the speaker shifts to the picture-as-object model when he accuses her of hypothetically killing him through arcane practice involving "pictures made and mard". These would apparently be used in supernatural ritual, the "wicked skill" of line five, which would involve some sort of voodoo-like defacement or other abuse of the picture, something like the needle-through-the-wax-figure routine.

The earlier-mentioned tears may equally be performing such an effect, though the later action is more intentional from her, requiring more conscious effort on her part, or at least the personal projects it as being such. At this point it is clear that we are not dealing with intangible images but rather with painted representations which the woman has the potential for using in some undefined variety of black or supernatural arts.

The persona then returns to the picture-as-image usage by connecting the departure he has decided upon with the loss of the image of him in her eyes: "My picture vanish'd, vanish feares / That I can be endamag'd by that art" (10-11). The "art" referred to is apparently the art of witchcraft ("that art," not this "art"), which can not be enacted without the physical object.

The picture vanishes because he denies her of himself, the

object that would make the image, just as he will deny her any further images of himself by departing. The persona's departure from the scene causes Baumlin some difficulty:

One would think that such pictures are charm-like guarantors of the poet's continued presence, if not in the language or textual space, then at least in the lady's memory and imagination. And yet the poet discovers nothing but the frailty of such self-representations, images that survive (and thus sustain both the lady's memory and fidelity) only so long as he generates them by means of his own bodily presence.

But the persona is something of a wizard or artist himself; as poet, he is able to side-step the problem of presence. He does this by relying on the shift between the two types of picture. In the last reference to picture, the persona synthesizes the two senses which he has been keeping distinct: "One picture more, yet that will bee, / Being in thine owne heart, from all malice free" (13-14).

The picture in her heart is both image and object, and thus does constitute the absent presence of the persona. It is not a picture that can endanger the persona, because the mistress can not physically get at it without first killing herself. It is also an image, because if it were literally an object, it would have already killed her.

Baumlin's assertion that the picture fails is thus invalid in that the picture does remain, no matter what the supposedly regretful mistress does to be rid of it. This is similar to the picture-in-heart conceit of "The Dampe": the persona puts the beloved of "Witchcraft by a Picture" in the uncomfortable position of having no option other than to endure his absence.

Again, the effect on the mistress is cautionary—don't cry or otherwise try to keep me here. It seems to me that the poem is more interested in assuaging the grief of parting than in demanding the faithfulness Baumlin attributes to it. Moreover, the reader is in the position of voyeuristically observing the persona's manipulation of the scene and granting chagrined approval to the persona for the strategy of his argument.

One benefit of treating the poem in its reflexive context is that this forces our attention back to the poem, instead of outward toward the critics' various preferences. Close reading shows that the spell the mistress has been attempting to cast is one that intends to keep the persona from leaving. She does this by burning his picture in her eyes and drowning his picture in her tears. This is the reach of her art and the limits to which she can "perform" her "will."

The burning is logistically placed in her eyes by an otherwise leaden "there" at the end of the first line. The drowning takes place "lower," and is noticed by the persona when he looks down to "espie" his picture. Is the picture then in two different places, both in the eyes and some undefined nether location? Is the distance of separation only between the eye and the tear? Why does he "fixe" his eye on hers, but has to "espie" the lower picture?

In his study of the impact of the visual arts on the Renaissance mind, Farmer observes that Donne recognized the priority of the visual sense. He suggests that we should and often do imagine visual analogues to Donne's metaphors. The priority of sight is corroborated by Ferry who suggests that this was a basic assumption of the rhetors of the Sixteenth Century: "words are not consistently distinct from nonverbal things... that reading is not clearly differentiated from seeing".

If we follow this wisdom, we are encouraged to look for sight-play in the scene. Yes, the picture is replicated, and he can legitimately look her in the eyes to see it, but he must covertly look down to see it again, thus suggesting that the lower picture is located where he is not allowed to look. This hint derives from a recognition that "espie" connotes a transgressive act.

The picture may be in the tear dropping from her eye, but there is nothing that limits the location to her cheek, where he would be legitimately allowed to look. Instead, it is probable that the persona looks much lower, down to her genitalia, where his gaze would be prohibited and where he would find a different "teare," homonymously the same as the lacrymal droplet and the opening or fissure that constitutes her vagina.

The womanly art that would keep the persona present, her witchcraft, is in part dependent on her "lower" abilities, these probably referring to her body, and by association to her obvious sexuality, which intimates the more captivating place the persona covertly espies. As a speaking picture, the persona sees himself, or the representative part thereof, i.e. his penis, drowned by the mistress' transparent tears.

Regardless of how graphically the reader wishes to interpret the scene, doubtless it is sexual action or the possibility of it that keeps the persona near. This is quite reasonable, for what would be the most obvious art that would keep the lover present if not the art of love? It is also apparent that the persona implies disdain for this kind of art that would bind him, especially as it is in contrast to the art that he practices, the art of poetry.

Although the more erotic reading may strain credulity, it is an available and emphatic version of the same concept which may be obtained in a more innocent reading, namely, that she would control him through her arts.

In this case the art in the poem—the pictures—and the art of the poem—the persona's strategem—stand as a hedge against unwanted reactions. Rather than fail because the picture does not guarantee continued presence, which is not what it overtly attempts to do, the persona's use of picture, and the speaking picture of the poem itself, does succeed in the dual task of quelling grief and ensuring faith. The persona's mistress is prevented from continued crying, and she is unable to do her image of him any harm.

As Londoner, scholar, and man-about-town, John Donne was certainly familiar with the late Elizabethan and Jacobean theatre. A contemporary refers to him as a "great frequenter of Playes." In his poetry he makes overt reference to Marlowe's *Tamberlain*, causing Donne's biographer, R. C. Bald, to suggest probable influence. Later in life, Donne intervened in a slander suit on the behalf of Ben Jonson, who was accused of having libeled Inigo Jones.

Although in his poetry Donne makes little specific use of theatrical events, it is worth speculating on how the experience of the theatre might have had an effect on Donne's consciousness, and thus how it might inform the poetry.

Clearly, Donne's poetry can not be interpreted as "theatre," although we should take into account the staged quality of his verse, the imaginary scene which allows the poems' personae the occasions in which they articulate their roles in poetic measure. Donne is frequently dramatic, if he does not specifically refer to the theatre.

Although much has been made of Donne's relationship to the arts, and both baroque and mannerist camps have claimed his poetry, surprisingly, no one has surveyed the references to pictures in the poetry, and only a few (such as Cunnar and Duncan) have made much use of these images.

These, I claim, are reflexive metaphors positioned in the poetry with the partial effect of enhancing the poetry's literariness, its *literaturnost*. As symbols of art, they implicate the poem in the context of artistry, and they suggest that the poem is primarily a performance of art instead of an argument for or against a particular theme.

Art in this sense is commemorative, a testimonial to the timeless and presumably faithful love that the persona raises at the time of apparent separation. As in other Donne poems, the imminent separation requires a response from the persona, partly to quell doubts and fears in the mistress, and partly to encourage a resolute faithfulness from her.

Donne's habit is to rely on concepts of artistry to accomplish these ends. His most anthologized poem, "A Valediction Forbidding Mourning," replicates this theme. Art is seen in Donne's mind as a provisional warning against impermanence and unfaithfulness.

By convincing the mistress to discontinue the unwanted behaviour, Donne is in effect using art to appeal for a kind of grace from the mistress. For Donne, art is the means by which he attains grace and is an insurance policy in the face of uncertainty. It is through the dual performance of writing and reading that he achieves a kind of salvation.

Chapter 10

Shakespearean Tragediennes in the Early Oil Days of Pennsylvania

In the October 13, 1865 edition of the *Titusville Morning Herald,* a surveyor placed the following announcement:

Risk the penny to gain the fortune, Shakespeare says, There is a tide in the affairs of men which taken at the Flood Leads on to Fortune. Omitted, all the voyage of their lives is bound in shallow and miseries.

That *Julius Caesar* could be quoted to promote land leases for the speculative oil rush indicates the degree to which Shakespeare was in the minds and hearts of nineteenth-century common folk. At the time the sales pitch appeared, there were nearly 15,000 people in Pithole City. It was said to be the third largest mail drop in Pennsylvania, but scarcely a year before, only a few scattered farmers—the Holmdens, the Moreys, and the Andersens—lived in the area.

In September 1865, fifty hotels lined the streets in Pithole City along with banks, saloons, whorehouses and theaters. That drama sold in this environment is difficult for many to believe; that Shakespearean performances were sold out is even more incredible.

The printer's office at Pithole kept records of the number of programs printed for dramatic performances at the Murphy Theater. These records show that drama was alive and well even in the oil boom town of Pithole as audiences of more than a thousand packed the second floor of the Murphy Theater whenever Shakespearean plays were performed. This essay explores the Shakespearean presence in the early oil days in the boom towns of Titusville and Pithole City and specifically it focuses upon the roles played by local acting companies, travelling combination groups, and Shakespearean actresses.

After the discovery of oil by Colonel Drake in northwestern Pennsylvania, it was not long until speculators, roustabouts, coopers and many others rushed to the region. The focal point was Titusville, but wildcatters struck oil throughout the area. Not much was known about oil or where it could be found, but thousands upon thousands of people rushed to the region to make their fortune. Oil boom towns arose, taking their names from the fortune which lay beneath them—Pithole City, Grease, Petroleum Centre and Oil City—just to name a few.

Despite the promise of wealth, many of the towns quickly disappeared, and the history of the region is nearly erased. The Drake Well Museum has done a good job of preserving aspects of the oil search; and hidden in this history lies another history which tells of drama, theaters, and opera houses constructed in many of the oil boom towns.

Chief among these ghost towns was Pithole City, and chief among the theaters of those days was the Murphy Theater. While other folks were gambling on striking oil, William Murphy thought it was better to invest in a drama hall than an oil well. At a cost of over $30,000, he erected a first-class theater which was said to rival those in Philadelphia and Boston (*TMH*, July 3-4, 1866).

The location at First Street had the advantage of placing the theater on a knoll overlooking the boggy streets which led to over five hundred wells lower in the valley. One may credit Murphy for having stage scenery, notable costumes, and an orchestra pit which housed twelve musicians.

Special velvet-covered boxes, common to theaters at that time, seated those who were willing to spend $8 for the entertainment. For $1.50, the audience sat on benches in the orchestra area or for fifty cents one could sit in the balcony. The September 8, 1865 edition of the *Titusville Morning Herald* described the theater as having a commodious gallery, a dress circle, six private boxes to be carpeted and fitted with damask curtains, a full orchestra box, a stage 30 by 40 feet, with a full set of scenery, and a splendid drop curtain made of satin and an interior handsomely painted and decorated throughout, and lighted by chandeliers from Tiffanys of New York City. It is contemplated to have a rich drop curtain painted, representing a scene characteristic of the oil region.

No known sketches or photographs of the theater exist, with the exception of a panoramic shot of Pithole City in which the theater is seen in the upper left-hand corner of the photograph. Not much detail of the theater is shown, but one can see that the building dwarfs every other structure in the town.

No doubt the theater was located on the second floor, and some commercial business was housed on the first floor. This detail can be inferred from an eyewitness, who expressed gratitude that it was good that the "planking and supports were strong" because "a heavy crowd attended last evening" (*PDR*, December 11, 1865). Most of the information regarding the theater is found in the *Pithole Daily Record*.

We do know that during the winter season, the theater remained somewhat comfortable. On January 27, 1865, the temperature dropped to a minus 18 degrees, but the theater, currently playing *The Angel of Midnight*, had a "good audience." The playhouse, like Pithole City itself, lasted a little more than a year; and when the oil bubble burst, the drama hall was sold to J. T. McCaslin, who moved the building to Pleasantville.

A record of Shakespearean performances at Pithole City and Titusville during the mid 1860's has never been compiled. Not much help can be obtained from playbills, although a few playbills of that period are housed in the Drake Well Museum. By far the best record of dramatic performances, including Shakespearean productions, may be found in two newspapers—the *Pithole Daily Record* and the *Titusville Morning Herald*.

Two reporters for the *Morning Herald* from Pithole City, known as "Pit Jr." and "Pit Jr. Cub," described the daily events. Their accounts, of course, focused upon new wells, well flow, depths at which oil was found, and the ever-abundant fires; but both men appeared to love the night life and reported regularly on the drama in the town. Pit Jr. Cub's descriptions of the performances often ran to several hundred words. It is from these sources that we can determine that the following Shakespearean plays occurred in the oil region during the 1865 and 1866 period:

November 8, 1865, Bliss Opera House, *Othello*
November 9, 1865, Bliss Opera House, *Othello*
November 17, 1865, Murphy Theatre, *Taming of the Shrew*
November 24, 1865, Murphy Theatre, *Hamlet*
November 28, 1865, Murphy Theatre, *Othello*
November 30, 1865, Murphy Theatre, *Othello*
December 1, 1865, Murphy Theatre, *Macbeth*
December 2, 1865, Murphy Theatre, *Macbeth*
December 19, 1865, Murphy Theatre, *Romeo and Juliet*
December 20, 1865, Murphy Theatre, *Romeo and Juliet*
December 22, 1865, Murphy Theatre, *Romeo and Juliet*
January 8, 1866, Bliss Opera House, *Richard III*
January 27, 1866, Bliss Opera House, *Macbeth*

What could account for the popularity of drama and Shakespearean plays in particular? Certainly the foremost reason for the rise of drama was the phenomenal influx of people. In his article on the population of Pithole City, Joseph Murray wrote that more than 10,000 people came in less than a four month period (*TMH,* August 22, 1934).

Likewise, Titusville grew from a town of 2,500 to more than 10,000 during this same time. In addition, in 1866, the railroads extended lines from bigger cities of the east and connected to the smaller towns in northwest Pennsylvania; consequently, the way was being prepared for traveling amateur-professional combination companies to put on performances in many of the towns in the oil region.

However, dramatic performances in Pithole and Titusville throughout 1865 were entirely produced by regional actors, resident stock companies, and theatrical entrepreneurs such as William Murphy. The glory days of local stock companies had arrived, with no fewer than three resident play groups offering entertainment in the region: the George O'Harra and George A. Hill troupe worked at Crittenden Hall in Titusville and at O'Harra's Opera House in Pithole City; a second company established by Evans, Doyle, and Ryan performed at the Bliss Opera House; and a third troupe was under the direction of William Murphy at the Murphy Theater. For the most part, these resident stock companies functioned as Alfred Bernheim has described them:

They were a complex of fairly permanent companies, each a continuous producing unit, each independent, functionally, from all others, and each attached to a specific theatre which it controlled and at which it played for a major part of each season.

One might quarrel with Bernheim's use of the word "permanent," because permanency in the oil region often meant as long as the nightly tips were plentiful or as long as other theater managers did not offer more pay. In addition, a number of the theater managers in the oil region allowed the actors within their group to perform limited engagements at rival theaters.

This courtesy was particularly true for Shakespearean performances at the Bliss Opera House and the Murphy Theater. These arrangements can be seen in the casts of the Bliss Opera House and those at the Murphy Theater, especially as they relate to women. Kate Rynar, Susan Dennin, and Anna Levering, for example, gave Shakespearean performances at the Murphy Theater in Pithole City as well as the Bliss Opera House in Titusville.

While one can only conjecture why these stars were permitted to perform at a rival theater, it is apparent that women had the upper hand over the managers of the theaters. The contracts which the theater owners used in order to commit the actors to a particular theater were frequently of little value.

By looking to what was occurring in the oil region at the close of 1865, we can see why resident companies were replaced by touring companies. When the theater season of 1866 opened, the local stock companies were under a great deal of strain; disarray was evident both at Titusville and Pithole City. Several stars left the area for more money and the amenities found in cities such as Albany and Cleveland, while other actors suffered under the strain of nightly performances at the Murphy Theater.

The local theater managers competed for stars, and when contractual obligations occurred, the managers promoted the stars with quarter-page advertisements in the newspaper. But this competition to obtain stars often brought disappointment, as can be seen in Edwin Forrest's expression of regret to owners of the Bliss Opera House that he had to cancel a performance at Titusville because of an engagement in Dayton, Ohio (*TMH*, January 12, 1866). The disintegration of the local stock companies also can be seen in a notice from the Erie Dispatch, which was published in the January 5, 1866, *Titusville Morning Herald*:

Bliss Opera House, Titusville, has brought its season to a sudden close, but from what cause we are unable to say. The management of the establishment has been for a few weeks past in the hands of Mr. Evans. Sam Ryan, we understand, has gone east. The remainder of the company will probably distribute themselves about the country to the best advantage. We have an uncollected claim against the establishment which we hope they will not forget.

The poignant reply of the *Herald* was, simply, "We assure you that Mr. Evelyn Evans is a busted apple dumpling. You won't get nary red" (January 5, 1866).

If Titusville, the "Queen City" of the oil region, was having difficulty with resident actors, then what occurred at the Murphy Theater in Pithole City was even more stark. Many of the actresses left the forlorn backwoods of Pithole, with its muddy streets and brawling night life. In addition, Murphy's leading man,

Mr. Lovelace, died of a heart attack, while another actor left his company to become a Methodist minister. The players were disappearing so fast that Murphy had to close his theater under the guise of "remodeling."

His determination of bringing "legitimate theater" to the

oil region brought with it a schedule that was nothing less than grueling. No other theater could match the productions at the Murphy Theater.

Besides the Shakespearean plays noted above, Murphy produced *Faint Heart Never Won Fair Lady, The Stranger, Lady of Lyons, Camille, East Lynne,* and *Black Eyed Susan* as well as many others. When the theater season opened in 1866, however, Murphy could no longer brag about his theater offering only "legitimate theater." Like the many opera houses in Pithole City, the Murphy Theater entertained the citizens with clog dancing, fiddle playing, and a string of melodramas.

In his work on the theater, Oscar Brockett speaks of the dramatic disappearance of resident companies, suggesting that the rise of the star system hastened the decline of local stock companies (409). By June, 1866, the travelling combination troupes had replaced many of the local stock companies in the oil region.

The boom and bust periods of the oil market also had much to do with the populations within the towns shifting. For example, Pithole City in fall 1865 had nearly 15,000 residents, but by spring 1866 the streets were nearly deserted. Under the conditions that they faced, managers and theater owners found that it was easier for them to become booking agents for national troupes than to secure actors on their own.

It was reported on more than one occasion that Evans and Murphy went to Pittsburgh or Albany to persuade actors to come to the oil region, but their attempts often failed. Jack Poggi has suggested that the balance of power between the local managers and the stars had shifted, so that the managers were required to do all that was necessary in order to obtain the star (6). The stars preferred to bring their own supporting actors so that they could control the quality of the production.

By summer 1866, the conditions had so changed that when theater troupes arrived in town, they brought their own scenery and costumes, put on a dramatic production for one night, and swiftly moved to the next town. From then on, the resident theater groups were generally confined to the small towns not served by the railroads.

The fate that the local stock companies would soon experience could not be imagined by anyone in the theater during fall 1865. Then the resident drama companies were highly successful, and theater managers were flush with cash. Murphy's receipts for one night were more than $900. In each month, November and December, 1865, Murphy made more than $21,000.

The success of his theater can be seen in C. C. Wicker's Cash Book Accounts, as well as from eyewitnesses who reported that Shakespearean performances were frequently sold out. Pit Jr. Cub said that standing room only was available on many occasions (PDR, December 5, 1865). A typical night's entertainment is shown in Pit Jr. Cub's remarks about Murphy's Theater in early December:

Murphy's Theater is still the great attraction...Miss Bridges, in her winning way, provokes applause at every turn...Mademoiselle Brignole, the charming danseur, has a house full of admirers every night, and nothing but her repeated appearance will satisfy the beholders...only when her delicate figure is exhausted by fatigue will her beholders be satisfied...go and see Mr. Jeffrey's as the Young Man...to see him is to laugh (*TMH*, December 1, 1865).

Thus, on one night the audience could see *Macbeth*, Mademoiselle Brignole's dance routine, and Mr. Jeffrey's skit of a "Young Man"—all for fifty cents, if one sat in the balcony.

What was Pithole like and who made up this audience of a thousand or more? Many visitors said that lawlessness was rampant, that saloons were attached to every building, and that the women were as plentiful as the oil wells. On Sunday mornings, French Kate's notorious girls rode naked on horseback from the shanties on Prather Street and paraded their wares throughout the town as well as the drilling sites which were scattered throughout the valley.

More than three thousand teamsters inhabited the town as well as coopers, oil-well drillers, lumbermen, pickpockets, scalawags, and con men of all sorts. It was this group of people predominantly who packed the Murphy Theater and patronized Shakespearean plays.

It could certainly be said that both actors and actresses were well received in Pithole. But the audiences in the oil region especially loved the performances of the Shakespearean tragediennes—Miss Eloise Bridges, Miss Susan Dennin, Miss Anna Levering, Mademoiselle Brignole, Mrs. Kate Rynar, Miss Mary Anderson, and Miss Anna Dickinson.

Miss Bridges' performance of Lady Macbeth on December 1 and 2, 1865, at Murphy Theater was so outstanding that teamsters and oil roustabouts showed their appreciation to her by giving her more than $500. *The Titusville Morning Herald* thought the audience was too unruly and lectured it on how to applaud:

A little taste in the manner of expressing our approbation would speak volumes. The simple clapping of the hands is sufficient to express the most exquisite delight and satisfaction with the performance while it does not offend the most delicate; but rude boisterous stomping and screaming so often, yes invariably witnessed in our public gathering, is absolutely disgraceful (January 3, 1866).

One source reports that after the performance of *Macbeth,* a gentleman from the audience gave Miss Bridges a $500 bill. It was noted that Miss Bridges' "Give me the daggers" speech while she was dressed in a negligee was absolutely riveting. Pit Jr. Cub simply writes that after her expression of gratitude to the audience, a gentleman tossed checks worth $500 and a note which read, "Please accept the enclosed, a slight testimonial of appreciation of you as a lady, socially and professionally" (*TMH,* December 11, 1865). Commenting upon her acting, Pit Jr. Cub wrote,

Macbeth was up, and the character of Lady Macbeth, as taken by Miss Bridges, we have never seen surpassed. In the scene with her husband, in which an ambitious woman's nature brooks no excuse, not even the pangs of remorse, Miss Bridges' 'give me the daggers' made the audience shudder (*TMH,* December 11, 1865).

Several nights before, when Murphy's Theater was playing *Othello,* Miss Bridges' portrayal of Emilia "provoked applause at every turn" (*PDR,* November 28, 1865). Having additional engagements in Cleveland, Miss Bridges departed Pithole City in early December, but years afterward the Shakespearean Club of Titusville spoke of her acting ability.

Murphy advertised the holiday performance of *Romeo and Juliet* and fully expected Evelyn Evans, who had played the role of Hamlet, to be the star attraction as Romeo. For whatever reason, Evans left town, and it appeared that *Romeo and Juliet* would be cancelled. Susan Dennin, who was slated to star as Juliet, took the lead role of Romeo, while Anna Levering substituted for Dennin as Juliet.

Many thought that disaster loomed. Murphy ran several quarter-page ads in the newspaper. Whether it was out of curiosity or love of Shakespeare, Murphy's Theater was especially crowded. Pit Jr. Cub reported that "Dennin met storms of applause last night" (*TMH*, December 22, 1965).

Throughout the years, there would be other actresses who would play male parts, but Susan Dennin had the honour of being the first lady to portray a male in Pithole City. There were critics, of course, especially the reporter who wrote for the *Oil City Register*. He was at a loss to know how to evaluate her performance. On the whole, he thought it was not proper for a lady to perform a male role, but Pit Jr. Cub wrote enthusiastically,

She was elegantly dressed and the pretty face and deep voice of 'Sue' as Romeo produced an entertainment that could scarcely fail to please the most fastidious. Her performance was worthy of renown—she gives the character all the fire of a youthful lover, resolved to dare all for his love (*PDR*, December 20, 1865).

In light of Miss Dennin's performance, it was only proper that an oil-field audience would call for her to come to the front of the stage after her performance. Many felt that on that night, Miss Dennin had pluck and vigor, qualities which the teamsters and roustabouts appreciated.

No actor or actress in the oil country had more of a following than Mademoiselle Brignole. Indeed, she received more press than any other actor. Starring in minor roles in order to complete the cast, Brignole had her own cheering section in the drama house. She first appeared at the Metropolitan Theater in Pithole City and later at the Athenaeum.

When Murphy saw her dance routine, he offered her a contract to appear exclusively at his theater. The press indicated that she was astonishingly beautiful, "a rare delight to look upon," a moral woman, and a good Catholic. The Irish Brotherhood worshipped her and showed their appreciation by throwing coins into her skirt after each performance. "Brig," as she was affectionately called, played minor Shakespearean roles but mainly excelled as an added attraction to the night's performance.

A man named Nicols, who had circulated scurrilous handbills throughout the town, charged that she had previously been engaged by the saloons as something other than a singer, Brig left town in early January with her two children and headed for Albany.

The *Pithole Daily Record* had a policy of not allowing personal retorts to be published, but their love for Brig was such that they published her side of the story: "if I am the low scoundrel which Nicols and his chums of the 'Varieties' would make me, then he is a mean poltroon in seeking to live with me." Her departure, like that of Miss Bridges, was another death blow to the Murphy Theater.

Anna Levering was described as very young, but her talent in acting in supporting roles was said to be first-rate. She performed mainly in plays such as *Camille* and *Faint Heart Never Won Fair Lady*, but she had a limited number of Shakespearean roles. Her performance as Juliet was especially commendable.

Pit Jr. Cub writes, "Juliet did admirably, especially in the scene where she receives the news of the death of Tybalt, and the banishment of Romeo and again in the scene where she takes the sleeping potion" (*PDR*, December 20, 1865). After the Murphy Theater closed, Anna Levering performed at the Bliss Opera House in Titusville and returned to the oil region when the lavish Parshall Opera House was built.

Her stature as a serious actress grew over the years when

she acted in the theaters in Albany, Buffalo, Cleveland, Pittsburgh and Dayton.

Mrs. Kate Rynar was among those stars who first performed at Murphy's Theater. Her performance as Kate in the November 16 performance *of The Taming of the Shrew* was hailed as outstanding. *Morning Herald* thought her performance was the finest that Pithole had seen to date. The theater was packed, and the crowd especially loved the "playful teasing" of the shrew (*PDR*, November 17, 1865). It would appear that Kate's husband Harry did not particularly like the environment at Pithole City.

Despite the fact that Murphy wanted Kate to stay, she went to Titusville and starred at the Bliss Opera House and never returned to Pithole. In the production of *Othello* in early November, Kate portrayed the part of Emilia and allegedly stole the show. *Morning Herald* reported that the play was repeatedly interrupted by applause for Kate and later indicated that the strength of the drama was owing to her performance (November 9, 1865).

With the arrival of travelling theater troupes, two actresses in particular stand out. Miss Mary Anderson played Juliet; the *Herald* lauded her performance, saying, "a more beautiful interpretation would be difficult to imagine." The critic went on to say that, "very few, if any, tragediennes who have visited this city have left a more favorable impression on the audience," and praised her "aptitude of interpretation" and "natural manner" (*TMH*, October 14, 1879). Many in the audience asked her to perform on an additional night, but her schedule prevented her staying in Titusville.

Anna Dickinson, like Susan Dennin, acted a male role in a Shakespearean play. Her performance of *Hamlet* at the Academy of Music in Titusville, made the town buzz. A reporter for the *Titusville Morning Herald* said, "*Hamlet* has been played worse than last night—and with equal justice it must be said that it has been played infinitely better" (May 12, 1882). The reporter's lengthy review of the performance grudgingly states that "the house was full, the audience applauded greatly, and she put much feeling into the part."

The problem for the reporter was that Anna Dickinson was making "a great sensation and much money," and she was likely to "triumph in the theatrical world with a big bank account at the end of it" (May 11, 1882).

The success of Shakespearean performances in the early oil region was owing in large measure to those women who made their living in acting. Thousands of men—mostly those who would be considered rugged by today's standards—chose a Shakespearean drama over brothels and striptease shows. The actresses moved audiences with their stirring character portrayals, and many of them were briefly worshipped. How else can we account for one of them receiving over $500 for one performance?

During these early oil times, the citizens of Titusville erected a statue of Shakespeare in their city park, and on that occasion the mayor cited Shakespearean performances as having contributed to the moral well-being of the community (*TMH*, May 29, 1872). He specifically mentioned the performances by the actresses who played Portia, Lady Macbeth, and Kate.

In Portia, he saw a model for judges and attorneys; in Kate, he saw the proper role of a woman; and in Lady Macbeth, he saw how the "overzealous advocates of women's rights could learn the fate of a strong-minded woman." A modern audience may not have agreed with the mayor's sentiments.

Chapter 11

Political and Social Criticism in "The Calme" by John Donne

John Donne's poem "The Calme," though well known as a literary piece, may also be considered as a historical document. The poem, in addition to another of Donne's works entitled "The Storm," recounts his personal perspective on his involvement in England's naval expeditions against the Spanish in 1597. In contrast to its predecessor "The Storm," which relays Donne's own account of battle, "The Calme" describes the time of peace that often follows war.

However, though the conception of peacetime would generally dictate a sense of relaxation as well as a relishing of accomplishment, Donne's speaker finds no content in this "calme."

In fact, the poem's narration seems buried in images of discomfort and despair with this current peaceful situation. While the poem conveys this sense of uneasiness in the "calme" itself on a physical level, one may notice that many references to political, religious, and social commentaries litter the poem as well. Thus, although Donne's description of the "calme" as an entity in itself stands well on its own under analysis, it is crucial that its function as a metaphor for these social criticisms be recognized as well.

Once enlightened with this insight, the reader can easily extricate these metaphors from their physical representations in the poem. The symbols of the storm and "the calme" themselves are certainly the most ubiquitous examples of this theme of multilevel commentary. In line 4, Donne's speaker claims "Storms chafe, and soon wear out themselves, or us," which, when interpreted literally, might imply a "storm" in a physical sense, as in a torrent at sea that might "chafe" a ship, or in a more metaphorical implication, supporting the reading of the storm as a military force that could "wear out" an opponent.

In either case, this storm is an indisputably destructive force, though the former type is omnipotent, being a force of Nature, while the latter represents an ostentation of power among human beings. However, on a more implicit level, this "storm" could intimate a political body, such as Parliament or a system of courts, that, by extensive abuse of power, might oppress the public with excessive expectations, including irrational tariffs and laws. In this way, the "storms" would certainly possess the capabilities to "wear out themselves, or us".

This symbolism continues in the next line of the poem, though the importance of the metaphor is now transferred to the insecurities following the trauma of the storm: "In calms, Heaven laughs to see us languish thus". The oppression and stress of the storm are followed quickly by a period of peace, here interpreted as more of an emptiness than a time of rest. And here looms heavy religious symbolism, in which the embodiment of religion "laughs" at the foolish tendency of human beings to relax their collective guard and allow themselves to "languish" as a race, both physically and morally.

This negative religious representation becomes all the more paradoxical and ironic as one considers some of Donne's more pious works, such as his "Holy Sonnets" and "The Litanie." The images in these other poems, when compared with the metaphors prominent in "The Calme," provide quite a contrast. Nonetheless, these unmistakable images pervade the poem, supplying an ominous, hopeless tone.

This religious theme appears in lines 11 and 12 of "The Calme," in which the speaker claims: "As water did in storms, now pitch runs out;/ As lead, when a fir'd church becomes one spout." These lines combine the religious metaphor with the physical images of storm and calm to sustain a feeling of despondency with a sense of sosme sort of impending doom.

The speaker claims the time of the storm corresponds with a kind of fluidity not present in its aftermath, comparing the flow of water during the storm with the running of "pitch" having the consistency of "lead," for which the church itself serves as a "spout," naming religion as a chief agent of this idleness attributed to "the calme." These repeated images display an unmistakable discontent with society and, especially, one of its key defining elements: the church.

Donne combines this theme of religious discontent with a feeling of social despair and hopelessness evident in the following lines:

Only the calenture together draws
Dear friends, which meet dead in great fishes' jaws,
And on the hatches, as on alters, lies
Each one, his own priest, and own sacrifice. (23-26)

Here the speaker makes the grim claim that the only way to reunite oneself with loved ones is through death, and a ghastly one at that, being driven mad by the sense of isolation and hopelessness caused by the raging waves of the sea, and casting oneself into the jaws of "great fishes." One could even argue the point of sacrilege against Catholicism from these lines, using as evidence the images of sacrificing oneself at the "alter" of the sea, as well as the concept of one being "his own priest," both of which directly conflict with the sacred Catholic house of worship and the need for tutelage and confession for acheivement in religion.

These lines also suggest that Catholicism has become decentralized, even isolating, and, ultimately, a futile effort in weathering "the calme." As the poem approaches its conclusion, the speaker presents the reader with one of the most potent religious images of the entire work, comprehensively summarizing this theme in a few lines:

Fate grudges us all, and doth subtly lay
A scourge, 'gainst which we all forget to pray.
He that at sea prays for more wind, as well
Under the poles may beg cold, heat in hell. (47-51)

Here again Donne's narrator combines religious imagery with reality to achieve his goal: a metaphor for hopelessness. "Fate" in this case might imply some force of Nature, but more likely suggests the supernatural, namely the Catholic Divinity. Nevertheless, this force "grudges" all of humanity. The phrase "doth subtly lay/ A scourge" itself conjures up images of contrast between the words "subtly" and "scourge," thus remaining consistent with the thematic content of the poem.

The depiction of hopeless, scurrilous prayer suggested by the desire for wind, or action, at sea comparing to wishes for cold at the North and South Poles, and "heat in hell," pursue this cohesion as well by presenting the institution of religion as worthless as far as its contribution to the alleviation of this sense of despondency. Donne combines this harsh religious imagery with political commentary in an interesting recitation of a list of historical and mythical figures.

Lines 33-36 site the misfortunes of characters such as Christopher Marlowe's Bajazet, the Biblical Sampson, and Emperor Tiberius, all of whom possess a common theme in a loss of power through treachery and deceit, to which the speaker compares his ships that "languish" now without power nor purpose. Ironically enough, there is an achievement in these hopeless prayers, as they cannot help but be answered with the results for which they sarcastically parley.

This idea of "the calme" paradoxically symbolizing a chaotic void of despair is not limited solely to the political and religious realms of Donne's speaker; the social world is catastrophically affected as well. In the following lines, the narrator combines physical and social aspects in order to achieve this end:

Earth's hollowness, which the world's lungs are,
Have no more wind than the upper vault of air.
We can nor lost friends nor sought foes recover,
But meteor-like, save that we move not, hover. (19-22)

Here the speaker extends this feeling of despair to include even the entity of Earth itself, depicting it as being lifeless and without air or breath. Again, the motionless, languid imagery of the calm dominates the social aspect of the poem, as the speaker compares himself and his cohorts to meteors, "save that we move not," leaving them nothing to do but "hover" idly. This concept of a physical-to-social comparison of immobility is repeated several times, including in line 10, where the speaker claims "our ships rooted be," much like the islands he used to seek. The speaker generalizes this sense of social despair: "How little more, alas,/ Is man now, than before he was? He was/ Nothing; for us, we are nothing fit".

Finally, the social aspect is centralized to focus upon the individual in the form of the speaker himself. He sees no moral difference in being in "a rotten state" with "hope of gain," than from that of longing for love, honour, or valor, as all are based on some level of personal greed and are, therefore, forms of corruption. There is no decipherable difference between living the remainder of life as a "despirate," or dying a coward, nor between predator and prey, as both are eventually rewarded with the same end: death.

Through the use of these metaphors, Donne is able to achieve multiple themes in "The Calme." He accomplishes the incredible feat of combining historical, physical, political, religious, social, and individual images in a single work to achieve a single goal: the expression of despair in his surroundings in just as many aspects; the articulation of dismay in finding oneself in "the calme" of life's aftermath and discovering the decay of all elements of one's life.

Yet, with all his imagery and parallels, Donne's speaker cannot express these concepts any more clearly than he does in the poem's final lines, ultimately declaring the paradox of human nature and its inability to rationalize what is beyond comprehension, hinting that the lack of which is, perhaps, the cause of its own discontent: "We have no power, no will, no sense; I lie,/ I should not then thus feel this misery".

Chapter 12

Under the Sign of Donne – John Donne

In The Fitzwilliam Museum in Cambridge, there is a painting by Stanley Spencer, "John Donne Arriving in Heaven". It is almost his earliest, done in 1911 when Spencer was an eighteen-year-old student at the Slade School of Art. It was exhibited the following year at the Grafton Gallery's Second Post Impressionist exhibition, although not particularly noticed in the hubbub and horror caused by the Cezannes or even by the paintings of the British group—Roger Fry, Duncan Grant, Vanessa Bell, and their soon to be nemesis, Wyndham Lewis.

There is certainly something of a Cezanesque proto-geometry to the painting's spaces, but in its subject and the generating idea for that subject it was quite unlike the others on those gallery walls. The figures are both their own tombstones and their resurrected bodies. They are at once stationary and in motion, here and there, in prayer and expectation—John Donne just happening by.

The painting was prompted by Spencer's receiving a copy of Donne's Sermons from his fellow Slade students, Gwen and Jacques Raverat, and in particular by the phrase, to "Go to Heaven by Heaven," which Spencer interpreted as going past Heaven, alongside it, heaven here being Widbrook Common, a place near Cookham, where Spencer spent most of his life, receiving and painting heavenly visitors.

Suddenly coming upon that painting prompted a series of questions that resulted in this partial inventory of twentieth century Donne signs and sightings. Among them—where was Donne in the literary/artistic imagination at the start of the century during the years immediately before the 1912 Grierson edition and in the decades that followed? Who read him, painted him, thought about him? What have been the terms of the engagement?

And behind those questions—why Donne? This investigation is more exploratory than polemical. The cast of characters is so varied, the Donnes invoked so multiple (love poet, dandy, satirist, religious poet, polemicist, priest), and the responses so various, that gathering the materials and making them speak to each other is in itself a useful enterprise.

For it is remarkable that a writer so word specific as Donne, so much a figure (even as a composite of many figures) of a time, of a space, of readily identifiable ways of being and seeing, can inhabit so many different times and spaces and not only enter, but grain-of-sand-like, disturb the imaginations of so many and so diverse readers. Of course, even in the seventeenth century, Donne was there and elsewhere, both in London and at and through the firmament, space travel in the not so very distant future.

Donne turns up surprisingly frequent]y, although certainly not as often as Shakespeare, who is far more thoroughly embedded in subsequent literature as a data bank of allusions, as a set of texts to remake, which, of course, happens with every production on stage or film (and in other media, as well, in opera or musical, from Verdi's Macbeth or Thomas' Hamlet, to Kiss me Kate, or Play On, the recent jazz version of Twelfth Night) and, most important, as an inescapable cultural presence.

As a synecdoche for the literary imagination, for creativity itself, and as the source for iconic representations of the human condition, his figures at once mythical and recognizable, Shakespeare seems to demand response. There has rarely been, for example, so profound an engagement by one writer of another as by Joyce of Shakespeare, not only in Ulysses but also in Finnegans Wake.

Joyce certainly admired Donne, too, especially the Donne

who "is Shakespearian in his richness," as Arthur Power records Joyce remarking in an account of his conversations with Joyce, but unlike the case of the Shakespeare encounter there was little at stake there and few traces in the Writing.

Moreover, it is usually Shakespeare's Hamlet or his Rosalind one talks about, less often "Shakespeare himself" (a phrase that is as much trope as historical identity); the biographical Shakespeare remains, for the most part, monumentally anonymous. But it is Donne in his texts, this strange yet still somehow contemporary figure from the past, whom the later writer greets, trying on his language and looking inside his imagination.

It is an audacious language, certainly, and it inscribes a vision no less so, but it is oddly transportable over the centuries, its time and place specifities notwithstanding. Donne's syntax of desire, which allows, too, for loss—of love, of God, of self—is somehow renewable in its own terms. The encounter happens less in the manner of a Bloomean agon or an overreaching than simply as a willingness to listen, to re-imagine, to make over as one's own.

In many of the encounters recorded here, it is not Donne as the name for high art whom we meet, but Donne as a writer who has to be read. There is a psychology to map and a linguistic system to parse that remain ongoing provocations, resources, and recourses.

There is an apt and very recent example of just such imaginative listening by the Canadian poets Doug Beardsley and Al Purdy, in their The Man Who Outlived Himself: An Appreciation of John Donne. Indeed, one could believe that the book's publication had been staged by Donne, for its title briefly stood in for the obituary of one of its authors. Al Purdy died on Friday, April 21, 2000, but his death had not yet been announced when the newspaper review appeared on April 22.

This not quite posthumous book (who has outlived whom?) consists of an ongoing conversation about Donne, "the strangest poet in the English language," and of twelve of his poems, followed by a rewriting of five of Donne's elegies in which Donne's language merges through translation, adaptation, and explanation with Purdy's and Beardsley's ("blood transfusions from Donne to us"), and this is followed by a poem from each to Ann More. "I vision her as a girl so tender / and heartbreaking in the way she was / you couldn't look at her without tears / and I can't write about her / without a peculiar kind of love," Purdy wrote, concluding

How far do the elements of lovers go
slingshot as far as the new millennium?
Her body trembling among the outer planets
when he touched her
remained on earth among her dying children.
But that isn't it either;
you say her name Ann More
and both of them
Ann and her lover
John Donne
flash quicksilver in the mind mirror
—her madman, her iconoclast her 'genius'
with microscope brain
and the girl who might have suspected all this
but knew it didn't matter much
beside the tenderness and laughter
a kind of formula we humans have
for making whole our broken lives (109)

Joining those who attempt to imagine Ann into being, Purdy writes to her both as and through Donne and he does get something of the Donne quicksilver and the interplanetary spaces. In the book's conversations, however, the emphasis is mostly on Donne the soliloquist, who is something of an attitude taker, nearly all intellect, someone who has "difficulty taking his eyes off himself", but who is also capable of being carried away in ecstasy, even if, as Purdy suspects, he may be only performing ecstasy. Purdy and Beardsley are attentive to that ecstasy, but entirely in the realm of the secular. They do not hear or see what Stanley Spencer did.

What Spencer saw, of course, was heaven and he saw it with Donne's eyes. He certainly had read more of the second prebend sermon on Psalm 63 (preached at St. Paul's Jan. 29,

1626) than the one line he alluded to in the painting's title. The sermon's soaring operatic conclusion has heaven in nearly every line (in one patch 20 times in 14 lines); indeed the whole passage is behind the painting: "for all the way to heaven is heaven.

And as those angels, which come from Heaven hither bring heaven with them and are in heaven here. So that soule that goes to heaven, meets heaven here." Spencer also read the poems as well as the sermons and many of his paintings suggest an ongoing meditation on Donne and, more to the point, a Donnean meditation on eros, God, and the wondrous materiality of our life on earth.

This is his only painting with Donne as subject, but an implicit Donne, the apostle of eroticized divine love and of sex made holy is a presence in nearly all he painted and in many of his writings (sermons he called some of them) on art, life, religion, and love.

In a series of paintings called "Beatitudes of Love," Spencer described "the twinned and unified souls of two persons [the two figures in each painting]. The composition turns the two into one person and becomes a single organism.... They are more genuine than any religious paintings I have ever done....

The religious quality I had been looking for and had never found in my work hitherto, now in my sex pictures showed itself for the first time.... In all my sex experience I notice the same degree of emotion as in religious experience." He described "Beatitude: Contemplation", as "a husband [a Spencer self-portrait] and wife... engaged in contemplation of each other, as if expressed by their rapt gaze, as though they would never stop looking" (quoted in Collis, 141).

Of another painting, he remarks, "I had just drawn a composition of Christ choosing the disciples. To make it convincing I had to pilfer from one of my sex pictures an incident where a man is choosing a girl. His gesture was just right. I could take some of my sex pictures and transpose them into religious ones, and no one would know they had ever been otherwise" (Collis, 143). And it was not just sex, it was all the activities of daily life that carried the divine, from the cowls (ventilating shaft covers on a brewery) in "Mending Cowls, Cookham" to the armchair Christ sits on in a late painting, "Christ in Cookham." They are presented as items in a transfigured but still workaday world where "the events must seem as real as going shopping." "I am always wanting," Spencer continued "to establish a union between myself and what is divine and holy."

The most widely known Spencer painting, "The Resurrection, Cookham", depicts a heaven quite like the one Donne arrived at a dozen years earlier, but more populated, closer to the centre of town. "As it is heaven," Spencer wrote, "there is no hurrying to be off.... they are at home before they have got right out of their graves ["as soone as it is out of my body [it] is in heaven" in the words of that sermon]....

In the bottom right-hand corner is another `me,'... the collapsing tombs interlock like the pages of a book. I love the pages of a book, an open book, and so I am where I love to be." And that body as book, body in book figure connects via Donne to another Spencer painting, "Love Letters":

Study our manuscripts, those Myriades
Of letters, which have past twixt thee and mee,
thence write our Annals, and in them will bee
To all whom loves subliming fire invades,
Rule and example found.

Spencer and his beloved, though divorced, wife Hilda wrote to each other from the twenties until her death in 1950 (he had divorced her in 1937), nor did her death stop his highly erotic letters. In this painting done shortly after her death, the two are in their letters, are of their letters. "Then as all my soules bee / Emparadis'd in you, (in whom alone / I understand, and grow and see"; "A Valediction of my name, in the window"), Spencer, had he been Donne, might have written.

What he had written to her twenty years earlier was, "I thought about a week agow [sic] that is about 460 quarters of an hour ago, that I would like to stick all mine and your letters... neatly all over the asbestos wall of the studio... what a marvelous feeling of communion of all our thoughts." Walls, windows, letters, bodies, books, John Donne redivivus, one might say, had that epithet not been applied to his acquaintance, Rupert Brooke. It was James Elroy Flecker who called Brooke "our Donne redivivus" in a review of Brooke's 1911 Poems. He was thinking of poems like "Dust" or "The Fish," or "Mummia."

Mummia
As those of old drunk mummia
To fire their limbs of lead,
Making dead kings from Africa
Stand pandar to their bed;
Drunk on the dead, and medicined
With spiced imperial dust,
In a short night they reeled to find
Ten centuries of lust
So I, from paint, stone, tale, and rhyme,
Stuffed love's infinity,
And sucked all lovers of all time
To rarefy ecstasy.

The "mummy" of "Loves Alchymie" hardly rarefied ecstacy, but Brooke's Donne is clad in rather pre-Raphaelite robes. "Dust" captures more of the Donnean desire and, in two of its lines, more of an echo of the voice, as it imagines the lovers dead, crumbled in their separate night, but with the possiblity of reunion remaining:

And every mote, on earth or air,
Will speed and gleam, down later days,
And like a secret pilgrim fare
By eager and invisible ways,
Nor ever rest, nor ever lie,
Till, beyond thinking, out of view,
One mote of all the dust that's I
Shall meet one atom that was you.

Brooke's Donnean manner may be too easily come by, but the echoes are often pleasing, "And Innocence accounted wise, / and Faith the fool, the pitiable. / Love so rare, one would swear / All of earth for ever well— / Careless lips and flying hair / And little things I may not tell" ("Sometimes Even Now...,"). Although there is more gesture than substance here as Brooke echoes the teacher and works the metaphor machine like an apt but not particularly inspired pupil, he does mark a significant moment in the history of Donne reception before the Grierson edition (his Donne was probably the Chambers edition, and encountered in what Dayton Haskin has documented as the newfound enthusiasm for Donne in the last years of the nineteenth century).

Brooke's letters show him reading Donne in 1907 and there are numerous other references, one a description of him setting off for Germany in 1912 with Baedeker and Donne in his pocket. He wrote three interesting reviews of the Grierson edition, the first, in The Nation for February 15, 1913, using the Spencer painting as its occasion: "One of the most remarkable of the English pictures in the recent Post-Impressionist exhibition depicts John Donne arriving in Heaven.

`I don't know who John Donne is,' a sturdy member of the public was lately heard to remark in front of it, `but he seems to be getting there.'" And, Brooke continues, with this new edition Donne is indeed "getting there." The Donne of this review "startles the soul from her lair with unthinkable paradoxes"; he is a love poet unafraid to "acknowledge that he was composed of body, soul, and mind."

In the next review, Brooke set the terms for the Herbert Read / T. S. Eliot Donne: "Donne feels only the idea. He does not try to visualize it. He never visualizes, or suggests that he has any pleasure in looking at things. His poems might have been written by a blind man in a world of blind men". Wrong, wrong, wrong, one is inclined to remark, but remarkably tenacious.

A late poem, "Safety," reads like a reprise of the separate planet Donne, the Donne of "The Sun Rising" and "The Good Morrow," but now in time of war: "Who is so safe as we? / We have found safety with all things undying, /... We have built a house that is not for Time's throwing. / We have gained a peace unshaken by pain for ever / War knows no power".

Some of these late poems confronting death and war are among his weakest, most notably the multiply anthologized, "The Soldier."

As Samuel Hymes observes, however, these poems do have a "value which one would not want to lose, for they tell us with terrible accuracy of the delusions of nobility which Brooke's generation carried into war." But many who carried Donne to war read those death inflected poems more profoundly than did Brooke. Owen is a good example and most strikingly, Edgell Rickword, who revealed a response very different from Brooke's variations on a Keatsian easeful death:

I knew a man, he was my chum,
but he grew blacker every day,
and would not brush the flies away,
nor blanch however fierce the hum
of passing shells; I used to read,
to rouse him, random things from Donne—
like "Get with child a mandrake root."
But you can tell he was far gone,
for he lay gaping, mackerel-eyed,
and stiff and senseless as a post
even when that old poet cried
"I long to talk with some old lover's ghost."
I tried the Elegies one day,
but he, because he heard me say:
"What needst thou have more covering than a man?"
grinned nastily, so then I knew
the worms had got his brains at last.
There was one thing that I might do
to starve those worms; I racked my head
for wholesome lines and quoted Maud.
His grin got worse and I could see
he sneered at passion's purity.
He stank so badly, though we were great chums
I had to leave him; then rats ate his thumbs.

Here Donne's lines are offered in defiance of death and yet are the very materials, in a species of verbal anamorphia, out of which Death is created. Rickword brought his Donne, the two-volume Muse's Library edition that he had been reading at Oxford, with him to the Front in late December, 1917, barely two months past his nineteenth birthday. Its echoes are not only audible in "Trench Poets" but in several other poems published in his first volume, Behind the Eyes (1921), notably "Advice to a Girl from the War," a grim recollection of "Go and Catch a Falling Star":

Weep for me half a day,
then dry your eyes,
Think! Is a mess of clay
worth a girl's sighs?
Sigh three days if you can
for my waste of blood.
Think then, you love a man
whose face is mud

Some years after his return to England, Rickword was still thinking about Donne. "Divagation on a Line of Donne's: `My verse the strict map of my misery'," which appeared in his second collection with the Donnean title, Invocations to Angels (1928), is both a commentary on the nature of Donne's poetry and a revisiting of that battlefield scene of death:

That tangled growth of intellect and passion,
where thought spread sensuous, mental love's last acts,
where doubt's exhuberance even doubt defied,
thrust skywards in the noon-day of ambition.
Till in a flash which humbled that rich Earth
Donne saw Time's handiwork on the bodies of men,
and Death, squat in each wrinkle as a trench,
sniping the careless heads of Love and Mirth.
He wooed God "like an angel from a cloud",
preaching: but sometimes the more faithful pen
revived a metaphor that had trapped a wench
and shames the dandy in the wimpled shroud.

"The most modern of all poets," Rickwood called Donne, and it is precisely this sense of Donne's contemporaneity that links the diverse voices assembled here.

Lytton Stachey also enters the picture. He reviewed the

Grierson edition, indeed before Booke did (he may well have been responsible for getting Brooke to read Donne), his own interest in Donne going back well before 1905. It was in that year that he wrote a set of poems anatomizing his despair over losing the battle to Maynard Keynes for the affections of their fellow apostle, Hobhouse. Their titles: "The Exhumation," "The Conversation," "The Speculation," "The Resolution." Strachey was a biographer and essayist, not a poet, but these poems do catch the Donne sound and image with a sort of spectral fidelity, for example, "The Exhumation," especially its concluding lines:

Oh, what rash fancy did your spirit move
To resurrect my long-expired love?
What was there in that corpse that you should break
So much thick stone asunder for its sake?
But when you stooped your lips down, and at last
Touched—oh, touched what?—did you not shrink aghast
To see in one swift second disappear
That vision, like the body of Guinivere,
And all the rich alembic of my lust
Turn in a moment to a little dust?

Donne remained an interest, an intellectual resource all his life. There's an amusing anecdote of Carrington preparing herself for a trip with Strachey in 1916, boning up on her Donne. In the event, it rained a great deal and so they stayed inside, Strachey reading, Carrington painting. She did a wonderful painting of half of this scene: Strachey is lying down, his Donne volume closed but held carefully as if he were weighing it in his exquisitely shaped hands.

At about the same time across the Atlantic, Hart Crane, a poet who not only learned how to read Donne but to write him from inside his language and yet never to sound imitative or derivative, was, in his words, "runn[ing] joyfully toward John Donne!!!" Crane found Donne "a wonder, speaking from my own experience".

"I am fond of things of great fragility," he wrote, "and also, and especially of the kind of poetry John Donne represents, a dark, murky, brooding, speculative vintage, at once sensual and spiritual, rather the beauty of experience than innocence". The transformation, transmutation really, is fascinating. Crane refers to specific lines—The "Second Aniversary" 's "Thou shalt not peepe through lattices of eies, / Nor heare through Laberinths of eares"—and all of "The Expiration" as illustrating what he wanted to do as a poet: "What I want to get is just what is so beautifully done in this poem ["The Expiration"], an `interior form', a form that is so thorough and intense as to dye the words themselves with a peculiarity of meaning, slightly different maybe from the ordinary definition of them separate from the poem. If you remember my `Black Tambourine' [he is writing to Sherwood Anderson in 1922, the year after the publication of this early poem], you will perhaps agree with me that I have at least accomplished this idea once".

The interests of a black man in a cellar
Mark tardy judgment on the world's closed door.
Gnats toss in the shadow of a bottle,
And a roach spans a crevice on the floor.
Aesop, driven to pondering, found
Heaven with the tortoise and the hare;
Fox brush and sow ear top his grave
And mingling incantations on the air.
The black man, forlorn in the cellar,
Wanders in some mid-kingdom, dark, that lies
Between his tambourine, stuck on the wall,
And, in Africa, a carcass quick with flies.

In Donne's "Expiration"—kiss, go, ghost, death, kill, word—carry their "ordinary meaning" but at the same time are "dye[d]... with a peculiarity of meaning," that is, de-and-reformed in metaphor. Crane's poem, like Donne's, 12 lines long, is not about kisses and lovers, but about black poets and musicians in the cellars of the white world cut off from the myth makers who mingle incantations on the air. But it too stays entirely inside its metaphor (as in that Frost line that defines poetry, "like a piece of ice on a hot stove, the poem must ride on its own melting"), no talking animals, just gnats, roaches, and flies."

'Make my dark poem light, and light'... is the text I chose from Donne sometime ago, as my direction", Crane wrote to Allen Tate, referring to the line, minus the "heavy," that comes from the same stanza in Donne's Metempsychosis in which he launches at Paradise. "I have always been working hard for a more perfect lucidity, and it never pleases me to be taken as willfully obscure and esoteric." But he was so taken; metaphysical, he was often called, and whatever that word means, it does seem to link these two apparently so different poets.

The connection that Crane felt between himself and Donne has more to do with deep structure than surface detail. That was certainly the way the poet and critic-teacher, Josephine Miles, approached the issue of the Donne legacy in her 19 71 essay "Twentieth Century Donne": "What 17th century metaphysical, what Donnian traits could be useful to the present?" What she found was a tradition she called "the poetry of concept countered by concept" within a structure that is both "exceptive and limiting... not merely and but but and yet, with implicative ifs and concessive thoughs".

Her terms are different from Crane's (he figures only briefly in her examples, for his handling of time) but, like him, she locates her investigation within the articulation of the poem's elements, its language and thought (Yeats thus becomes the truest heir with other examples drawn from Auden, Eliot, Cummings, Stevens, Warren, but not from too many at the time of her writing).

What she was looking for was less what a twentieth-century poet might want to take from Donne, or how such a poet might read, respond, or echo him, than what Donne and his contemporaries had "deposited" in the language that had survival power (language here conceived almost as a geological stratum—a Burgess shale of teeming syntactic forms), so that coming across W. S. Merwin's "Fear," for example, she sees "the survival [there] of the skeleton of exceptive and adversative concept... as a wonder worth remark, a suggestion of the surviving power of Donne's thought in the 20th Century".

Thus, despite the interest shown in Donne by Brooke, de la Mare, Elinor Wylie, Dylan Thomas, the Fugitives, among others (connections that George Williamson had identified in his 1931 essay "Donne and Today," where his argument had chiefly centered on the Donne/Eliot link, Miles concludes that "few... have tried for or achieved that combination of values which makes for a whole likeness rather than a scattering of likenesses."

Both Miles and more recently Arthur Clements in his Poetry of Contemplation construct a Donne (for one he's a conceptual, for the other a contemplative poet) then look for modern likenesses. I am more interested in the encounter of poet to poet and in the turns of the ensuing dialogue.

However, at the same time, I want to identify the multiple uses to which he has been put, the way he turns up as name, allusion, cultural reference, or simply turn of simile, in undertakings that may or may not resemble his. Or even in the way a Donne figure is suddenly reborn whole in "Natural History," a poem E. B.

White sent to his wife, Katherine Angell, in 1929: "Thus I, gone forth, as spiders do, / In spider's web a truth discerning, / Attach one silken strand to you / For my returning." Donne as source for Charlotte's Web?

The Donne with whom Miles opened her essay was the Eliotic Donne, the Donne she had grown up with, "direct sensuous apprehension of thought," the immediacy of the odor of the rose, terms that she realized were inadequate as she reread and rethought the poems.

It has become a familiar refrain, that mischievous paragraph in the 1921 "Essay on Metaphysical Poetery" (one paragraph and all that fuss!). And the few echoes in the poetry are also familar (they are not so much allusions as nods in the direction of; Eliot talked about Donne far more than he used him).

The canonization narrative and the counter narratives, how Eliot needed his version of Donne for his version of Eliot, are familiar, too. But one of the real silences of that narrative is the absent book on Donne. There were the 1926 Clark Lectures,

"On the Metaphysical Poetry of the 17th Century," and the 1931 "Donne in Our Time" essay, which offered, it should be emphasized, a considerably nuanced version of the 1921 argument. Thought and sensibility are still fissured but the emphasis now is on language; there is less about the mind of England and more about the natural, conversational style that made it possible for subsequent poets to think in lyric verse.

There was, as well, an abbreviated version of the Clark in the 1933 Johns Hopkins Turnbull lectures. There were plans to publish these as The School off Donne but that never happened. Visions and revisions notwithstanding (and there were several), and Eliot's insistence that the lectures not be quoted without permission, there was no book (the lectures were only published a few years ago). Eliot finally gave the rights to the title to A. Alvarez, whose book The School of Donne appeared in 1961.

Eliot's view of Donne, of course, was not his alone. Rupert Brooke had anticipated it and Herbert Read echoed and somewhat modified it two years later in his 1923 essay, "The Nature of Metaphysical Poetry," published in the Criterion. But in many ways more interesting than his intervention in Donne criticism, is the volume of poetry Read published the same year, Mutations of the Phoenix.

The epigraph of the title poem is to Shakespeare's rather than to Donne's phoenix. But the mythical bird mutates and in one section "burns spiritually among the fierce stars and in the docile brain's recesses," giving to the phoenix riddle something of a Donnean sense of last things: "But vision is fire, Light burns the world in the focus of any eye. The eye is all: is hierarch of the finite world. Eye gone light gone, and the unknown is very near."

Two other poems in that volume are explicit in their Donne references, indeed one is about Donne, spoken by him, "John Donne Declines a Benefice." The other, "The Analysis of Love," has as its epigraph, "The Ecstasy" 's "great prince in prison." Its analysis of love and lust is Read's not Donne's, but at moments is strikingly Donnean in form as Read works through Donne's language to argue against it:

In vain I have searched the visible earth
For any symbol of our love:
Doves, elephants and Abelards
Have seemed too empty of our mood.
They are too finite in their wooing
Linked by ambitious bonds:
I court you in the commonplace
And a wonder is in our path.
Rather we are like a plant's cells
Invisibly one:
And then you are universal;
I too: our minds,
Not cramp'd by figured thought
Unite in the impersonal beauty we possess.

By the close, however, Wordsworth has replaced Donne:

Link me with circumstance if you must,
But live to triumph all the same;
We'll be insensate when the whirl
Of circumstance is past

And the ending is almost a refutation of Donne:

This mental ecstacy all spent
In disuniting death;
And the years that spread
Oblivion on our zest.

"John Donne Declines a Benefice," is quite different. It uses Donne's letter to Morton taken from Walton's Life as an epigraph and is a meditative monologue in which "Donne" ponders his refusal. To a certain degree it is pastiche (Donne speaks "Donne"): he talks of God who is "to man... a magnetic North, a call / For conscience to settle toward"; flesh is "throughshine," at another point, "hydroptic," the space of timeless radiance is "an intangible fire / That does not stain those white souls black," "the body [is] left, a wickless mass / Of inchoation," a word that occurs in the sermons, but not in the poems.

The monologue is imagined as happening moments after the letter is written, but will it be sent? Has he convinced himself of the refusal? The offer is appealing, "If but the propulsion for such scheme / Were generate in this complex frame!" And then, too, he muses, what if Morton departs "And I am outcast in a wrangling world / Where an evolved soul's of no avail, / Save for the delight of wits." Finally, fearing to "fade into age, / Full of dissembling sanctity," he is determined, "I'll not! I'll not! / Quick! To Morton! The will is set!" (159-64).

Much more than Read, however, William Empson is the poet-critic who is pretty nearly Donne's best reader and a good poet, too, in some considerable measure because of Donne. Empson was an undergraduate at Magdalene when Eliot gave the Clark lectures, and he worked a recollection of Eliot's coffee circle talk to the undergraduates into Seven Types of Ambiguity, but claimed in later years that he had never actually attended the lectures on the grounds that as an undergraduate he attended no lectures.

No other critic so directly challenges my conviction that Donne will say anything that the poem requires, truth value of little concern. Empson's Donne means what he says, you had better believe him. This is not the place to examine Empson's critical writing about Donne and, too, the Donne presence in his poetry has been well explored by Christopher Ricks. There are, however, a few points worth emphasizing.

For Empson and Donne "the metaphors are not reduced to a blank obedience but are allowed to ask for themselves a richer presence," in Ricks's fine phrase. Both poets think in science, if not as scientists. Ricks point to "To an Old Lady" as a poem which "makes the most serious use of the spacemanship which Empson learnt from Donne"

Years her precession do not throw from gear.
She reads a compass certain of her pole;
Confident, finds no confines on her sphere,
Whose failing crops are in her sole control.
Stars how much further from me fill my night.
Strange that she too should be inaccessible,
Who shares my sun. He curtains her from sight,
And but in darkness is she visible.

In his 1935 note to the poem, Empson fretted about not getting all he wanted in: "the unconfined surface of her sphere is like the universe in being finite but unbounded, but I failed to get that into the line". However, in the prefatory note to the 1955 Collected Poems he observed:

"By the way, I have been much disturbed by recent theories that the universe is not, after all, finite though unbounded, as the earlier poems here often require it to be; but I retain my confidence that the sane old views we were brought up upon will come back into favour." This is not so different from Donne's lament over lost coherence in "An Anatomy of the World," which one finds echoed in another poem, where Donne's inch that was a span becomes Empson's title, "Earth has Shrunk in the Wash".

There is, no doubt, a greater degree of irony in Empson's remark about "the sane old views" than in Donne's, but for both what the writing requires is primary, and even if old views are disturbed the intellectual excitement of the new is always present.

Like Donne, Empson listens to the "eternal silence of the infinite spaces" and asks "where is the darkness that gives light its place?" ("Letter I," 19). Sometimes he even sounds like Donne or as Donne might have sounded some three hundred years later, as in "This Last Pain":

This last pain for the damned the Fathers found:
'They knew the bliss with which they were not crowned.'
Such, but on earth, let me foretell,
Is all, of heaven or of hell.
Man, as the prying housemaid of the soul,
May know her happiness by eye to hole:
He's safe; the key is lost; he knows
Door will not open, nor hole close.
'What is conceivable can happen too,'
Said Wittgenstein, who had not dreamt of you;
Feign then what's by a decent tact believed
And act that state is only so conceived,
And build an edifice of form
For house where phantoms may keep warm.
Imagine, then, by miracle, with me,
(Ambiguous gifts, as what gods give must be)

What could not possibly be there,
And learn a style from despair.

The "edifice of form" to warm the phantoms, the miraculous in possibility's despite, the style learned from despair—these get at something essential in Donne's writing as well as in Empson's.

It is not only for poets writing in English that this encounter has been crucial. Joseph Brodsky claimed he learned English in order to be able to translate Donne and when he left the Soviet Union for England in 1972 he had a copy of Donne in his pocket.

At his 1964 trial (it was at hard labour after that, when he wrote the 200+ line "Elegy to John Donne"), he was asked his profession, "I am a poet," he answered. Not a good answer: "Tell us why you refused to work," the judge demanded. "I did work. I wrote poems," said Brodsky. "Elegy to John Donne" is in some measure a justification of that claim. "John Donne fell asleep, and all around him slept. The pictures slept, the wall, the floor, the bedding." In the elegy, the world sleeps, God sleeps, Donne sleeps, his poems sleep:

..., all lay sleeping.
All was asleep. The window, with its snow,
the white slope of the rooftop like a blanket,
its ridge and the whole quarter lie asleep
slit open by a window mortally.
A boat sleeps in the port. The snow and water
under its hull sleep wheezily and cough
merging far-off with heavens, long asleep.
John Donne lay sound asleep. The sea slept with him,
the chalky shore asleep above the sea.

The snow keeps falling... on the speaker in his Archangel exile (Archangel!... there are no coincidences), on the imagined London of the past poet's life and death. It's a difficult poem, a dialogue of poet to poet—Donne/Brodsky—it's not always clear who speaks, who listens, who weeps, who reads the tears. Is it the cherubim who weep? Paul? Gabriel? "No, it is I, John Donne. `Tis I, your soul." Thus elegist becomes subject (something of a "Lycidas" turn):

... You climbed the roof-top's ridge.
You saw the ocean, all the lands far off,
and Hell you saw by image, and then real.
And God you saw, then hastened back again.

Through Donne, Brodsky is a poet both living and dead: "For though we can with others share our life, whom can we find to share death equally?" Later, in the West, his poems still caught the Donnean sense of miracle, for example, "25.XII.1993" published in 1999:

For a miracle, take one shepherd's sheepskin, throw
In a pinch of now, a grain of long ago,
And a handful of tomorrow. Add by eye
A little bit of ground, a piece of sky.
And it will happen. For miracles, gravitating
To earth, know just where people will be waiting,
And eagerly will find the right address
And tenant, even in a wilderness.

Those last lines Donne would certainly have approved.

In some sense all poetry is translation—from the inchoations of the silent self to the fixity of language, from past texts to present remakings, from language to language. Like Brodsky, Yehuda Amichai learned his own voice in part through these acts of translation and for both Donne was a crucial space to pass their words through. In several of Amichai's poems, Donne is the silent middle term in the act of transumption/translation.

The eleventh-century poet-philosopher Shlomo Ibn Gabirol (Avencebrol as the West knows him) is the subject of a poem about poetry and pain that concludes, "But through the wound in my chest God peers into the universe. I am the door to his apartment."

Or "Jerusalem, 1967," where the phrase "Yehudean desert," plays on his own name and place and the name of the twelfth-century poet, Yehuda Halevi, whose line, "My heart is in the East and I am at the edge of the West," becomes in Amichai's poem, "I played the hopscotch of the four strict squares of Yehuda Ha-Levi: My heart.

Myself. East. West". Amichai reading Donne and reading

Halevi; Donne reading Halevi? Quite possibly since Halevi's "Ode to Zion" was one of the most widely available Hebrew poems for several centuries after his death.

Throughout Amichai's poetry one hears echoes, not of lines or words, but, as with Empson, of ways of seeing, being, saying: for example, further on in "Jerusalem, 1967": "And already the demons of the past are meeting with the demons of the future and negotiating about me," or most strikingly (as Edward Hirsch has pointed out) in "A Pity we were such a good invention":

They amputated
Your thighs off my hips.
as far as I'm concerned
they are all surgeons. All of them.
They dismantled us
Each from the other.
As far as I'm concerned
they are all engineers. All of them.
A pity. We were such a good
And loving invention.
An aeroplane made from a man and a wife.
Wings and everything.
We hovered a little above the earth.
We even flew a little.

Another title could be "A Valediction Demanding Mourning." And one might describe "Travels of the Last Benjamin of Tudela," as, in some measure, Amichai's Metempsychosis, the poet now the fourth of these Benjamins and living on Tudela Street in Jerusalem: "My body will be dismantled and my soul will glide out to sea, and its shape is the shape of my body in which it lay and its shape is the shape of the sea, and the shape of the sea is like the shape of my body".

Like the vagrant soul, Donne turns up in all sorts of places, in Borges's encounter with Biathanatos, which turned him into an avid Donne reader, in Philip Larkin's "Poem about Oxford: For Monica:" "It holds us, like that Fleae we read about. In the depths of the Second World War," in Bob Dylan's "Sister," "we die and were reborn and then mysteriously saved" ("Wee dye and rise the same, and prove Mysterious by this love" as "The Canonization" would have it). Not surprisingly, it is mostly the poets who have read Donne with greatest intensity, but there are novelists, too, in this narrative—Virginia Woolf, for example.

She, as did all Bloomsbury, read her Donne. In a 1931 diary entry, she lists things that make her happy: music, walks, writing, "and interestingly at Donne of a morning." The following year, indeed the very day that the invitation to deliver the Clark Lectures arrived, an offer she refused, she recorded receiving as a gift a book with Donne's autograph and notes (it was the first 1605 edition of Alberico Gentilis, Regales Disputationes Tres).

She made detailed reading notes on his poems and her characters read and know Donne from her earliest novel onward. He appears in several of the essays and has one of his own, "Donne after Three Centuries" in the second Common Reader in 1932, where she attempted to find out how "his voice... strikes upon the ear after this long flight across the stormy seas that separate us from the age of Eizabeth."

She found a writer of contradictions, one who could not see the whole, who particularized, who diminished, who stared intently at detail, who at times is like us, but at others inconceivably remote, who, to the end, "retained the incorrigible curiosity of his youth," one whose "obstinate interest in the nature of his own sensations still troubled his age and broke his repose," who even in death, "must still cut a figure and still stand erect." It is his nonconformity that she valued most, his "queer individuality," her sense of him (as of her self?) as eccentric, as at once inside and out.

As interested as Woolf was in Donne, he does not seem as deeply implicated in her writing as he is in Djuna Barnes's Nightwood, where he enters the "Watchman, What of the Night?" section of that novel. There the transvestite Dr. Matthew-Mighty-Grain-of-Salt-Dante-O'Connor, talks Browne and Burton, cites Montaigne and uses as a major text in his discourse on the night the lines from a Donne sermon: "We are all conceived in close prison, in our mothers' womb we are close prisoners all. When we are born, we are but born to the liberty of the house—all our life is but a going out of the place of execution and death.

Now was there ever any man seen to sleep in the cart, between Newgate and Tyburn? Between the prison and the place of execution, does any man sleep? Yet he says, men sleep all the way.

How much more, therefore, is there upon him in a close sleep when he is mounted on darkness." And in the transmigrations of his imagination, O'Connor sometimes sounds like the repository of the deathless soul's wanderings in Metempsychosis: "What an autopsy I'll make... a kidney and a shoe cast of the Roman races; a liver and a long spent whisper, a gall and a wrack of scolds from Milano, and my heart that will be weeping still when they find my eyes cold, not to mention a thought of Cellini in my crib of bones".

The uses to which Donne is put are sometimes profound, sometimes superficial. Vikram Seth, for example, takes his title, An Equal Music, and his epigraph from the sermons: "And into that gate they shall enter, and in that house they shall dwell, where there shall be no cloud, nor sun, no darkness nor dazzling, but one equal light, no noise nor silence, but one equal music, no fears nor hopes, but one equal possession, no foes nor friends, but one equal communion and identity, no ends nor beginnings, but one equal eternity."

It is unlikely, however, that Donne imagined such music to have been audible on earth, even if he could have heard The Art of the Fugue. Epigraph and title are made to certify the novel's high intent, but other than upping the ante for musics powers, they don't (or Donne doesn't) really matter for the novel.

On the other hand, Updike's use of Donne in Bech at Bay is both subtle and conceptually crucial. Quotation and allusion matter less than the name, than Donne as book. In "Bech Noir" Donne presides over Bech's first murder, as Bech brings about the seemingly "accidental" death of one of his many imagined literary nemeses at the Rockefeller Centre subway station. A few minutes later "a dainty edition of Donne's Poems [is] pressed close to [Bech's] face as the news of the unthinkable truth spread." A bit later, this time at Times Square, the book falls open to "Death Be Not Proud."

Later, as the murders multiply and Bech waits for the return of Robin, his young sidekick with whom he has "known sin" (the plotting and planning of these accidents and induced suicides and occasional outright murders), he reads Froissart about the body count at Crecy and then, as a cleansing gesture, takes a dip into the little volume of Donne.

In a recent meditation on the nature of faith, Updike evokes a Donnean sense of last things, his vivid realization that "we were all poised above the chasm—suddenly quite vivid to me—of our eventual deaths," the sense that "one had been suddenly flayed of the skin of habit and herd feeling that customarily enwraps and deadens our deep predicament.

I later assigned this experience to a fictional character, a Jewish character, though it may be a Christian-specific form of harrowing." And to that character, Bech, he gave Donne's poems as a marker of the soul's intricacies and deceptions.

Two plays also offer a similar contrast and may help focus the still lingering and not really answered question "why Donne?"—Wallace Shawn's The Designated Mourner and Margaret Edson's Wit. In an elegant discussion of Shawn's play, Dayton Haskin explores whether it matters that it is Donne whose obliteration from human memory the mourner sets out to mourn? Is it Donne, in particular, or Donne as a name for poetry in general?

He finds that it is, indeed, Donne that matters, but not necessarily the familiar Donne, rather the Donne of excess, of bad taste and impertinence, the Donne who played Elizabeth Drury's designated mourner, a role, Haskin argues, Shawn takes for himself in the play; and also the Donne whose sermons were autobiographical acts, scripts with which his readers could recreate the lost original performances? The point I would underline here is that Donne matters in this play, that the questions Who is and What is Donne are the crucial ones.

It is precisely in these terms, however, that Donne does not matter for Edwon's Wit, despite the constant reiteration of his name and at least one of his texts, "Death Be Not Proud." To be sure, the body is a book and those anatomizing doctors read its parts with the scholarly attention that Professor Bearing had lavished on her Donne texts, both doctors and scholar eschewing the sentimental, the merely human.

But for all the niceness of the pointing (no melodramatic semicolons, only sighing commas), Donne is reduced to that "brilliant... guy [who] makes Shakespeare sound like a Hallmark card," and at the climax is trumped by Margaret Wise's Runaway Bunny ("shucks, said the little bunny, I might just as well stay where I am and be your little bunny") and displaced, too, by that culturally more assimilable Shakespeare and his flights of angels.

Donne here means "difficult writer," but not one that Edson seems to have read much of. I don't think Edson really likes Donne or his poems; still the debate she stages over how to read them, or at least one of them, does quite beautifully set up that extraordinary moment when her scholar heroine passes over that slight breath, the comma between life and death.

Life, Death—last things: Donne and Emily Dickinson are probably the two most spectacular death poets in English (a connection that has been made musically in John Adams's Harmonium, a setting of Donne and Dickinson poems). Although Dickinson often sounds like Herbert, one of whose poems she had copied in a notebook, the obsessive fascination with death rather recalls Donne. There is no real evidence that she read Donne, but one feels that she must have.

Yet Virginia Woolf's comment about Donne wanting to cut a figure even in death, which gets at the combination of death's head and dandy that has intrigued so many, does not describe Dickinson's more impersonal, less melodramatic encounters with death. It does, however, point exactly to what the mid-century American painter and poet Marsden Hartley saw and heard.

His "The Last Look of John Donne" works with the

familiar image that Donne had had painted so that he could contemplate it as he lay dying, but it is not quite as remembered; it is a little less smiling, less composed than the original effigy.

Hartley painted it in 1940, not long before his own death and in the direct frontal style that he was working in then, most notably in his portrait of fellow painter, Albert Ryder, who stares at the viewer with a Donne-like fierceness and whose white wool tuque suggests Donne's shroud. It was during this period that Hartley was also writing a sequence of poems called

"Patterns for Prayers," all suffused with a Donnean anguish, sensibility, and language. They reprise the Holy Sonnets; one begins "Look down ever-intimate one / see the bird of these ultimate and inevitable wishes cries out from its crucifixion in the sky," or

O lift me—majestic Sire
touch me with your quenchless
fire.
Keep me—O keep me from falling
down—down into the incredible
abyss
Of human helplessness.
Lend me one ray from the
inexhaustible sun
of your immeasurable love.
I would, like the gentle dove,
fly to some aspect of your
most generous heaven
and there be saved from dire
oblivion.

At the time that Hartley painted the portrait effigy, and with the concluding lines from Donne's "Oh my black soul..." echoing, he wrote a poem that brilliantly recapitulates the encounters I've been tracing here. There is a gesture of recognition, a question or two, an acknowledgment of shared sympathies, yet a registering of something else, of danger, of distance, of frozen light:

John Donne in His Shroud:
It was a smart caprice
to dress
you like this.
Was it a borrowed occasion
as some hire evening suits for a party?
And the white poppy
on top of your head,
does that mean now white
that once was red?
For red is the colour of a pagan wine
of brisk desire
and of flesh-fire—
white is for calm attire.
In any case, if it is character
is wanted in a face
I would say—look at
John Donne,
that will suffice,
fierce passion turned to ice
and frozen light.

The ars moriendi tradition that Donne inherited, replayed, eroticized is one link from then to now, so, too, are the intellectual curiosity, the cynicism, the "fierce passion," the linguistic extravagance, the insistent embodiment of the spirit.

Yet none of these equals Donne, who remains a multiple, unresolvable provocation. As the allusions accumulate, there is always another sighting to record or encounter to assess. He is certainly useful coin for those who want to trade on his name now that Shakespeare's stock is possibly too common. But for those who take him on, speak to and through him, receive the "blood transfusion" in Al Purdy's words, the results can be astonishing.

Chapter 13

John Donne's "The Sun Rising"

Critics of John Donne's "The Sun Rising" often note that the poem's displacement of the outside world in favor of two lovers' inner world serves to support its overall theme: the centrality of human love amidst a permanent physical universe. In an essay entitled "John Donne," Achsah Guibbory supports this reading of the poem, stating, "The world of love contains everything of value; it is the only one worth exploring and possessing.

Hence the microcosmic world of love becomes larger and more important than the macrocosm". "[T]he lovers' room," Toshihiko Kawasaki observes similarly, "is a microcosm because it is private and self-contained, categorically excluding the outer world".

As evident in this criticism, Donne's lovers seem to transcend the limits of the physical world by disregarding external influences, coercing all things to rotate around them instead. In Thomas Docherty's words, "[the lovers] become the world and occupy the same position of centrality as the sun. They become, in short, the still point around which all else is supposed to revolve, and around whom all time passes [...]". They create a miniature world that is more important than the larger universe within the realm of their bedroom, and their bodies are the gravitational centre.

Expanding upon the criticism of this poem in his analysis of Donne's poetry, James S. Baumlin concludes that "The Sun Rising" must not be interpreted literally. Rather, Donne's displacement of the outside world, in favor of the lovers' inside "microcosm," is a rhetorical technique used to argue for the strength and energy of mutual love. "Actually," Baumlin writes, [...] the reader knows that the world *does not* literally go away, that the sun's orbit *does not* contract to the bedroom of the lovers; but as one reads, one observes how the beliefs, emotions, and values of the lovers themselves undergo a sea change. Hyperbole may lack the power to change the external physical world; still it changes the private world of the lovers, a world of emotion and experience that proves stubbornly resistant to logic, though marvelously—miraculously—open to language.

Indeed, this analysis is valid if readers assume with Baumlin that while the poem's logic operates inadequately, its rhetoric works "miraculously." But, is the persona's reliance on language to transcend the physical world able to succeed? Or, does the language of "The Sun Rising," like the logic, fail to communicate the theme that many scholars have recognized?

The rhetoric of Donne's persona does seem, upon a first reading, to locate the lovers at the centre of the universe successfully while it subordinates all surrounding objects. And the poet's use of hyperbole is convincing enough if readers immediately assume that Donne intended to oppose logic and to define the universe's purpose through the transcendent qualities of language.

Yet the inconsistencies in rhetoric that the poem manifests, what one scholar has deemed "a tangle of contradictions and reversals," make this commonly accepted interpretation unstable (Brown 110). While Donne's speaker may dislocate the outside world only for the extent of "The Sun Rising," he is still unsuccessful at convincing critical readers that internal love can symbolically replace the physical world if logic is subordinated to language.

The persona establishes several binary oppositions and seems to favor a certain hierarchy within the rhetorical structures he creates. As the poem progresses, however, he begins to misspeak, seemingly forgetting the earlier language of his discourse. Ultimately, the persona's reorganization of language, his attempt to push rhetoric beyond the limits of logic, fails; for, upon condensing the world around his lover and himself, he calls back those objects that he initially excluded. The poem dismantles itself through the inherent contradictions of the persona's rhetoric, leaving the reader unconvinced that language permits love to transcend the outside world.

In the first stanza of "The Sun Rising," Donne's persona creates several binary oppositions that indicate the poem's ultimate but unsuccessful argument: love exists independently from and superior to the physical world. The persona, questioning the sun, asks contentiously,

Busy old fool, unruly Sun,
Why dost thou thus
Through windows, and through curtains call on us?
Must to thy motions lovers' seasons run? (1-4)

The substantial oppositions present in these lines are confinement versus openness and eternity versus momentariness. As for the former, the persona objects to the sun's intrusion "Through windows" and "through curtains." Windows and curtains separate him and his lover from the outside world, from the knowledge that their love exists within a mundane, physical realm. And if the "Busy [and] unruly" sun permeates these modes of exclusion it will undermine his desired confinement, devitalizing his love as it intrudes upon his room.

His reasoning leads into the other significant opposition of the poem's introduction: eternity / momentariness. The "lovers' seasons" are placed against the sun's seasons, and the persona's disputatious tone suggests his efforts to subordinate everyday, natural motions to ceaseless love. He continues, "Love, all alike, no season knows, nor clime, / Nor hours, days, months, which are the rags of time".

All in all, the introductory stanza of "The Sun Rising" reveals the persona's motive to engage in mutual love within a confined realm that is free from the time constraints of the physical universe.

While in the first stanza the persona declares the physical world's inferiority to love, he also suggests the social sphere's necessary absence from his microcosm. He rhetorically pushes the sun away, telling it to "go chide / Late schoolboys, and sour prentices, / Go tell court-huntsmen, that the king will ride". Indeed, the sun is commanded to seek these individuals because its search will render the persona free from its "motions."

Yet he also demands the sun to pursue these people because he knows its "chid[ing]" and "tell[ing]" will keep them away from his room. The first stanza, then, presents a figurative opposition to everything in the outside world—from the sun and the "ants" to children and the king—in order to convince the audience that the language of love is capable of consummating this act.

However, the persuasive language of the first stanza begins to break down early in the second stanza, as the persona seems to forget the love ideals that he is seeking. In particular, his celebration of love's eternity versus his condemnation of the outside world's momentariness loses its potency, for he is overtly unable to escape time constraints—even through the use of language.

Remarking on the simplicity of escaping the sun's intrusive beams, the persona states, "I could eclipse and cloud them with a wink, / But that I would not lose her sight so long" (13-14). By closing his eyes, he excludes the external world from his internal world of love. This aspect of his rhetoric is still convincing, for readers can understand that the eye acts like the window of the first stanza, separating an internal sphere from an outside sphere; and, the "wink"—the curtain—prevents the sun from intruding.

However, readers cannot be convinced that the persona continues to favor (or, can continue to favor) the ideal of love's eternity. The assertion "so long" at the end of line fourteen demonstrates that he is unable to create a language that is independent from the physical world.

As he defined it earlier, his internal world of love knows no "hours, days, months, which are the rags of time," but in expressing his fear that closing his eyes would cause him to lose sight of his love for a certain amount of time—for "so long"—he tacitly admits that his microcosm must obey external rules. His inside sphere and the outside world have a "tomorrow late" and a "yesterday," and through admitting this the persona evinces the inability of rhetoric to transcend the physical, momentary world and to exist apart from external influence.

The last two lines of the second stanza and the first two lines of the third stanza continue to manifest the persona's language dismantling itself. Besides the eternity / momentariness opposition that breaks down because of the persona's inability to dismiss time constraints from his world of love, lines nineteen and twenty also demonstrate his failure to exclude the social world from his microcosm, an important opposition that he develops in the first stanza.

After telling the sun a second time to depart and engage with the social sphere, he comments, "Ask for those kings whom thou saw'st yesterday, And thou shalt hear, all here in one bed lay" (19-20). Whereas earlier the persona commands the sun to leave because he wishes to live with his lover uninfluenced by time (which, as discussed, is an unsuccessful endeavor) and to remain uninterrupted by the outside, social world, here the poet claims that the social sphere is in his bed.

Perhaps disclosing this weakness of his rhetoric more distinctly, the persona states of his lover and of himself, "She is all states, and all princes, I, / Nothing else is" (21-22). In "John Donne, Undone,"

Thomas Docherty, comments on the first line of this passage: "Sexual relation fades into commercial relation here, and the female herself becomes mediated as a symbol of the market-place itself, [...]". Indeed, the persona follows the putative seventeenth-century social paradigm of female inferiority when he claims that his lover is territory while he is the prince of that territory. Again, he is unable to utilize a language that can transcend the external world; in this instance, a dominant social ideology pervades his rhetoric, and his world of love cannot escape the outside structure once again.

Before the third stanza begins, two of the binary

oppositions that the persona establishes in the first stanza have broken down. While he attempts to engage in a convincing discourse on the potency of love, the persona's rhetorical attachments to eternity and to social exclusion work within governing structures that he is unable to avoid; therefore, his argument for these ideals is not firmly grounded.

He endeavors to use language in order to assert love's superiority to the external world, but by acknowledging time limitations and the social sphere he ultimately supports the structures that he hopes to undermine. The last stanza of "The Sun Rising" consummates the destruction of his attempt. As previously mentioned, the persona establishes a confinement openness opposition, favoring to be enclosed within a microcosmic world of love. However, this idea is dismantled when the persona summons everything in the external world to his room:

In that the world's contracted thus;
Thine age asks ease, and since thy duties be
To warm the world, that's done in warming us.
Shine here to us, and thou art everywhere;
This bed thy centre is, these walls, thy sphere. (26-30)

Here, the most evident contradiction in the persona's reasoning is his contraction of the external world into his internal world. As noted earlier, he claims that love knows no time and exists independent from external influence. Through this assertion, the persona confines himself and his lover willingly, expelling the sun and rejecting the cultural sphere with the notion that his love surpasses these aspects of the physical world.

Yet the buttress of his final argument, which he presents syllogistically, is the assumption that his microcosmic world of love *is* the whole world. In lines twenty-seven and twenty-eight the persona reasons that since the sun is obligated to illuminate the world, it must shine on him and his lover; thus, he thinks that his microcosm is everything. His bed, he asserts in the final line, is the centre of the universe; his walls are its borders.

The persona's argument ends with the assumption that

the entire physical world occupies his microcosm. He and his lover are the centre of this new sphere, and their love transcends the physical limitations of the outside world. But upon critical analysis, this rhetoric is unconvincing. He brings openness into his closed world, implicitly subverting his ideal to remain isolated from outside influence.

Throughout the progression of "The Sun Rising," Donne's persona has made claims that undoubtedly break down as he continues to speak. In the final instance, the confinement that he favors in his internal world of love, as opposed to the openness of the macrocosm, is undermined because he insists that the external world exists within his microcosm.

Ultimately, the persona's attempt to utilize a language that will communicate love's transcendent qualities is a failure—not a "sudden creative power" as Lisa Gorton asserts with other critics—because the structures that he hopes to escape are inherently incorporated in that language (par. 17). He tries to embrace the ideals of eternity, social solitariness, and confinement; however, in this verbal enterprise, he incorporates the ideas that he is reacting against into his rhetoric. As a result, his argument loses force—his language is unsuccessful.

Chapter 14

John Donne and Elizabethan Economic Theory

Few poets of Donne's time — or for that matter any time — show his understanding of contemporary economic theory and use it as a body of metaphor in their poetry. It has of course been argued that there was in fact no such thing as Elizabethan economic theory; even the so-called Gresham's Law was not thought up by Queen Elizabeth's financier but was actually the creation of a nineteenth-century Scot. Economic theory in English is usually held to begin with Adam Smith, although several recent historians have pushed the beginning of scientific thinking about economics back to the late 1660s.

However, in the later sixteenth and earlier seventeenth centuries, a number of English writers worked the ground between theory and practice, most notably John Hales, Gerard Malynes, Edward Misselden, and Thomas Mun. Many financiers such as Sir Thomas Gresham also made, in their letters and working papers, what might be called direct contributions to the evolving field of study; and of course philosophers such as Sir Francis Bacon and Thomas Hobbes put in their two cents, worth.

None of these have any particularly impressive achievements in what we would call imaginative literature, and this essay began with an inquiry into just what early modern economic concepts might have first percolated down into the poetic mind.

I should make clear at the outset that I am not speaking of the simple use of figures of speech derived from the concept of usury. Countless Elizabethan writers employed this metaphor, which had been current since the later Middle Ages. Shakespeare's Sonnet 4, for example, addresses the fair youth as mindlessly engaging in usury, but this use of the metaphor shows no special understanding of the economics behind the practice.

By contrast, Donne's writing shows how a late Renaissance poet, certainly no financial wizard himself, was able to use ideas from economics with considerable sophistication. Donne is one of the first English poets to sense the vast economic changes coming over Europe in general and England in particular, and the first to work them into the understanding of intellectual experience.

Perhaps the best place to centre the discussion is that aspect of economics that has always been of the most immediate interest, currency. This was not only the most written-about aspect of the English economic picture, but it was also one of Donne's favorite sources of metaphor. By 1600 there was general agreement that the main problem of the English economy was the shortage of money, which seemed to go hand in hand with rising prices, what the Elizabethans called "the dearth."

It was as if the supposed law of supply and demand had been somehow suspended: even though there was abundant food, produce, clothing, and crafted goods, prices still rose steadily throughout the later sixteenth century and even more rapidly in the first quarter of the seventeenth century.

Money of course means coin, and there was never enough to go around. John Hales, writing in 1581, wonders at the paradox of plenty within shortage of money: "There was never more plentie of cattell than there is nowe, and yet [it] is scarcitie of things which commonly maketh dearthe. This is a mervelous dearthe, that in such plentie cometh, contrary to his kynd."

Popular literature and sermons tended to blame venal merchants and the consumer's vain desire for luxury as the twin sources of rising prices,, but there is no evidence to suggest that human nature in the later sixteenth century received a sudden infusion of greed that was previously lacking. And prices were not being driven up by the lavish spending habits of some of the wealthier classes, as the failure of the sumptuary laws would show. Toward the close of the century subtler minds began to sense that more strictly monetary difficulties lay at the source of the problem, difficulties that Donne alludes to in his poetry.

The first cause was thought to be the debasement of currency. Going into the sixteenth century, silver money had been essentially unchanged since the Conquest, and gold money had remained unchanged in quality since Edward III introduced the florin in the fourteenth century. But under Henry VIII the coinage had been debased steadily. The original Tower pound standard silver stood at five parts fine to one part alloy, but by 1544 it had fallen to one part fine to two parts alloy.

The gold standard had been 23.5 carats fine, but by 1544 it had fallen to 20 carats fine. Donne alludes to this adulteration as "changing that whole precious Gold/ To such small Copper coynes." Elsewhere he specifically alludes to the fineness of gold: "How is the gold become so dimme? How is/ Purest and finest gold thus chang'd to this?" While Elizabeth succeeded in stabilizing the currency, it still bought less and less, and the debasement of coinage came to describe the decaying quality of life: as Donne says, compared to our fathers, we are indeed debased men,

But this were light, did our lesse volume hold
All the old Text; or had wee chang'd to gold
Their silver.

Smaller and weighing less for our relative size, we are like lightweight coin, not even good silver, much less gold.

This view, that the dilution of the precious metal in the currency made it necessary to spend more in order to obtain the same goods, was in competition with an older view, which was that the currency itself had no intrinsic value, but only the value that the monarch gave to it. Deriving their position from Aristotle and St. Thomas, the medieval schoolmen had argued that the prince had the right to fix the value of money, terming this the valor impositus.

Elizabeth had never endorsed this theory but the Stuart kings would insist on it (in Charles's case, to disastrous effect). Thus the king's very image on the coin gave it monetary value. Not surprisingly, this theory is the source of one of Donne's favorite economic metaphors. The woman's impression in the lover's heart

Makes mee her Medall, and makes her love mee,
As Kings do coynes, to which their stamps impart
The value.

When the lover cries, his tears are like coins, "and thy stampe they beare,/ And by this Mintage they are something worth." In the same way, the metaphor applies to a saintly person like Elizabeth Drury, whose actions validate our own: "Shee coyn'd, in this, that her impressions gavel To all our actions all the worth they have." This metaphor can subsume even the poet's ability to write, as he identifies both himself and his subject as bearing God's stamp: "Did this Coine beare any other stampe, then his,/ That gave thee power to doe, me, to say this."

Donne seems to have found the metaphor useful for reasons perhaps more poetic than social, for certainly he was aware of the debate over what conferred value: in "The Canonization," telling the reader how to succeed in the world, he says to go "Observe the Kings reall, or his stamped face." But he was also well aware of economic realities, and more sophisticated views of how English currency acquired its value also found their way into his poetry.

To step back a moment: in the late Middle Ages, the search for more gold supplies became increasingly intense. While countries like Germany had their own mines and Italy had its valuable trade routes, the English never had access to as free supplies. (And in every European country, the difficulties of mining and commerce made alchemy seem like a workable alternative, although the successes, here were of course fraudulent — as Donne says, "oft Alchimists doe coyners prove.")

What ended the shortage of native English precious metals proved also to be the source of the dearth, and that was the infusion of massive supplies of gold from Spain and the New World. Donne repeatedly alludes to the influx of Spanish gold;writing in the persona of a starving poet, he says that Poetry indeed be such a sinne/ As I thinke That brings dearths, and Spaniards in." Donne knew that Spanish money looked rough, knew how it had become diffused through Europe, and knew that it brought not prosperity but ruin wherever it went:

Spanish Stamps, still travelling,
... are become as Catholique as their King,
Those unlickt beare-whelps, unfil'd pistolets
That (more than Canon shot) availes or lets;
Which negligently unrounded, looke
Like many angled figures, in the booke
Of some great Conjurer that would enforce
Nature, as these doe justice, from her course;
Which, as the soule quickens head, feet and heart,
As streames, like veines, run through th'earth's every part,
Visit all Countries, and have slily made
Gorgeous France, ruin'd, ragged and decay'd;
Scotland, which knew no State, proud in one day:
And mangled seventeen-headed Belgia.

Donne knew also that England was not exempt from the effect, and like others he thought that the main conduit was the "Crownes of France":

For, most of these, their naturall Countreys rot
I think possesseth, they come here to us,
So pale, so lame, so leane, so ruinous.

There is a distinct connection between the new money and the new insolvency:

Active Kings
Whose foraine conquest treasure brings,
Receive more, and spend more, and soonest breake.

Donne sees the danger in the influx of gold from the New World, a danger that has an ironic edge to it when he refers to his mistresses as being rich mines like the Indies: all the sexual jokes about digging in mines suggest trouble in monetary terms.

But the influx of gold from the New World did not drive

prices up simply because the wealthy became more ostentatious (with James's lively encouragement) or because of the new gold's evident purity. What a few Elizabethan economic writers grasped, and what Donne alone among the poets seemed to sense, was that within his lifetime, money itself had become a commodity.

After the relative shortage of specie in England in the fifteenth and most of the sixteenth centuries-relative, that is, to Spain and France — the abundance of new gold made goods cost more simply because there was more gold that could be paid for them.

Prices rose in direct proportion to the gold that was available, and as John Kenneth Galbraith has said, "these prices, not the tales of the conquistadores, were the message to most Europeans that America had been discovered. At work in a primitive but unmistakable fashion was the central proposition concerning the relation of money to prices — the quantity theory of money." In contrast, then, to other theories of value — value comes from the King's face, or the amount of alloy, or some basic greed quotient — this theory recognizes that the principles of commodification apply to money itself and not just to goods.

Or as Donne says in the clogged syntax of a verse letter, "Rarenesse, or use, not nature value brings." That is, scarcity or availability determines value, not nature or anything intrinsic. (The woman he is praising has made herself scarce by living in Twicknam, and by the end of the poem, Donne is predictably comparing her to a mine.)

So far the discussion has centered on problems of currency, but Donne's poetry also shows a general awareness of the interconnections between economic matters. A notion of credit, debt, and borrowing figure often in his description of love, and as always Donne take commonplace metaphors and reinvents them.

True lovers, for example, illustrate a constant movement toward a kind of intellectual balance of trade, in that they pay, lend, and pay out again, in a currency that is not debased and cannot decline in value:

They unto one another nothing owe,
And yet they doe, but are
So just and rich in that coyne which they pay,
That neither would, nor needs forbeare, nor stay;
Neither desires to be spar'd, nor to spare,
They quickly pay their debt, and then
Take no acquittances, but pay again;
They pay, they give,, they lend, and so let fall
No such occasion to be liberall.

The balance can be upset if one party pays ahead; thus if a man owes a letter to a woman he loves, he is on the road to bankruptcy:

nothings, as I am, may
Pay all they have, and yet have all to pay.
Such borrow in their payments, and owe more
By having leave to write so, then before.

This is an especially dangerous situation to be in if the woman is a man's main source of intellectual capital (Elizabethans used the term stock), and he has been spending it:

First I confesse I have to others lent
Your stock, and over prodigally spent
Your treasure.

Donne's financial metaphors repeatedly suggest that women are risky intellectual investments, not so much because they might be fickle or untrue (he admits this and moves beyond it) but because love ties up all the lover's mental stock or capital. The case appears in its most extreme form when two lovers believe their love is growing infinitely. In the quasi-fiscal operations of the loving intellect, this is a possibility: if one has laid out all he owns intellectually for the woman, and her love for him is not total, he cannot expect a return any greater than his own initial investment. This is the argument behind "Lovers infinitenesse":

all my treasure, which should purchase thee,
Sighs, teares, and oathes, and letters I have spent,
Yet no more can be due to mee,
Then at the bargaine made was ment,

If then thy gift of love were partiall,
That some to mee, some should to others fall,
Deare, I shall never have Thee All.

Suppose she did love him completely at one time. Other lovers then may come along, and with a larger investment of capital, create new value in her:

Or if then thou gavest mee all,
All was but All, which thou hadst then,
But if in thy heart, since, there be or shall,
New love created bee, by other men,
Which have their stocks intire, and can in teares,
In sighs, in oathes, and letters outbid mee,
This love may beget new feares.

The poem wittily concludes that as his own love grows every day, he cannot want all her love in return, for "If thou canst give it, then thou never gavest it," and he must abandon the metaphor of exchange altogether:

But wee will have a way more liberall,
Then changing hearts, to joyne them, so wee shall
Be one, and one anothers All.

In a more somber mood, Donne will say that the more intellectual capital we accumulate, the better we will be able to handle the final payout we all must make: we may, "If we can stocke our selves, and thrive, uplay/ Much, much deare treasure for the great rent day." Or to view the metaphor another way, when the woman one loves has died, the lover's interest rate grows at such a pace that he makes the final payout faster:

This death, hath with my store
My use encreas'd.
And so my soule more earnestly releas'd,
Will outstrip hers; As bullets flowen before
A latter bullet may o'rtake, the pouder being more.

The idea of life as a succession of payments or exactions seems to have been central to Donne's view of human behaviour, and especially to his view of love. The growth of true love most closely resembles rising taxes:

though each spring doe adde to love new heate,

As princes doe in times of action get
New taxes, and remit them not in peace,
No winter shall abate the springs encrease.

More complex is Donne's use of a taxation metaphor drawn from the royal subsidies. These levies for the prosecution of wars had been made since early Tudor times, but during Elizabeth's reign they came to be exacted for any unusual expense. During James I's reign, it became apparent that the parliamentary grants the King was receiving were enough to cover military expenses and reasonable household expenses, and the subsidies were actually going to cover James's extravagant largesse to his many favorites.

Thus among those close to the court, there was a very real sense that even though the country did not need the subsidies, they would never go away and would only go up. Coupled with this were gross inequities in the way the subsidies were assessed, with the middle and lower classes being assessed at full value and the wealthiest being assessed at only a fraction of their net worth. Donne would have understood the Leona Helmsley principle that only the little people pay taxes.

Donne pulls all of this into focus in "A Valediction: of the booke," which begins by saying that the book comprised of the love letters between him and his mistress will be an encyclopedia of knowledge about the mysteries of love. He then invokes his familiar idea of love's clergy, who will use this text to understand either "abstract spirituall love" or "Something which they may see and use", something represented by physical beauty. But this kind of love can be a trap, and the poem then turns on an intricate stanza describing love as a peculiar form of taxation:

Here more then in their bookes may Lawyers finde,
Both by what titles Mistresses are ours,
And how prerogative these states devours,
Transferr'd from Love himselfe, to womankinde,
Who though from heart, and eyes,
They exact great subsidies,
Forsake him who on them relies,
And for the cause, honour, or conscience give,

Chimeraes, vaine as they, or their prerogative.

Womankind now has the prerogative of exacting great subsidies, as the God of Love once did, subsidies they levy from the heart and eyes. In contrast to "abstract spirituall love," the love subsidized by the beauty that the eyes take in can devour the state, and the man who pays out the taxes will be forsaken. Such women use illusions of honour or conscience to justify their actions, which are as foolish and hopeless as their very right to exact the subsidies.

Donne's lover is like the wealthy nobility under Elizabeth and James, who resisted the subsidies and had themselves underassessed in order to avoid paying them. This type of taxation is a metaphor for misplaced love, the greatness of which can be reckoned best, the poem concludes, when the lovers are apart and not physically together. Here again Donne describes love in terms of economic metaphors that would appeal to the class to which he aspires and for which he writes.

Why did Donne find economic metaphors coming so readily to hand? And how did his understanding of the ideas behind the metaphors actually develop? No other major English poet of the time shows this kind of acquaintance with economics; as I have suggested, Shakespeare's sonnets using metaphors from usury show no particular understanding of interest, and as Marc Shell has shown, the monetary background of The Merchant of Venice is more that of the Middle Ages than of 1600.

R. C. Bald's biography of Donne traces en passant the routes by which Donne would have been exposed to thought on economics. His father was a prosperous ironmonger and coal merchant who contributed to the founding of Sir Thomas Gresham's Royal Exchange. He was active in the politics of the City and was an accomplished master of financial maneuvering, so adept in putting off a large debt to his father-in-law that William Cecil, Lord Burleigh once had to lean on him.

His son john attended the Inns of Court and saw the convoluted financial maneuvers of lawyers and suitors in Chancery and the Star Chamber, but probably young Donne's best opportunity to see the world of finance up close would have been the four years (November 1597?-February 1602) that he served as Secretary to Sir Thomas Egerton, Lord Keeper of the Great Seal. These would have given him an extraordinary education in fiscal policy and manipulation, especially since Egerton was often at odds with Burleigh, who had been a close associate of Sir Thomas Gresham and was one of the most powerful figures in Elizabethan and Jacobean finance.

One guesses that employment with Egerton must have involved handling a good deal of money, because Donne's poetry from this period is full of references to the appearance of coins, counterfeit, patched, soldered, and clipped. Most of these allusions are explained by Helen Gardner and Wesley Milgate in their editions, respectively, of the Elegies and the Satires; but thorough as these notes are, they still occasionally miss some witty turns on the physical alteration of money.

Two examples: Elegy XI, "The Bracelet," not only alludes to the practice of clipping (shaving the edges of coins to pick up small quantities of gold), but also puts it in its social context: "howsoe'r French Kings most Christian be,/ Their Crownes are circumcis'd most Jewishly" (27-28).

The point of the joke is not simply that clipping is a cutting or trimming like a circumcision, which would be a rather aimless metaphor, but that jews were blamed for clipping, and several times in English history, when clipping became rampant, all Jewry were arrested or expelled. Another: in Satire V, which treats Egerton's handling of "demands, fees, and duties,"

Donne says that "The mony which you sweat, and sweare for, is gon/ into other hands" (40-41), making a punning allusion to the practice of "sweating" coins. This was the practice of putting gold coins in a leather bag and shaking them, thus giving the coins the appearance of only normal wear while leaving a deposit of gold dust in the bag. One of the perks of being in any position that involved handling large amounts of money was the chance to sweat coin, finding gold without technically breaking the law.

Donne's postgraduate education in economics might be said to have begun with the disclosure of his clandestine marriage to Egerton's niece. Blocked from employment from the age of 30 to 43, Donne demonstrated the man of letters, minimal skills in handling money, but somewhere in his mind he must have continued to have speculative finance on his mind.

Going right to the top, with the grandest of the seventeenth-century investment schemes, in 1609 he sought the post of Secretary of the Virginia Company, as if they did not have enough problems without being managed by a poet. By 1611 he was a member of a select dining club that met at the Mitre Tavern; one member was Lionel Cranfield, who was already rising rapidly to become one of the most powerful financiers in England, and another was his business partner Arthur Ingram, whose shifty dealing would make him even wealthier than Cranfield.

One would give a great deal to know more about Donne's connections with Ingram, who was a projector, on the grand scale, although as one economic historian has said, "it can hardly be doubted that ethically his conduct in business often failed to reach even the low standards of his age." Ingram, Donne, and Cranfield were all members of the so-called Addled Parliament' of 1614, in which Donne served on a select committee that reviewed the King's right to impose certain customs duties.

Donne and Cranfield remained good friends the rest of their lives, even after Cranfield's fall; Cranfield sent his own doctor to Donne when he was ill in 1628, and, perhaps more significantly, he also sent money.

By his thirties Donne knew Francis Bacon, if he had not known him much earlier, for Bacon had also sought preferment from Egerton, and certainly it is difficult to imagine that Bacon's popular essays on business and economics would have escaped Donne's attention.

And investment projects involving colonial expansion continued to engage Donne personally, even beyond his 1622 sermon to the Virginia Company: late in his life, he worried much about his son George, who commanded the militia protecting the colonists on the island of St. Kitt's. In all, there would seem to be much connecting Donne's life with financial speculation in both theory and practice.

By far the greater part of my illustrations has been drawn from Donne's verse letters, elegies, satires, secular lyrics, and the two Anniversaries. This is itself an accurate reflection of the way that economic metaphors tend to drop out of Donne's work in the latter part of his life, and almost none appear in his divine poems.

Is it that the shifts and strategies necessary for survival and success in finance are pointless, when we know we are under the eye of God? Or is metaphor itself suspect, a means of exalting the writer's own spiritual hubris and personal pride in his handiwork? What is certain is that metaphors from economics or commerce appear only seldom in the poems and sermons that occupied Donne from his ordination in 1615 to his death in 1631.

But there is one final superb illustration of Donne's understanding of economic matters, and this is his funeral sermon for Sir William Cokayne in 1626. A greatly admired performance in the high Donnean sermonic mode, it uses four of his favorite themes: the certainty and finality of death; the hope for resurrection; the difficulty of praying with a single mind; and the final vision of rising into the pure light of God. The magnificence of the sermon's prose cadences has often been admired, and the paragraphs working out those four themes have been frequently anthologized and quoted.

Less well-known is the eulogy for Cokayne, and here Donne's personal involvement requires some delicate balancing. One of the wealthiest merchants in London, Cokayne had been an alderman and Lord Mayor, and for a private funeral his was lavish even by Jacobean standards. The funeral herald's order for the funeral gives the names of the principal mourners, and these include many of the most prominent English merchants and financiers of the time.

Of particular interest for this discussion is the presence of the Lord Mayor and five previous or future holders of the office, fourteen aldermen, and nine major figures in the City who had been knighted for their financial services to the crown. At one point in his sermon Donne notes that Cokayne's fellow merchants are seated in the choir, and for him this has a special significance.

It can be documented that at various times Donne had been directly involved in financial or legal dealing with three of them; at least five others had mutual friends in Ingram and Cranfield; two others had been masters of the Ironmonger's Company, of which Donne's father had been warden; and several of those present had held offices in the Virginia Company. Donne is speaking to businessmen he knows, in the context of business, and this will affect the remarks he is about to make.

For the merchants their relationship to Donne is also complex, and this too Donne is going to understand. They know that because of his own background, Donne is no stranger to the workings of finance; and because Cokayne's business affairs had been widely discussed in Court and in Parliament, they can also assume that he knows Cokayne's immense wealth had been built on sharp practices, and that ten years earlier his manipulations had brought the country to the brink of a massive economic recession. The problem for Donne is how to handle this ticklish situation in the sermon. In our time, it would be like having to deliver a eulogy for Charles Keating.

Donne's solution is the bold one of admitting Cokayne's under-handed dealings directly into the sermon, using the language of economics and trade that the merchants and financiers in his audience would understand. Cokayn's story needs to be recounted in order to see how Donne can praise him. At the end of 1612, upon the death of Lord Treasurer Salisbury, rather than appoint a new Treasurer, King James temporarily appointed a Commission for Treasury Affairs. The dilution of responsibility and authority was ready made for an entrepreneur like Cokayne.

Most of the commissioners were operating out of fairly blatant self-interest, and with bribes from Cokayne, they approved Cokayne's proposal to prohibit the export of undyed and undressed cloth; the ostensible plan here was to stimulate the dyeing and dressing industries, which had lined up behind Cokayne.

Broadcloth, the so-called white cloth, comprised the bulk of English export trade; Sir Edward Coke estimated it at 90% of all English exports. Most of the fabric went to the Low Countries and Germany, where established dyeing and finishing operations completed the manufacture of usable cloth.

The customs duties on the export of the unfinished cloth were 60,000 pounds a year, and Cokayne claimed that the dyed and finished cloth would yield revenues of five times this. The financial yield appealed to James, who was overspending wildly, but the plan also appealed to his vanity: he would become both the father of a new cloth trade and the country's economic savior. Overriding the Privy Council, he put the export ban into effect in July 1614.

The plan backfired almost immediately. The Dutch prohibited the import of dyed cloth and took up the slack with cloth from other countries. The export of undressed cloth fell 60%, and in the first three months of 1615, customs revenues, far from increasing, were down by 6,000 pounds, and the deficit mounted as the year went on. Now, the sale of broadcloth was the monopoly of the Merchant Adventurers, of which Cokayne was not a member, and one of his chief aims was to crack their monopoly. Thus as the national debt grew, in 1615 he secured their licence to export undyed and undressed cloth.

In the meantime, he did nothing to stimulate the dyeing trade; in fact he had avoided all along making any commitments to produce a specific amount of dyed cloth. Now with the licence to export white cloth, he had no incentive to produce dyed cloth, a point that Sir Francis Bacon made in a letter to James.

Cokayne soon began buying large quantities of white cloth at depressed prices, which he was to resell later when the market turned around. The doubledealing at the heart of the operation was apparent to everyone: in Parliament, Cokayne and his friends were said to be like watermen, who looked one way and rowed another. It was a clear case of a merchant so rapacious he was willing to throw the country into a depression in order to make his own fortune.

At this point Donne's friend Lionel Cranfield enters the picture. Since they had been dinner companions at the Mitre Tavern he had risen to be Surveyor-General of the Customs, and he had complete control of the figures. Just as important, he was a member of the Merchant Adventurers and knew the cloth trade.

In January 1616 the Privy Council summoned Cokayne to answer questions put by Cran-field, a blunt and hardheaded master of his books, and all the details of sinking exports, failing industries, and rising unemployment were laid on the table. James did nothing. A month later Bacon wrote to him asking how much longer he would continue these "experiments," that were ruining the health of the nation, but James showed virtually no interest in stopping the project.

Inertia had its rewards. In June Cokayne showed his gratitude with a grand banquet in his home, at which James was presented with a gold basin filled with a thousand pounds in gold pieces, while young Prince Henry was given five hundred pounds. At the end of the summer, when Cranfield pointed out that unemployment was double what it was when James came to the throne, James responded by endorsing Cokayne's scheme once again.

What finally stopped the scheme was Cokayne's overreaching attempt to merge his own New Company with the Merchant Adventurers. Under the pressure of Cranfield's figures, the King was also beginning to have his doubts about Cokayne's scheme, and he now wanted to broker a compromise between the two companies. Cranfield and Bacon both attempted to mediate, but the Merchant Adventurers wanted no part of it, even when the King denounced their recalcitrance.

Yet in the end they agreed to try to get along with Cokayne, and in January 1617 the King granted them all their old privileges, possibly being influenced by a bribe of 80,000 pounds they gave to him and the Lord Treasurer. Despite the quashing of Cokayne's scheme, though, for more than a year the country remained in an economic slump, and the whole affair had far reaching consequences in later sessions of Parliament. The drama of the scheme is depressingly familiar to modern readers, who have seen how trade imbalances can result in the collapse of not one but many industries. But for someone close to the Stuart court, the Cokayne affair had a kind of novelty.

It renewed discussion of how trade works, and it redirected concern about the influx of specie from the New World somehow going hand in hand with the dearth and the shortage of capital. More immediately for Donne, preaching a sermon in St. Paul's, the ironies must have been rich: the man for whom he is pronouncing the eulogy was stopped in his schemes by a friend of Donne's; and Cokayne's profit-taking and greed had been encouraged by the King, who had also given Donne his Deanship.

But there are even more intriguing links. Cokayne had left his wife and children after 1616, when their youngest child was born, but Donne had continued to correspond on friendly terms with Mrs. Cokayne, and in one extant letter he refers to "the perverseness of the father" in what appears to have been a fierce custody battle. Preaching an intellectually and emotionally engaging eulogy for a man whose character in many respects must have been antipathetic is precisely the challenge this preacher must have relished, although the sermon does show, as Arnold Stein dryly notes, "Donne working hard at his task."

Donne lays out his subject in such a way that he can glance at the particulars of Cokayne's life, feeling no need to make excuses, but omitting where he must, and all the while establishing his credentials to speak about a financier. Donne takes his text from John 11:21, Martha's lament to Jesus, "Lord, if thou hadst been here, my brother had not died." But he does not unfold the text until later, and instead begins with a line of reasoning that has an immediate and astonishing biographical relevance, as if to notify his listeners that the details of Cokayne's life may appear at any point: "God made the first Marriage, and man made the first Divorce". Explaining that he is referring to soul and body, Donne says that God makes their union indissoluble."

As farre as man is immortall, man is a married man still, still in possession of a soule, and a body too". Donne then lays out two main headings, that in spiritual things there is nothing perfect in this world, and that in temporal things there is nothing permanent.

The first part has three divisions, "the weakness of Man's best actions," the weakness of Martha, and the greatness of God's mercy in accepting our offerings; the second part has a similar three divisions, the transitoriness of things, the decay of the body, and, despite that decay, the assurance that God will take the body up to a glorious state. Most of these branches of the argument contain allusions to Cokayne's financial life; all build toward a final analysis of Cokayne's theory of wealth.

Beginning by looking at how weak our knowledge is, Donne makes a witty reference to know-nothing philosophers, comparing them to us and how little we know of our net financial worth: "We call that a mans meanes, which he hath; But that is truly his meanes, what way he came by it. And yet how few are there (when a state comes to any great proportion) that know that; that know what they have, what they are worth?"

After numerous examples of how flawed our faith is, he says even our prayer is flawed, the most glaring example being the use of prayer by the Catholics, who have turned prayer into a virtual commodity: "they wil antidate and postdate their prayers; Say to morrows prayers to day, and to dayes prayers to morrow, if they have other uses and employments of the due time betweene; where they will trade, and make merchandise of prayers by way of exchange".

Moving then to Martha's words, of all the many ways they could be taken Donne focuses them as a powerful exposition of the need for charity, the absolute imperative to resist condemning others, "whom thou wilt needs thinke lesse pure, or perfect then thy selfe". The reason for this rather unexpected interpretation of the text is clear if we think of the merchants present who had had financial dealings with the man in the coffin before them.

Donne's development of the second part of the sermon is briefer and all three sections are focused on business and Cokayne. The first division is the impermanence of all earthly things, and his example here is again suited to his audience: "Ayre condensed becomes water, a more solid body, And Ayre rarified becomes fire, and a body more disputable, and in-apparant. It is so in the Conditions of men too; A Merchant condensed, kneaded and packed up in a great estate, becomes a Lord; And a Merchant rarified, blown up by a perfidious Factor, or by a riotous Sonne, evaporates into ayre, into nothing, and is not seen". The merchant's condition is the human condition; we can become "packed up" into a great alderman and Lord Mayor, like Cokayne, or we can get bad advice and our fortunes disappear.

Donne now moves directly to Cokayne and the point upon which the mass of the whole sermon revolves. First, "God imprinted in him an industrious disposition" and more: "God enlarged him, and then he filled him; He gave him a large and comprehensive understanding, and with it, A publique heart". What Donne means by "a publique heart" is not the charity he saw in the story of Martha, much less the philanthropy and good works that many great merchants such as Gresham practised, but rather a view of the way money works.

Donne first distinguishes between making money through trade and making money through foreign exchange, and he directly addresses the merchants in the congregation: "You have, I thinke, a phrase of Driving a Trade; And you have, I know, a practise of Driving away Trade, by other use of money".

Cokayne belongs to the first, because he wanted to use domestic goods for export, applying to them a manufacturing process to create added value: "And you have lost a man, that drove a great Trade, the right way of making the best use of our home-commodity. To fetch in Wine, and Spice, and Silke, is but a drawing of Trade; The right driving of trade, is, to vent our owne outward; And yet, for the drawing in of that, which might justly seeme most behoofefull, that is, of Arts, and Manufactures, to be imployed upon our owne Commodity within the Kingdome, he did his part, diligently, at least, if not vehemently, if not passionately".

Donne accepts here the modem idea of driving trade outward, and he also appears to have accepted Bacon's idea — in contrast to James's — that the goal was to have more exports than imports and not merely balance the two. Donne's description earlier in the sermon of how God gives out eternal life suggests that He too would approve of a trade overbalance:

"Out of the surplusage of his inexhaustible estate, out of the overflowing of his Power, he enables his Executors to doe as he did; for Peter gives Dorcas this Resurrection too". But again, the crucial matter at hand in eulogizing Cokayne is that he advocated more than merely increasing exports, or what the Elizabethans called (rather infelicitously) "seeking vent": he sought through technology to build additional value into basic commodities.

As a defense of Cokayne's scheme in the cloth trade this is wonderfully highminded: he was not attempting to take over a monopoly for personal gain, but rather was pushing a theory of added value into the comparatively recent idea of building a surplus in foreign trade. The fact that Cokayne had never agreed upon a set amount of fabric he would have dyed and processed, that he could never be brought to make a promise about keeping up dyeing after the three-year agreement expired; and that he bought white cloth at depressed prices to sell later for huge profits, are only details that do not need to be considered, given the 'vehemence' of the theory.

If Donne has accounted here for Cokayne's motives, he has yet to account for the manner in which the whole ruinous scheme was allowed to continue, and that was the vain and foolish indulgence of the King. But here Donne can give some testimony straight from the horse's mouth:

I have sometimes heard the greatest Master of Language and Judgement, which these times, or any other did, or doe, or shall give, (that good and great King of ours) say of [Cokayne], That he never heard any man of his breeding, handle businesses more rationally, more pertinently, more elegantly, more perswasively; And when his purpose was, to do grace to a Preacher, of very good abilities, and good note in his owne Chappell, I have heard him say, that his language, and accent, and manner of delivering himselfe, was like this man [Cokayne].

Having made his own assessment of Cokayne's financial ideas, Donne now implies, by his emphasis on verbal style and manner, that economic considerations played no part in the King's assessment of Cokayne's worth. The validation is now complete: Cokayne had a good theory: he believed in it; and the King believed in Cokayne. It is as straightforward as that. Donne could not have avoided knowing what Cokayne's project had done to the economy. He also would have known that the chief opponent to the project was his friend Cranfield.

Obviously none of this can enter the eulogy, and instead Donne directs attention to the theory behind the project rather than the imperfect — some would have said crooked — application of the theory. When the disastrous consequences of the project appear in the sermon, they are sublimated into the private and personal rather than the public and social: "So great a Ship, required a great Ballast, So many blessings, many crosses; And he had them, and sailed on his course the steadier for them,. These crosses do not need to be mentioned, however, as the "Persons of this City", sitting by Donne will have no problem recalling them. A brief and moving description of the death itself leads Donne to his end, with two short paragraphs on the funeral.

As a bravura performance in its sections on the resurrection, the difficulty of prayer, and the frailty of the body, the sermon has been greatly admired, but I have focused instead on the metaphors Donne used to praise a man who had exploited a rapidly changing economic system. That Donne understood most of the basic principles in the evolving study of economics is evident; that he found in them material for his art is certain.

Chapter 15

Marlowe's Second City

When the London theatergoers of the 1590s made the short river trip to the South Bank, they left behind them a place which displayed certain fixed features (infrastructure, Protestant Christian ideology), and a place where the lives of the lawmakers and law-followers were affected by the political machinations of international relations and historical placement (tension between London and Spain, proximity to the economically and ideologically important Netherlands).

Where they went, to the Rose or the Globe, were places with fixed features (the walls, the stage, the galleries, Protestant Christian ideology) and where the lives of those who performed, those who were portrayed, and those who watched were affected by the political and religious machinations in England and abroad (the sensitivity of the Master of the Revels, dramatic fashion). They left the city of London and reconvened in a "second city," the theater.

In this paper I shall show how one of the satirical political dramatist's most cunning weapons was put to work in this "second city," and how the location of the amphitheaters - geographical, social, and ideological - paradoxically both intensified the potentiality of the damage this weapon could inflict, yet also cushioned the city of London from the influential power of the drama.

This weapon was simply one of the dramatist's characters: the figure of the male Jew - an outsider, a stranger, an objective commentator and subversive critic, willing to fight against the sociopolitical system represented on the stage. Robert Wilson, Shakespeare, Chapman, William Haughton, and Marston all wrote plays in which a Jewish or Jew-like character played a leading role; and in all these cases, the Jew carries out the function of social critic, sometimes passive and meek, often angry and loud. My familiar example will be the Jew of Malta, Barabas, and his slave, Ithamore.

As an outsider, in terms of religion, nationality, and (often enforced) professional occupation, the Jew on the late-sixteenth-century stage becomes the centre of a larger critique. He becomes the criticizer of the state of the city and of the ruling classes at large, and also the target of the audience's - both on stage and off - judgment against him. I will go on to investigate how such an alien figure can resemble a "hero," and in order to justify the suggestions of analogy and transference from stage representation to the "real world" that I will make, we should consider a little further the theater/audience/city relationship at the Rose in 1592.

That the amphitheaters were divided from the city, at a distance outside the walls, meant that the theatergoers could physically exit the contained city ideologies of London. Steven Mullaney blurs something of this simple yet important concept when he terms the suburbs "Liberties" as well as the real Liberties of the city.

What happened during the migration of persons between the two cities, London and amphitheater, is this: knowing themselves to be the very definition of the city (cities are described by population figures), and the subjects and therefore very perpetuators of ideology, the playgoers deconstruct the city of London without destroying it.

The city of London as an ideological concept in the minds of the theatergoers is kept in limbo. Once in the South Bank theater these subjects, pieces of the city structure, possess a vital distance from the city, and the subsequent reconstruction of their community is an affirmation of this group's own identity as different from the city, but inextricably of the city; they are able to leave London, reconvene, and avoid the city authorities, but their points of reference in play-making, their judgmental forces, will continually refer back to their conditioning as Londoners.

The very idea of the Jew on the late-sixteenth-century stage makes the use of this figure as an associate of the Christian audience alarming, cunning, and subversive. What is set up in The Jew of Malta is something that will be far less certain in The Merchant of Venice when it appears several years later. Barabas is a villain precisely because he is a Jew, and therefore the term "Jew" will suffice to presuppose all other villainous attributes.

Something of the status of the appellation might be gleaned from the episode in which Pilia-Borza and Bellamira arrange with Ithamore to get money from Barabas. Ithamore begins the demand letter "Master/Barabas -" (IV.ii.75-6). Pilia-Borza tells him "Write not so submissively, but threatening him" and so Ithamore restarts, "Sirrah Barabas" (IV.ii.77-8). When Pilia-Borza returns with the news that Barabas has supposedly only given him ten crowns instead of the demanded three hundred, Ithamore thinks of the most contemptuous way to demand more money. His letter begins "Sirrah Jew" (IV.ii.124).

Shylock, on the other hand, has reason for what he does. Whether it is good reason or not, it is certainly logical, and the Christians find themselves in need of a good (non-Venetian) mouthpiece to argue for their side. This mouthpiece, Portia, is another example of a figure from without who critiques the State she or he enters into, a State that to a greater or lesser extent marginalizes that character. Note that this critic is not impartial, not in the least objective; simply, that critic-figure must engage the audience, so that the audience effectively "sees" through her or his eyes.

This figure acts as a kind of guide to lead the audience through the stage world. This is the role played by Barabas. But Marlowe's weapon is so much more powerful, the relativity of the grievances so much more intriguing because, unlike Portia, Barabas is a hateful character, a Jew; yet he wins an audience's empathy.

Marlowe gives nothing away at the beginning. We surely cannot guess that soon we will consider seriously the appropriateness of the Jew's subversive message and methods.

The introduction of Barabas is a blatant taunting device - "in his counting-house, with heaps of gold before him". Barabas laments "what a trouble 'tis to count this trash!". He may signal to the audience in the yard as he says "The needy groom that never fingered groat / Would make a miracle of thus much coin," and goes on to lament the money-counting chore a second time (I.i.12-3).

In his little counting-house, rich and bitter, wealthy and boasting, perhaps wearing "the artificial Jewe of Maltae's nose" and traditional red wig denoting a traitor against Jesus, he is the archetypal villain. If the audience knows only that he is a Jew at this point, they know by line 49 that he is not just any Jew, but Barabas, aurally the same as the robber and murderer who was freed in Christ's place.

That the audience is aware of this name's relevance is confirmed by Barabas's instruction and ironic question to the merchant in the opening scene, "Go tell 'em the Jew of Malta sent thee, man; / Tush, who amongst 'em knows not Barabas?" We should make a distinction here between the use of the Jew as a representative of Barabas, and the use of the Jew as a representative of Judas.

Although standing for the anti-Christian race, this Jew of Malta does not stand for the specific betrayer, the damned Antichrist. A similar effect upon the audience of anti-Christianism, but not "Antichrist-ism," may occur when Shylock says of his daughter "Would any of the stock of Barabbas / Had been her husband rather than a Christian! - " (IV.i.293-4). Barabas names himself here, then, but that naming paradoxically takes away from specific identity, rather than adding to it.

It only places him in a category. Stephen Greenblatt has spotted a conflict of identity in Barabas, a tug-of-war between hidden psychology and what is openly declared. While plying an individuality through his self-alienating, and his exemplary "self-fashioning" behaviour, Barabas is also falling into the trap of becoming a personification of a concept, not of a human being. "Most dramatic characters - Shylock would be an appropriate example - accumulate identity in the course of their play; Barabas desperately tries to dispossess himself of such identity. But this steady erosion of himself is precisely what he has pledged himself to resist; his career, then, is in its very essence suicidal."

The erosion of identity of the antagonists is an ancient requirement for tragedy. Rene Girard seems absolutely correct when he writes that "violence invariably effaces the differences between antagonists." Barabas erodes his own identity through paradoxical self-nomenclature, disguises (apparel, drugs), and association (Ithamore, the Turks, the Maltese), and through violence he and his enemies are made all but indistinguishable. The audience will be left in a quandary: whether to support the admirable efforts of the disgusting Jew or the saving grace of the popish Catholics.

How the identity of Barabas is seemingly "fattened out," made particular, is by teaming him up with a partner in crime, who will shadow Barabas and imitate his evil. Ithamore is from "Thrace; brought up in Arabia" (II.iii.131). Barabas puts aside the slave he specifically terms "Moor" to choose one who will be credited with the traditional viciousness of a Turk, but with a punning name that reminds the audience of his region of upbringing, neighbour land to the Moorish North Africa; he is a double villain.

And Ithamore, like Barabas, is a critical outsider and a stranger in so far as he was not brought up where he was born and is now taken to a foreign land against his will. The Turk and the Jew are on England's stage, under the censuring eyes of the re-created "second city" spectators.

Ithamore possesses no loyalties in the conflicts that will occur, but is a pawn, a death-messenger. We could say that we are, ultimately, left with an infidel threat from a rich stranger and his servant, to a Christian strategic stronghold, the city of Malta.

This viewpoint estranges the Jew, makes foreign the compact Barabas-Ithamore army, and instructs the audience to take the evil natures of the Jew and the Turk for granted. In doing so the fact of their strangeness becomes at least as important as their specific nationality or religion; or rather their equal status as infidels puts to one side the apparently foregrounded scorn for "the Jew," per se. Marlowe gives the audience a fascinating choice over how to view the relationships here: either critical outsiders versus followers of anti-Christ or evil infidels versus Christians.

It is difficult to guess just how much the general theatergoing public knew or cared about the history of Malta and the legacy of the Knights of St. John. If reports of the situation in Malta were reaching England in the 1580s, as Godfrey Wettinger claims, the concern of the English that the strategically located island be sufficiently protected from the Turk must have been mixed.

Malta had not seen significant military action since the Turkish attack of 1565, the great Turkish invasions of Byzantium, Serbia, Morea, and elsewhere occurring in the fifteenth century. But the association of the Jew and the Turk was still a frightening anti-Christian force and the existence of a rich Jew in Malta was a horrendous thought, if we assume that to be rich is to be powerful.

Of course, it is also ideologically incorrect to cheer for the Spaniards represented on stage in 1592, and it is in the final act of The Jew of Malta that the audience's sympathies are tried. We may not expect an Elizabethan audience to be converted to the cause of Barabas; and neither should our modern sensitivities mislead us on the question of whether we expect them to object to the ferocity of Barabas's punishment when his entire estate was taken from him, for Barabas responds with disgusting verve.

To be sure, his murder of a friar and poisoning of a whole convent involve the comedy of the assassin set upon popish victims, and play with the tradition of the corrupt or suspect figure of the friar, but this part of the drama remains within the secure realm of the "play world." Where the audience's "real world" understanding of the figure will come from is the fact that the audience possesses a specific, analogical situation. It is located historically in 1592 and spatially outside the city walls.

Steven Mullaney notes the parallel of the theatrical

fictional and physical situation: Barabas outside Malta's walls, and the theater outside London's walls.

As I engage now with the analysis of a particular dramatic moment to put these proposals of place, relationship, and effect into practice, I should call a character witness to support my isolation of a scene for use as illustrative material. Yurim Lotman has said that "the analogy between painting and theatre was manifested above all in the organization of the spectacle through conspicuously pictorial means of artistic modelling, in that the stage text tended to unfold not as a continuous flux (non 'discrete') imitating the passage of time in the extra-artistic world, but as a whole clearly broken up into single 'stills' organized synchronically, each of which is set within the decor like a picture in a frame." The time-abstracted picture on which Mullaney, and now I, dwell is presented to the audience in the theater's frame, and shows Barabas thrown "o'er the walls".

He wakes from the drugs he has taken to feign death and stands alone, the single unheard middle-ranking professional. He is at this moment both physically and socially (as a Jew and a foreigner) an outsider. As such he is free to begin to decide on a way to reenter the city on his own terms, using the double level of identity that each audience member possesses - that of individual subject to the city, and ideological reinventor when outside the city boundary.

He must use his knowledge of the city (his "inextricable link") and also his distance (outside of the walls) to create the critical act - the player attempting a "re-semblance" of the personal character that exists without the structure and stricture of the city law.

This display of potentially subversive originality can be seen by an ideology locked within a city only as acting an unnatural part. In the South Bank theater the concept of the suburbs and of the danger of individual mental and physical liberty at this point becomes most highly charged. The whole purpose of creating a text of laws and proclamations within a jurisdiction is to ensure conformity and equal behavioral acts from its subjects.

If the subject leaves that jurisdiction, she or he is free to reassess laws. Exiting an ideology (or even more simply exiting a safe, if oppressive community) to create such an original, de-legalized character produces a being who must in the end, like Barabas, be "all alone" (V.i.61); alone but with a charismatic power that dissatisfied Londoners might yearn for in this dark economic period.

This character's deconstruction of the city body (by the removal of himself) is a way to reanalysis and affirmation of his serf as potential whole thinker and act-er; it is an analogue of the audience's deconstruction of the city structure and reestablishment in the theater.

Multiple or en masse recognition of the place of the oppressed individual subject, possible only in the theater, is the beginning of the route to a common effective reaction against the city from without. It is the first step on a subversive path that leads right to the lawmakers and monarchs of the city or realm being critiqued.

It appears at first, then, that individuality is encouraged through the subjects' exiting from London, that we are seeing individuals in the audience being excited by the strongly individual character of Barabas. But in fact the theater creates a world in which the playgoers are homogenous analogues to the Jew. They may have a personal reaction to Barabas's display, but this reaction is a product of communal fashioning - it is the theater audience's reaction as a whole.

This is not an encouraging concept for the human narcissistic and independence-loving psyche, but it would be, for many critics, the quintessential metamorphosis of the audience, allowing a common reception to dramatic stimuli, and so creating a serious anti-authoritarian, united force. Paul Yachnin, in his useful essay, "The Powerless Theater," denies this possibility:

In the theater of the period, political meaning was depoliticized, either by being contained within the aesthetic form as merely the indeterminate subject of imaginative representation or by being made the product of the audience's reception of the text rather than the product of the text itself.

The stage's representation of the operations of power was normally not allowed to coalesce in the kind of univocal and authorized meaning which might be seen as an attempt to intervene in the real world.

Like Barabas's naming of himself at the beginning of the play, the playgoers' renaming of themselves as a theater crowd does not create specific identity; it only shifts their membership affiliation between two related categories, London city and theater city.

It is this two-fold, interdependent audience identity, I would argue, and not the weakness of drama and theater itself, which lessens dramatic political power. For in 1592 the stage was still potentially dangerous.

In the theater of Marlowe, the aesthetic form of political action is not embellished or softened into an "indeterminate object of imaginative representation," but is cold, rapid display - the siege of the town cannot even be shown on the stage, it is so factual and real; the scaffold of Barabas's death is built and mastered as a new stage of death - simple, clean, quick, deadly, subversive, political.

We must reconsider the widespread concern among critics to try to prove power inherent within the theater and dramatic performance, to find a "univocal and authorized meaning which might be seen as an attempt to intervene in the real world." The play is all power game, all control mechanism, manipulating the audience; the play world is already in the real world, and should affect it.

Where the problem lies, why the should is not a will, is in the fact that the audience in London city and the audience in theater city cannot entirely dislocate themselves, and a univocal meaning (or even an over-simplified authorization: to fight, to overturn, to die) falls however potently onto the ears of an audience fashioned too much by just that real world and ultimately unable to go out of the theater and act against it. It is not "the audience's reception" that we should be concerned with, but audience retention, necessary for audience action.

Thomas Cartelli's proposal that "in The Jew of Malta

Marlowe provokes only minimal resistance to the enjoyment his version of burlesque affords" does not matter. It is not enough for the play to be "a collective fantasy getting out of hand." The play can assume all the powerful roles in the world. But for the playgoers to accept Barabas as their permanent hero, their subversive role model, they must reject London's ideology wholesale - not only its suppression of domestic protest, but also the long-assumed hatred for the "infidel."

It is with such an ideologically cleared mind that the theatergoers subsequently would have to return to London, if they were to effect change in their personal situations as a result of the play. But such a reaction against what has largely become accepted, even if questioned, ideological norms are a lot to ask.

We must investigate further how Marlowe wheedles his critical Jew into the favor of the audience, and moreover how this can only remain a local effect, one that disintegrates with the breaking-up of the audience at the end of the play. Calymath enters to the wakened and vengeful Barabas, who proclaims "My name is Barabas; I am a Jew". The dramatic irony of the line is hilarious, for the audience can see that he is a Jew; even in the fictional image Calymath should be able to see that he is a Jew.

Barabas even reveals his name before the obvious statement. And finally, as if teasing, as if he knew all along, Calymath recognizes Barabas's fame: "Art thou that Jew whose goods we heard were sold / For tribute-money?"

"The very same, my lord," Barabas replies (V.i.73-4). Barabas, now outside the walls, now alone in a personal quest for revenge against the city, appears through this irony to be rebuilding the identity that he falsely set up at the beginning, a shield of nomenclature from behind which to fight. This self-reintroduction by Barabas so late in the play, rapidly followed by his plan for taking the city, should be the ultimate piece of effective "self-fashioning."

But as Stephen Greenblatt reminds us, "Naming oneself is not enough; one must also name and pursue a goal. [Marlowe's] heroes do so with a splendid energy that distinguishes their words as well as their actions from the surrounding society. The Turks, friars, and Christian knights may all be driven by 'The wind that bloweth all the world besides, / Desire of gold', but only Barabas can speak of 'infinite riches in a little roome'." But even this is not good enough. Barabas is talking in riddles. His "infinite riches" are, of course, unattainable, and this will be proven at the end of the play - at the end of all life.

As Cartelli insists, this scene certainly "provokes" the audience. The niggling fact that the Maltese city that wronged Barabas is one governed by Spanish-ruled Catholics makes its undermining - in the fiction of this play - a not unattractive proposal for the London audience. And undermining is literally what the Turks and Barabas do. They reenter the city via its sewers; they take revenge on the city emblematically in that they return through the channels that should only allow effluent to leave the jurisdiction - they are therefore dangerous excess to the city's safety, the city's political filth infecting the city structure.

Back inside the Maltese city, Barabas and the Turks avenge as iconoclasts, usurping the figures of supposed justice, rising up "dirtily" from physically - and by metaphor socially - "below" the city. The actor on stage is setting an example for the audience, but the message is not stable. As Michael Goldman has said, "We are made sharply aware of the actor both activating an icon and altering it"; manipulation is the name of the game.

Scene ii of the final act opens with the assault having succeeded. Magically, off-stage, in the "theatrical space without," the city of the Spanish crusaders is violated. Hanna Scolnicov writes:

The founding of Rome [in Ovid's Fasti] is described as a cutting-off and consecrating of a particular space. According to Eliade, city walls were originally erected not for military protection but as a magical defence, for they marked out from the midst of a "chaotic" space, peopled with demons and phantoms, an enclosure, a place that was organised... provided with a "centre."

The sacred circle, cut off and delimited, consecrated and imbued with strength and significance, is highly suggestive in relation to the theatrical space. If the theater is its own "organised" space, it is truly a "second city": a walled, organized location of life-stories, parts of which others experience, relate, or miss completely.

There is more. The idea of magical defense reflects the reliance of the theater on illusion - the illusion of protection (that the Essex conspirators trusted to), of autonomy, and of power within the theatrical (architectural) space. The theater is an alternative not only to the geographical city space but also to the city ideology. It is a "sacred" alternative to the religious requirement of the official ideological apparatus; the trend to contrast the theater with a church or with schools, theaters being places of ungodly learning, was perhaps a more profound observation than many contemporary writers realized.

We are shown that Barabas's method of entry has left the city walls physically intact. His self-enclosure in the city is his suicidal version of "the constant attempt by characters within the plays to control, imprison, and wall up one another, while maintaining to themselves the fiction of breaking boundaries down." Intention-success (performance of the intended action) is possible, but purpose-success (achievement of the desired end) is ultimately not. The overthrow of the oppressor does not result in finality; revolution is not a stable condition.

So, ultimately, despite all the promise, the theatergoers are not given a way to hold the city from within. The Machiavellian element may be involved in the successful siege, but is really confirmed with typical Marlovian sleight-of-hand in the successful princehood and protection of the fortress by Ferneze.

The power of drama gulls the audience. Barabas's victory is temporary, even illusory. His greed will cause a final self-destructive attempt at gain and glory and the Catholic Christians will regain the city; their sacred wall - the Religious State Apparatus - remains intact too. The two enclosures, city and theater, remain discrete and undamaged.

Rebecca W. Bushnell is near to the mark with her summary of Tamburlaine I and II and The Jew of Malta as "plays that explore the craving for power and the strategies of usurpation. None of these plays concerns the exercise of power as tyranny; instead, each play displays the spectacle of ambition." She continues:

In The Jew of Malta, when Barabas is installed as governor, he seems momentarily confused; like Tamburlaine, he understands only need and not its fulfillment, so when he seeks "for much, but [can] not compass it," it is because he cannot bear to be "compassed". Having achieved authority, Barabas almost immediately collapses, and one of his own "engines" backfires on him. In the logic of representing ambition in these plays, the conclusion is not morally motivated; the action just grinds to a halt when desire is exhausted.

Stephen Greenblatt has blamed Barabas's failure on "his desire to avoid the actual possession of power." Indeed, by keeping the horizon of his power struggle exactly that - an ever-escaping sight ("infinite riches") - Barabas avoids having to hold on to the reality of power, avoids the inevitability of having to impose limits on his power (hence the dreadful mistake inherent in walling himself in the city). Tamburlaine similarly sees infinite space left to conquer as he peruses a map in his final hours of life. Peter S. Donaldson says of Tamburlaine's reception of the tactile crown:

The crown is necessary here not because Tamburlaine has any real sense of the earthly fruition he claims it represents, but because one must turn to something from the chaotic reflection of man's essence in nature, from warring elements, wandering planets, reflecting inner weariness and aimless oscillation. Marlowe mentions the "wondrous architecture" of the world, but what he presents is not an ordered universe, but rather one that mirrors the disorder of a fragmented self. To aim at the crown is really to turn away from the chaos of nature to a realm of willed coherence. The speech passes from images of fragmenting "natural" energies to the stable but ironic self-icon of the crown.

Barabas is the alternative power seeker. His "willed coherence" is strong, but his "aimless oscillation" is revealed in his final fall into the cauldron. Barabas does have a real sense of the earthly fruition that he claims his power signifier - money - represents, but he cannot grasp the reality of power itself.

The chase is more thrilling - and less tiresome - than holding on to the struggling catch called the power of rule. His ordered intention is reflected in his carefully constructed execution scaffold upon the stage; but his desire for avoidance of final power - the purpose-success - makes this scaffold another "self-icon," the rebuilt ("revolutionary," reinstating, return to the original) power structure.

What is provided for the audience is only the suggestion that from without the city can be challenged. There is no dramatic force that can scale the walls and overturn this "real world." In the end political subversion is within the power of the theater, but it cannot be converted to revolution inside the city by the audience, who must be the agents of any such process. But we may not like this ending. It is depressing. So we come back at it with dramatic subversion like the Isle of Dogs affair, or the incidents surrounding The Play of Sir Thomas More.

Or we cite the Dutch Church libel, with its "Machiavellian Marchant," its "Paris massacre" and its marginal "Tamburlaine," a prime example of a political text born of social and political dissatisfaction, of the force of knowledge of foreign affairs, and of the power of Marlowe's particular seminar in subversion at the "school of abuse" called the Rose.

But the Dutch Church Libel was a sheet pinned up in the primary city (London), that having stated its dramatic influences from the second city of performance (the Rose), remains a text that hints at revolutionary, subversive, individualistic possibility, yet in reality confirms only nationalistic and xenophobic homogeneity. Full of plans and threats - like Barabas - the text has lost its ability to turn into action somewhere in the "passage" between the theater and the streets of London.

Chapter 16

Marlowe's Cambridge Years

Faustus asks, and the question Marlowe wrote for his hero echoed the uncertainty over religious beliefs and practices felt by many of Queen Elizabeth's subjects. Indeed, in writing Doctor Faustus, Marlowe reflected the growing debate among Protestants that grew progressively more intense at his university during his years there. For unlike Oxford, Cambridge in the later 1580s was the battlefield on which the Calvinist and anti-Calvinist advocates played out their strategies, and the young Marlowe was surely an impressionable witness.

To appreciate the impact of this experience on him, we should know something of what he encountered as an undergraduate—the broad areas of disagreement that separated the various Protestant positions, the intense quarrels over religious doctrine, and the powerful impression created by influential churchmen. And we should keep in mind that what may seem today to be minor differences took on importance because, to a true believer, such matters could prove decisive in the salvation of one's soul; the risks were very high.

Disagreements in matters of religion were, of course, nothing new to the English of the 1580s, for the populace was still feeling the effects of the Reformation—divided not only into Catholics and Protestants but also into varieties of Catholicism and Protestantism. Some Catholics considered themselves primarily English subjects and placed loyalty to the monarchy above obedience to the pope; others believed that true Catholicism could not be practiced without accepting the pope's primacy of place. Among Protestants, too, the varieties of religious beliefs and practices as well as the intensity with which they were held defined the spectrum of English Protestantism in which the members of the Church of England could be more or less Calvinists.

Quite naturally, many felt bewildered, alienated from their God. For some, the loss of the spiritual comfort afforded by the Catholic belief in Purgatory, or in the effectiveness of prayers for the deceased, or in the practice of Confession was made even more painful by the desecration of churches and by the elimination of ritual elements from the service. Moreover, the government understandably feared that religious radicalism would lead to political ferment and social unrest.

Those who claimed to be church reformers, some even preaching a new doctrine of egalitarianism, could make use of the tensions in society caused by economic problems such as inflation and social dislocations such as land enclosure to heighten the strains between rulers and ruled, between the wealthy and the impoverished. Elizabeth's administration happily adopted Archbishop Cranmer's Forty-two Articles, though now reduced to thirty-nine, since they were drafted in such a way that they could accommodate a variety of religious convictions.

As Powell Mills Dawley has pointed out, the queen's "original settlement of religion had been constructed to rest on the broadest possible base of agreement on the essentials of Christian doctrine rather than on the precise and rigid theological definitions familiar in sixteenth-century confessional systems."

And so some matters were deliberately left unsaid or stated vaguely in an attempt to head off controversy. But in its effort to be all-encompassing, the Elizabethan settlement was rendered susceptible to influences from all directions, especially of those Reformed writings that issued from Geneva. The initial efforts of the English Calvinists to correct what they saw as errors or abuses in the Church of England were focused on matters of polity and ritual.

While they were prepared to accept episcopacy—on condition that the bishops were "godly"—the suspension of Grindal as Archbishop led a significant number in the late 1570s to press for an alternate presbyterian system similar to that of Geneva, in which the clergy were elected by church members and matters of administration were shared by ministers and laymen.

And they argued for the need to cleanse or purify the ceremonies of the church service from what they claimed were the remnants of Popish customs—including such matters as the wearing of surplices and vestments, the location of the altar, and the practice of kneeling at prayer. According to Patrick Collinson, although these remained contentious issues, the energy to sustain an active fight for such changes was exhausted before the 1590s: the reformers were outmaneuvered, and the death of the Earl of Leicester, one of their most influential supporters, proved a heavy loss.

In addition, attention in the 1580s had been shifting from these operational concerns to doctrinal and philosophic matters that were closer to the heart of the differences between Calvinist and anti-Calvinist views. Nicholas Tyacke has neatly summarized how the balance of power changed throughout the decade:

In the early and middle years of Elizabeth's reign Calvinism keyed in fairly convincingly with political reality. To begin with, the existence of a large body of English Catholics lent credence to the identification of Protestants with the elect. Later, as relations with Spain deteriorated, Calvinism was transferable to the international plane, and Englishmen were now portrayed as chosen by God to do battle for the true religion. But as political circumstances eased, so the way was opened for undermining Calvinism from within.

In the course of the 1590s the external threat from Spain appeared to diminish and the prospect of an internal revolt by English Catholics seemed increasingly remote. A united Protestant front was, therefore, less essential. At the same time English Calvinist teaching was itself becoming more extreme, in line with continental religious developments.

Now questions of grace and salvation came to the fore—questions that would be of particular interest to the young Marlowe: Who were those elected to be saved? How could they know? How could salvation be assured? Could it be won or lost? Were some born reprobates, inevitably to be damned, and if so, when did God make this determination and why?

These are indeed what were called "deep points." During the 1590s English Calvinism had been very much in the ascendant, and nowhere was that ascendancy more obvious than at Cambridge University. Symptomatic of the situation is the publication in 1590 of William Perkins's Armilla Aurea... I which~ asserted the doctrine of absolute predestination against its critics....

Paradoxically, however, the propagation of such views also helped fuel the anti-Calvinist sentiment. The differences between English and Continental Protestantism were becoming increasingly difficult to ignore, and the hostility between those who held opposing points of view intensified. Through these quarrels, through public debate and preaching, ministers on both sides grew more outspoken, their skills sharper and more finely honed.

As Patrick Collinson has remarked:

Calvinist assumptions... were challenged, as they would not have been ten years before, by the reaction against Geneva which was gathering force amongst a party of avant-garde divines in Cambridge, and this nascent English "Arminianism" would lend orthodox, Calvinist puritanism a new "theological distinction."

Conditions were ripening for the forceful confrontations of the 1590s—the issues were more difficult and serious, the opponents more practiced and determined. Enter Christopher Marlowe. On this scene of religious strife, Marlowe began his Cambridge University career as a student of divinity at Corpus Christi College in early December 1580.

His programme in his first year would have involved attending lectures in rhetoric (Quintilian, Hermogenes, and Cicero), preparing lessons for his tutor, studying the Old and New Testaments, and attending chapel sermons. Marlowe's arrival in Cambridge coincided with the period when William Perkins became known by his preaching as the most popular and effective spokesman for the extreme Calvinists. Perkins had received his B.A. in 1581 and his M.A. in 1584; in that year he was elected a fellow of Christ's, a position he was to hold for the next decade, and he was appointed lecturer at Great St. Andrews in the town.

Perkins rapidly established himself both as a preacher and as "the most outstanding systematic Puritan theologian of his time." Marlowe's career at Cambridge spans these years: he completed his undergraduate studies in 1584 when he was awarded his B.A.; and he continued in residence, with some periods of absence, until March 1587, when he filed his application for admission to the M.A. degree. His interest in the Faust story must have followed hard upon, for The Tragical History of Doctor Faustus was written sometime between 1588 and 1592—with many scholars giving it an earlier rather than later date.

Since Perkins was among the most powerful voices at Cambridge during Marlowe's career there, we should consider what Calvinist principles he emphasized and how his presence may have influenced undergraduate attitudes. From first-hand accounts we know that he was an impressive and memorable teacher: according to Samuel Ward, who was trained at Christ's, "in expounding the Commandments Perkins~ applied them so home, I that he was~ able almost to make his hearers hearts fall down, and hairs to stand upright."

And in 1584 his appointment as lecturer at Great St. Andrews gave Perkins the opportunity to address an audience of both students and townspeople in Cambridge. His technique was clearly impressive. Even after the Civil War his fame was remembered.

Ultimately, two aspects of Perkins's manner account for his wide appeal—his arguments were constructed by a precise and logical method that applied the new Ramist principles of organization then in vogue, and his language was simple, direct, and moving. Perkins was so deeply persuaded of the importance of his mission and his words were chosen so carefully that a listener would find "his conscience so convinced, his secret faults so disclosed and his very heart so ripped up that he said, 'Certainly God speaks in this man.'" Naturally, Perkins's success aroused the anti-Calvinist opposition and, feeling threatened, they began a counterattack. It is this controversy that provided the background for the debate Marlowe would dramatize in Doctor Faustus.

But actually such tensions were nothing new among those holding differing views of what constituted the true doctrine of the Protestant church. Spokesmen for various points of view in the University had been sparring with one another throughout the 1580s, jockeying for lead position, attempting to attract converts, and vying for influence in the highest reaches of the English Church.

An especially vivid instance of the intensity of the conflict between the two parties can be seen in the bitter quarrel that, after long smoldering, finally erupted in 1595-1596 between William Barrett and Peter Baro, the Lady Margaret Professor of Divinity, on the one hand, and the heads and dons of the more Calvinist-oriented colleges on the other.

Baro was accused of having "for the space of these fourteen or fifteen years, taught in his lectures, preached in sermons, determined in the Schools and printed in several books divers points of doctrine... contrary to that which hath been taught and received ever since her Majesty's reign, yet agreeable to the errors of Popery."

Ironically, the views of Barrett and Baro were actually closer to the letter of the Thirty-Nine Articles than were the theological positions of their opponents. Nevertheless, Perkins and his followers argued that their Calvinist opinions correctly expressed the spirit of the doctrines of the Church of England rightly understood, and that only those holding their views could think of themselves as true members of that Church. Their influence was so strong that Barrett was actually forced to recant and Baro was eased out of his position.

Indeed, later church historians acknowledge the importance of Baro's role in curbing the growing power of the Calvinists: "this Doctrine finding many followers... might have quickly over-spread the whole University had it not been in part prevented and in part suppressed by the care and diligence of Dr. Barse i.e., Baro and his Adherents."

Marlowe's *Doctor Faustus* directly engages these controversies. His plot roughly follows the story-line of the English Faustbook, but the issues it raises are not discussed in this source.

The theological significance of Dr. Faustus's choices can perhaps best be understood by referring to what Perkins himself wrote in a work that, as Ian Breward notes, "grew out of sermons in the 1590s, when a fresh outbreak of popular interest in the discovery and detection of witches would make it a very topical treatment."

According to Perkins, the practice of witchcraft is like the sin in Eden of desiring to become a god, motivated by a longing either to win "credit and countenance amongst men" or, "not satisfied with the measure of inward gifts received, as of knowledge, wit, understanding, memory and suchlike,... to search out such things as God would have kept secret." This is what Marlowe describes as the "world of profit and delight, / Of power, of honour, of omnipotence": his hero wants "to practise more than heavenly power permits." Now "having commencde" |sic~—or taken his degree—Faustus would exceed "Emperours and Kings," for they

Are but obeyd in their seuerall prouinces: ..... But his dominion that exceedes in this, Stretcheth as farre as doth the minde of man. A sound Magician is a mighty god: Heere Faustus trie thy braines to gaine a deitie.

(lines 88-93)

To describe him in Perkins's words, Marlowe's Faustus is "not satisfied" with the achievements of his education. Had he been a student at Cambridge, for example, his programme of study—disputations in divinity on such topics as free will, justification, and grace; systematic and analytic sermons on biblical passages; and the presentation and defense of theses—would have trained him in such matters as God would not have kept secret from us.

To conduct these disputations, analyses, and defenses, the

study of logic or dialectics was prescribed in the undergraduate curriculum in the third and fourth years.

Aristotle was the required text; as Faustus says, he would "live and die in Aristotles workes" (line 35). But in his very next words Faustus quotes a precept of the controversial French reformer, Peter Ramus, who advocated revising the traditional scholasticism of the university curriculum that blended Aristotle with St. Thomas Aquinas.

By their efforts, the Ramists attempted to simplify and clarify the methods of the scholastics and to systematize the reasoning processes-especially on the correct way to establish truth through logic. Perkins, for one, retained the scholastic method for discussing questions of divinity, but he was a Ramist in his arguments.

For analyzing matters of church doctrine his preferred method was an orderly, step-by-step sequence of questions and answers. As described by Peter Helyn, who was perhaps rephrasing Thomas Fuller's words, "when he was a Catechist of Christs Colledge in Cambridge Perkins~ did lay the Law so home in the ears of his Auditors that it made their hearts fall down, and yea their hair to stand almost upright."

Catechisms were a common element in teaching the principles of the reformed churches: "a huge number appeared in England between 1558 and 1660, frequently written by those with puritan sympathies, aimed not only at supplementing or replacing the brief catechism in the Prayer Book, but also seeking to provide godly householders with material with which to edify their family and servants."

Perkins offers a fine example in his Foundation of Christian Religion Gathered into Six Principles (1590), in which he carefully makes the fine distinctions that will help one think correctly on religious matters:

Question: What state shall the wicked be in after the day of judgment?

Answer: In eternal perdition and destruction in hell-fire.

Question: What is that?

Answer: It stands in three things especially: first, a perpetual separation from God's presence; secondly, fellowship with the devil and his angels; thirdly, an horrible pang and torment both of body and soul arising of the feeling of the whole wrath of God, poured forth on the wicked for ever, world without end; and if the pain of one tooth for one day be so great, endless shall be the pain of the whole man, body and soul for ever.

Faustus makes use of just this kind of catechism when he first talks with Mephostophilis. For the most part, his lines are a series of questions to which Mephostophilis provides the answers: "Tell me what is that Lucifer thy Lord?" (line 307), "Was not that Lucifer an Angell once?" (line 309), "How comes it then that he is prince of diuels?" (line 311), "and what are you that liue with Lucifer?" (line 314), "Where are you damn'd?" (line 318), "How comes it then that thou art out of hel?" (line 320).

Despite all of his advanced studies and perceptive questions, Faustus is completely unaware of his ignorance and blinded by his self-conceit. In his opening soliloquy in which he debates the merits of various fields of endeavor, Faustus rejects Aristotelian logic as a subject worthy of his attention and considers medicine as a possible career. But once again, his aspirations are blasphemous. Faustus could be satisfied as a physician only if he had the god-like power to grant immortality—to "make man to liue eternally / Or being dead, raise them to life againe" (lines 54-55).

Medicine, it appears, is too restrictive for one with his ambitions. And, after thinking about it, he determines his disposition is also unsuited for the law, for Faustus has neither the patience nor the interpretative skills to interest himself in what he calls "paltry legacies." Faustus even admits that he cannot distinguish "a petty case" from much more important instances—for example, under what circumstances a father may disinherit a son: "Ex haereditari filium non potest pater nisi."

This topic is, in fact, one discussed not only by Justinian but also by Protestant clerics: in spiritual terms, when and under what conditions does God decide to disown his child? Faustus is like the man described by Perkins in a sermon delivered in 1593: a sinner in his first estate... hath a veil before his face so that he seeth nothing. The wrath of God and the curse due for sin, hell and damnation seeking to devour him he seeth them not... but rusheth securely into all manner of sin, the night of impenitence and the mist of ignorance so blinding his eyes that he seeth not the narrow bridge of this life, from which if he slide he falls immediately into the bottomless pit of hell.

Unable to reason properly and, as Perkins describes it, "not resting content with the condition of men," hoping to be "a mighty god" (line 92), to be "on earth as Ioue is in the skie" (line 108), Faustus rejects Jerome's Bible for "Negromantike bookes" (line 80). In the play each of these subjects has its advocate, the Good Angel naturally promoting the joys of Bible study and the Evil Angel recommending the advantages of black magic.

Whether they are reflections of Faustus's own mental processes or independent of them, these allegorical figures objectify the inner conflict in the hero; through them the contest for his soul is dramatized. And what at first seems most important is that they emphasize his freedom to choose. If Faustus were born to be damned, as he might be in a Calvinistic universe, he is surely ignorant of it, for he believes he can exercise his own will. Yet he admits that the rewards promised by the Evil Angel are irresistible. Since Faustus is actually the type of person who is drawn compulsively to what is blasphemous, daring, and imprudent, it is not at all clear that his choice is so free after all.

The A-text, in lines that do not appear in the 1616 edition, emphasizes how greatly his decision is a consequence of his character: not your words onely, but mine owne fantasie, That will receiue no object for my head, But ruminates on Negromantique skill.

(lines 136-38)(29)

The force of his own nature compels him to the study of magic, and he is unable to resist: "Tis Magicke, Magicke that hath rauisht mee" (line 143) Faustus signs his pact with the devil, providing, as Perkins explains, "the ground of all the practices of witchcraft:... a league or covenant made between the witch and the devil wherein they do mutually bind themselves to each other." Faustus reminds himself repeatedly of the price he will ultimately pay if he continues, and he realizes, at least in a part of his mind, that reformation and repentance are more than "vaine fancies" (line 441).

But Faustus lacks faith, and that is essential for salvation. Acknowledging that in his case "the god thou seruest is thine owne appetite" (line 448), he rightly concludes that he "must... needes be damnd" (line 438).

His inability to give up the pursuit of magic or break his agreement with Lucifer, then, can explain, according to anti-Calvinist teaching, why he is ultimately damned or, according to Calvinist teaching, why he was born damned. As Perkins reminds his congregation, "The decree of God |in rejecting some~ is secret, because it ariseth only from the good pleasure of God, unsearchable."

The ending of the play merits especially close attention, for it focuses explicitly on the conflicting Calvinist and anti-Calvinist views. According to the Old Man, Faustus can still be saved: he has only to "call for mercie and auoyd dispaire" (line 1323). Just such a line of reasoning would be held by Perkins's opponent, Peter Baro, who argued that "to each and every man God desires to give grace sufficient for salvation, for Christ died for each and every man."

Though some may choose to resist it—"the grace which is offered they thrust from them" in Hooker's words—saving grace is available to all. The Old Man's encouragement to Faustus would certainly support such a reading: "I see an Angell houers ore thy head, / And with a violl full of precious grace, / Offers to powre the same into thy soule" (lines 1320-22). It is only by rejecting the grace that is freely offered that one becomes a reprobate: as Baro explained, "Men shut themselves out of heaven, not God."

In its ending the text of the play can be made to support the non-Calvinist view that Faustus can still attain salvation by an act of faith, by repentance and prayer. But Faustus's faith proves too weak and insufficient: "I do repent, and yet I do dispaire" (line 1330). He cannot believe he can be forgiven by the God he "hath abjurde... whome Faustus hath blasphemed." According to the Old Man, Faustus is "accursed" (line 1377) because he "excludst the grace of heauen" (line 1378).

But Faustus has always thought of himself as beyond common humanity. Since to his mind superlative and excessive actions are the hallmarks of his nature, his offenses must naturally be so great that he "can nere be pardoned, / The Serpent that tempted Eue may be sau'd / But not Faustus" (lines 1402-404). As Wilbur Sanders has observed, "We are watching a man... locked in a death embrace with the agonising God he can neither reject nor love. It is the final consummation of the Puritan imagination." Much as he may desire it, Faustus's conception of himself prevents him from achieving justifying faith.

The anti-Calvinist, emphasizing the hero's need to turn to God and believe in his forgiveness, can, of course, be countered by stressing those elements that make Faustus seem more a Calvinist paradigm. Read in that light he is quite simply one born a reprobate who will feel God's "heavy wrath." He was damned from birth: "You starres that raignd at my natiuitie, / whose influence hath alotted death and hel" (lines 1474-75).

In the final judgment his fate was not determined by Faustus's deeds or lack of faith. According to Perkins, the decision who shall be saved and who condemned is God's alone; it "hath not any cause beside his will and pleasure." The saving drop of Christ's blood is denied him as it is to all reprobates who, in the words of Perkins, are punished with eternal confusion and most bitter reproaches.... They have fellowship with the devil and his angels. They are wholly in body and soul tormented with an incredible horror and exceeding great anguish, through the sense and feeling of God's wrath poured out upon them for ever.

Can one fix the ultimate, responsibility, however? Is Faustus a Calvinist reprobate, a being born to be damned, one so fixed in his ways that from birth the course of his life is a foregone conclusion? As Alan Sinfield succinctly expresses this point of view: "Marlowe's Faustus is not damned because he is wicked, but wicked because he is damned." Or on the contrary, is Faustus an Arminian soul, a free agent exercising volition who refuses the grace that is freely given?

In the words of Roma Gill, "Marlowe's God is more long-suffering than the God of the Elizabethan church and continues to extend mercy and forgiveness to Faustus long after the traditional God would have turned away." Clearly, in either case, the spiritual failure in the hero's character is a crucial element in the outcome, but in the final analysis, the issue remains unresolved and unresolvable. Both Calvinist and anti-Calvinist views are sustained throughout the action.

In no small measure Marlowe's experiences at Cambridge helped shape his hero who is neither clearly redeemable nor reprobate: ultimately, the play cannot be reduced to a straightforward theological text.

The reasons for what Norman Rabkin would call its "complementarity," however, are surely personal and practical as well as religious. We need not read Doctor Faustus as reflecting quite so extreme a psychological crisis as Wilbur Sanders, who holds responsible "those disordered forces in Marlowe's own imagination which lead him either into hectic exaggeration or into moralistic excess."

Yet we should acknowledge that the young playwright was not only reacting to the fierce debate between Calvinists and anti-Calvinists he had witnessed as a Cambridge undergraduate but also incorporating into the poetry something of his own personal reaction to this debate.

While a divinity student he had, after all, heard some of the most forceful and unforgettable presentations of the extreme Calvinist position: even as an old man, Peter Helyn could still recall that William Perkins would "pronounce the word Damne with so strong an Emphasis that it left an echo in the ears of his hearers a long time after. When designing his play in the late 1580s or early 1590s, Marlowe must have also taken into account political and aesthetic considerations. He was surely aware of the long-standing government prohibition against those who "handle in their plaies certen matters of Divinytie and of State unfitt to be suffred." Indeed, perhaps as a consequence of the Martin Marprelate imbroglio, the authorities were once again feeling the need for more forceful control over the stage: in November 1589 the Privy Council requested that Archbishop Whitgift appoint a "fytt persone well learned in Divinity" to assist the Master of the Revels in screening plays "to geve allowance of suche as they shall thincke meete to be plaied and to forbydd the rest."

The performance history of Marlowe's effort clearly indicates that it did not defy the censors, however much it might have ruffled the feathers of one or another religious position. And whether the result of his practical good sense, of his instincts as an artist, or of some combination of the two,

Marlowe must have understood that a work that engages in so hotly contested a subject would surely attract the public, just as he must have realized that any play with a clear-cut or consistent theological message would be in danger of turning into a sermon, didactic, undramatic, and dangerous. The energy of his work, its power to draw an audience, would be generated by playing off the possibility of salvation against the fear of absolute damnation, an anti-Calvinist world-view, expressed through the Good Angel, in conflict with a Calvinist hero, a born reprobate.

And this combination would enable him to create a memorable character. After all, a protagonist presented purely in a Calvinist light, one who can do nothing to assure his own salvation, is merely a victim—rather like the pathetic figure of the de casibus tradition. And the other alternative, a protagonist who is completely responsible for his damnation, is liable to appear merely wicked or foolish—rather like the title character in a Senecan-styled tragedy.

A hero of either stamp could arouse little interest. In the final analysis, then, Marlowe's drama can be appreciated as the product of a number of forces—the controversy between Calvinists and anti-Calvinists that must have impressed him deeply during his years at Cambridge, the expanding power of state censorship, and, surely not to be underestimated, his own personal, poetic, and artistic instincts.

Chapter 17

The Progresse of the Soule

During the last year of his residence in the household of Sir Thomas Egerton, Donne began the composition of a longer and more elaborate satirical poem than anything he had yet attempted, a poem the personal and historical significance of which has received somewhat scant attention from his biographers.

The Progresse of the Soule. Infinitati Sacrum. 16 *Augusti* 1601. *Metempsycosis. Poema Satyricon* was published for the first time in 1633, but manuscript copies of the poem, by itself and in collections of Donne's poems, are extant. That he never contemplated publication is clear from the fact that he adopted the same title, *The Progresse of the Soule,* for the very different *Anniversaries* on the death of Elizabeth Drury.

Starting from the Pythagorean doctrine of metempsychosis, it was Donne's intention, in this poem, to trace the migrations of the soul of that apple which Eve plucked, conducting it, when it reached the human plane, through the bodies of all the great heretics. It was to have rested at last, Jonson told Drummond, in the body of Calvin; but the grave and dignified stanzas with which the poem opens show clearly that queen Elizabeth herself was to have closed the line of heretics whose descent was traced to the soul of Cain, or of Cain's wife:

This soul to whom Luther and Mahomet were
Prisons of flesh; this soul which oft did tear,
And mend the wracks of the Empire and late Rome,
And lived when every great change did come.

Writing to Sir Thomas Egerton in the following February,

Donne disclaims all "love of a corrupt religion." Yet, during the preceding year, he had been busy on an elaborate satire, delineating, from a Catholic standpoint, the descent and history of the great heretics from Arius and Mahomet to Calvin and Elizabeth. There can be little doubt that the mood of mind which found expression in this sombre poem was occasioned by the execution of Essex in the preceding February. Nothing, for a time, so clouded Elizabeth's popularity as the death of her rash favourite.

Up to the time of the outbreak, Egerton himself had been reckoned of Essex's party; and Wotton, through whom Donne had first, probably, been brought within the circle of Essex's influence, was one of those who went into exile after the earl's death. It would have been interesting to read Donne's history of heresy, and characters of Mahomet and Luther, great, bad men as he apparently intended to delineate them; but the poem never got so far. After tracing through some tedious, not to say disgusting, episodes the life of the soul in vegetable and animal form, Donne leaves it just arrived in Themech,

Sister and wife to Cain, Cain that first did plough

The mood in which the poem was conceived had passed, or the poet felt his inventive power unequal to the task, and he closed the second canto abruptly with a stanza of more than Byronic scepticism and scorn:

Whoe'ere thou beest that readest this sullen writ,
Which just so much courts thee as thou dost it,
Let me arrest thy thoughts; wonder with me
Why ploughing, building, ruling and the rest,
Or most of those arts whence our lives are blest,
By cursed Cains race invented be,
And bless'd Seth vex'd us with astronomy.
There 's nothing simply good nor ill alone;
Of every quality comparison
The only measure is, and judge opinion.

Chapter 18

His Love Poetry

It is not difficult to distinguish three strains in Donne's love poetry, including both the powerful and enigmatical elegies and the strange and fascinating songs. The one prevails in all the elegies (except the famous *Autumnal* dedicated to Mrs. Herbert, and the seventeenth, the subject of which may have been his wife) and in the larger number of the lyrical pieces, in songs like "Go and catch a falling star," "Send home my long stray'd eyes to me," or such lyrics as *Woman's Constancy,*

The Indifferent, Aire and Angels, The Dreame, The Apparition, and many others. This is the most distinctive strain in Donne's early poetry, and that which contrasts it markedly with the love poetry of his contemporaries, the sonneteers. There is no echo of Petrarch's woes in Donne's passionate and insolent, rapturous and angry, songs and elegies. The love which he portrays is not the impassioned yet intellectual idealism of Dante, nor the refined and adoring sentiment of Petrarch, nor the epicurean but courtly love of Ronsard, nor the passionate, chivalrous gallantry of Sidney.

It is the love of the Latin lyrists and elegiasts, a feeling which is half rapture and half rage, for one who is never conceived of for a moment as standing to the poet in the ideal relationship of Beatrice to Dante or of Laura to Petrarch. *Das ewig Weibliche zieht uns hinan* is not Donne's sentiment in these poems, but rather

Hope not for mind in women; at their best
Sweetness and wit, they 're but mummy possest.

But if Donne's sentiment is derived rather from Latin than

from Italian and courtly poetry, it was reinforced by his experience, and it is expressed with a wit and erudition that are all his own.

And, in reading some, both of the elegies and the songs, one must not forget to make full allowance for the poet's inexhaustible and astounding wit and fancy. "I did best," he said later, "when I had least truth for my subject." Realistic, Donne's love poetry may be; it is not safe to accept it as a history of his experiences.

The *Elegies* are the fullest record of Donne's more cynical frame of mind and the conflicting moods which it generated. Some, and not the least brilliant in wit and execution, are frankly sensual, the model of poems such as Carew's *The Rapture;* others, fiercely, almost brutally, cynical and satirical; others, as *The Chain* and *The Perfume,* more simply witty; a few, as *The Picture,* strike a purer note. A strain of impassioned paradox runs through them; they are charged with wit; the verse, though harsh at times, has more of the couplet cadence than the satires; the phrasing is full of startling felicities:

I taught my silks their rustlings to forbear,
Even my oppress'd shoes dumb and silent were;

and there are not wanting passages of pure and beautiful poetry:

I will not look upon the quickening sun
But straight her beauty to my sense shall run;
The air shall note her soft, the fire most pure,
Waters suggest her clear, and the earth sure.

This turbid, passionate yet cynical, vein is not the only one in Donne's love poetry. Two others are readily distinguishable, and include some of his finest lyrics. In one, which is probably the latest, as that described is the earliest, Donne returns a little towards the sonneteers, especially the more Platonising among them. Poems like *Twickenham Garden, The Funerall, The Blossom, The Primrose,* were probably addressed neither to the mistresses of his youth, nor to the wife of his later years, but to the high-born lady friends, Mrs. Herbert and the countess of Bedford, for whom he composed the ingenious and erudite compliments of his verse letters.

Towards them, he adopts the hopeless and adoring pose of Petrarchian flirtation (of Spenser towards lady Carew or Drayton towards mistress Anne Goodere) and, in high Platonic vein, boasts that,

Difference of sex no more we knew
Than our guardian angels do;
Coming and going we
Perchance might kiss, but not between those meals;
Our hands ne'er touched the seals
Which nature, injured by late law, sets free;
These miracles we did; but now alas!
All measure and all language I should pass,
Should I tell what a miracle she was.

Less artificial than this last strain, purer than the first, and simpler, though not less intense, than either, is the feeling of those lyrics which, in all probability, were addressed to his wife. To this class belongs the exquisite song:

Sweetest Love, I do not go
For weariness of thee,
Nor in hope the world can show
A fitter love for me.

In the same vein, and on the same theme, are the *Valediction: of Weeping:*

O more than moon,
Draw not up seas to drown me in thy sphere;
Weep me not dead in thine arms, but forbear
To teach the sea what it may do too soon;

and the more famous *Valediction: forbidding Mourning,* with its characteristic, fantastical yet felicitous, conceit of the compasses:

Such wilt thou be to me who must,
Like the other foot, obliquely run;
Thy firmness makes my circle just,
And makes me end where I begun.

The seventeenth elegy, "By our first strange and fatal interview," may belong to the same group, and so, one would conjecture, do *The Canonization,* "For Godsake hold your tongue and let me love" and *The Anniversary.* In these, at any rate, Donne expresses a purer and more elevated strain of the same feeling as animates *The Dream, The Sun-Rising* and *The Break of Day;* and one not a whit less remote from the tenor of Petrarchian poetry. At first sight, there is not much in common between the erudite, dialectical Donne and the peasant-poet Burns, yet it is of Burns one is reminded rather than of the average Elizabethan by the truth and intensity with which Donne sings, in a more ingenious and closely woven strain than the Scottish poet's, the joy of mutual and contented love:

All other things to their destruction draw,
Only our love hath no decay;
This no to-morrow hath nor yesterday.
Running it never runs from us away,
But truly keeps his first, last, everlasting day.

Of the shadow of this joy, the pain of parting, Donne writes also with the intensity, if never with the simplicity, of Burns. The piercing simplicity of

Had we never loved sae kindly

was impossible to Donne's temperament, in which feeling and intellect were inextricably blended, but the passion of *The Expiration* is the same in kind and in degree, however, elaborately and quaintly it may be phrased:

So, so, break off this last lamenting kiss,
Which sucks two souls, and vapours both away.
Turn thou ghost that way, and let me turn this,
And let ourselves benight our happiest day;
We ask'd none leave to love, nor will we owe
Any so cheap a death as saying "Go."

The Ecstacy blends, and strives to reconcile, the material and the spiritual elements of his realistic and his Platonic strains. But, subtly and highly wrought as that poem is, its reconciliation is more metaphysical than satisfying. It is in the simpler poems from which quotations have been given that the diverse elements find their most natural and perfect union.

Chapter 19

Letters and Funerall Elegies

The more normal and courtly moods of Donne's mind in these central years of his life are reflected in the *Letters* and *Funerall Elegies*.

Of the former, the earliest, probably, were *The Storm* and *The Calm*, whose vivid and witty realism first set Donne's "name afloat." When Jonson visited Edinburgh, he entertained Drummond by reciting the witty paradoxes of *The Chain* and the vivid descriptions of *The Calm:*

No use of lanthorns: and in one place lay
Feathers and dust, today and yesterday.

The two epistles to Sir Henry Wotton beginning "Sir, more than kisses letters mingle souls" and the above mentioned "Here's no more news than virtue," were, probably, both written in the same year, 1598. An interesting and characteristic reply to the first by Wotton is preserved in one or two manuscripts, but has never been published.

The Burley MS. contains another to Wotton in *Hibernia belligeranti,* written, therefore, in 1599. That on Wotton's appointment as ambassador to Venice was composed five years later. To Goodere and to the Woodwards and Brookes, he wrote quite a number, in the same last years of the sixteenth century, not all of which are yet published.

Those to more noble patrons, generally ladies, were the work of Donne's years of suitorship. He seems to have written none after he took orders. The long letter to the countess of Huntingdon, beginning "That unripe side of earth, that heavy clime" is assigned to Sir Walter Aston in two manuscripts; and the three short letters, to Ben Jonson and to Sir Thomas

Roe, first printed in 1635, are pretty certainly not Donne's at all but Sir John Roe's.

The moral reflections in these letters are elevated, and are developed with characteristic ingenuity. The brilliance with which a train of metaphysical compliments is elaborated in such a letter as that to the countess of Bedford beginning "Madam—you have refined me" is dazzling. But neither Donne's art nor taste—to say nothing of his character—is seen to best advantage in the abstract, extravagant and frigid conceits of these epistles and of such elegies as those on prince Henry and lord Harington. The strain of eulogy to which Donne suffers himself to rise in these last passes all limits of decency and reverence.

To two feelings, Donne was profoundly susceptible, and he has expressed both with wonderful eloquence in verse and prose. He has all the renascence sense of the pomp and the horror of death, the leveller of all earthly distinctions; and he can rise, like

Sir Thomas Browne, to a rapt appreciation of the Christian vision of death as the portal to a better life. But his expression of both moods, when he is writing to order, is apt to degenerate into an accumulation of "gross and disgusting hyperboles." In an elegy on Mrs. Bulstred, which, apparently by an accident, is divided into two separately printed poems, *Death I recant* and *Death be not proud,* these moods are combined in a sonorous and dignified strain.

But the finest of Donne's funeral elegies is the second of the *Anniversaries,* which he composed on the death of Elizabeth Drury. The extravagance of his praise, indeed, offended even Jacobean readers, and the poem was declared by Jonson to be "profane and full of blasphemies."

It is clear, however, that Donne intended Elizabeth Drury to be taken as a symbol of Christian and womanly virtue. He may have known something of the Tuscan poets' metaphysic of love, for Donne is one of the few poets of the day who had read "Dant."

It cannot be said that he succeeded in investing his subject with the ideal atmosphere in which Beatrice moves. *The First*

Anniversary is little more than a tissue of frigid, metaphysical hyberboles, relieved by occasional felicities, as the famous

Doth not a Teneriffe or higher hill
Rise so high like a rock, that one might think
The floating moon would shipwreck there and sink?

The *Second,* however, is not only richer in such occasional jewels but is a finer poem.

With the eulogy, which is itself managed with no small art, as, for example, in the recurring cadences of "She, she is dead," the poet has interwoven a *meditatio mortis,* developed with the serried eloquence, the intense, dull glow of feeling and the sonorous cadences which we find again in the prose of the sermons.

Chapter 20

Religious Verses

Of Donne's religious verses other than the funeral elegies, the earliest, *On the Annunciation and Passion falling in the same year,* was written, according to the title given in more than one manuscript, in 1608. *The Litany* was composed in the same year as *Pseudo-Martyr;* and it is interesting to note that, though the Trinity is followed, in Catholic sequence, by the Virgin, the Angels, the patriarchs and so forth, there is no invocation of any of these, but only commemoration.

The two sequences of sonnets, *La Corona* and *Holy Sonnets,* belong, apparently, to the early years of his ministry. One of the latter, first published by Gosse from the Westminster MS., refers to the recent death of his wife in 1617; and *The Lamentations of Jeremy* would appear to be a task which he set himself at the same juncture. The hymns *To Christ, at the Authors last going into Germany, To God, my God in my Sickness* and *To God the Father* were written in 1619, 1627 and 1631 respectively.

There is a striking difference of theme and spirit between the "love-song weeds and satiric thorns" of Donne's brilliant and daring youth and the hymns and sonnets of his closing years; but the fundamental resemblance is closer. All that Donne wrote, whether in verse or prose, is of a piece. The same intense and subtle spirit which, in the songs and elegies, analysed the experiences of passion is at work in the latter on a different experience.

To be didactic is never the first intention of Donne's religious poems, but, rather, to express himself, to analyse and lay bare his own moods of agitation, of aspiration and of humiliation in the quest of God, and the surrender of his soul to Him. The same erudite and surprising imagery, the same passionate, reasoning strain, meets us in both.

Is the Pacific sea my home? Or are
The Eastern riches? Is Jersualem?
Anyan, and Magellan, and Gibraltar,
All straits (and none but straits) are ways to them
Whether where Japhet dwelt, or Ham, or Shem.

The poet who, in the sincerities of a sick-bed confession, can spin such ingenious webs for his thought is one of those who, like Baudelaire, are "naturally artificial; for them simplicity would be affectation." And as Donne is the first of the "metaphysical" love poets, he is, likewise, the first of the introspective, Anglican, religious poets of the seventeenth century. Elizabethan, and a good deal of Jacobean, religious poetry is didactic in tone and intention, and, when not, like Southwell's, Romanist, is protestant and Calvinist but not distinctively Anglican.

With Donne, appears for the first time in poetry a passionate attachment to those Catholic elements in Anglicanism which, repressed and neglected, had never entirely disappeared; and, from Donne, Herbert and his disciples inherited the intensely personal and introspective tone to which the didactic is subordinated, which makes a lyric in *The Temple,* even if it be a sermon, also, and primarily, a confession or a prayer; a tone which reached its highest lyrical level in the ecstatic outpourings of Crashaw.

Chapter 21

His Position and Influence

The relation of Donne to Elizabethan poetry might, with some justice, be compared with that of Michael Angelo to earlier Florentine sculpture, admitting that, both as man and artist, he falls far short of the great Italian. Just as the grace and harmony of earlier sculpture were dissolved by the intense individuality of an artist intent only on the expression in marble of his own emotions, so the clear beauty, the rich ornament, the diffuse harmonies of Elizabethan courtly poetry, as we can study them in *The Faerie Queene,*

Hero and Leander, Venus and Adonis, Astrophel and Stella or *England's Helicon,* disappear in the songs and satires and elegies of a poet who will not accept Elizabethan conventions, or do homage to Elizabethan models, Italian and French; but puts out to discover a north-west passage of his own, determined to make his poetry the vivid reflection of his own intense, subtle, perverse moods, his paradoxical reasonings and curious learning, his sceptical philosophy of love and life.

It cannot be said of Donne, as of Milton, that everything, even what is evil, turns to beauty in his hands. Beauty, with him, is never the paramount consideration. If beauty comes to Donne, it comes as to the alchemist who

glorifies his pregnant pot,
If by the way to him befall
Some odoriferous thing, or medicinal.

From the flow of impassioned, paradoxical argument, there will suddenly flower an image or a line of the rarest and most entrancing beauty.

But the tenor of his poetry is witty, passionate, weighty

and moving; never, for long, simply beautiful; not infrequently bizarre; at times even repellent.

And so, just as Michael Angelo was a bad model for those who came after him and had not his strength and originality, Donne, more than any other single individual, is responsible for the worst aberrations of seventeenth century poetry, especially in eulogy and elegy.

The "metaphysical" lyrists learned most from him—the conquering, insolent tone of their love songs and their splendid cadences.

In happy conceit and movement, they sometimes excelled him, though it is only in an occasional lyric by Marvell or Rochester that one detects the same weight of passion behind the fantastic conceit and paradoxical reasoning. But it is in the complimentary verses and the funeral elegies of the early and middle century (as well as in some of the religious poetry and in the frigid love poems of Cowley) that one sees the worst effects of Donne's endeavour to wed passion and imagination to erudition and reasoning.

And yet it would be a mistaken estimate of the history of English poetry which either ignored the unique quality of Donne's poetry or regarded its influence as purely maleficent. The influence of both Donne and Jonson acted beneficially in counteracting the tendency of Elizabethan poetry towards fluency and facility.

If Donne somewhat lowered the ethical and ideal tone of love poetry, and blighted the delicate bloom of Elizabethan song, he gave it a sincerer and more passionate quality. He made love poetry less of a musical echo of Desportes. In his hands, English poetry became less Italianate, more sincere, more condensed and pregnant in thought and feeling. The greatest of seventeenth century poets, despite his contempt for "our late fantastics,"

And his affinities with the moral Spenserians and the classical Jonson, has all Donne's intense individuality, his complete independence, in the handling of his subjects, of the forms he adopts, even of his borrowings. He has all his "frequency and fulness" of thought.

He is not much less averse to the display of erudition, though he managed it more artfully, or to the interweaving of argument with poetry.

But Milton had a far less keen and restless intellect than Donne; his central convictions were more firmly held; he was less conscious of the elements of contradiction which they contained; his life moved forward on simpler and more consistent lines.

With powers thus better harmonised; with a more controlling sense of beauty; with a fuller comprehension of "the science of his art," Milton, rather than Donne, is, in achievement, the Michael Angelo of English poetry. Yet there are subtle qualities of vision, rare intensities of feeling, surprising felicities of expression, in the troubled poetry of Donne that one would not part with altogether even for the majestic strain of his great successor.

Chapter 22

The History of His Poems

Reference is made elsewhere to Donne as a preacher. Here, we are concerned with him as poet and prose artist. The history of his poems is involved in the difficulties and obscurities of his biography. Only three were published in his life time, *The Anatomy of the World* (1611, 1612); the satirical lines *Upon Mr. Thomas Coryat's Crudities* (1611); and the *Elegie on Prince Henry* (1613). In 1614, when about to cross the Rubicon, Donne thought of hurriedly collecting and publishing his poems before the doing so could be deemed an actual scandal to his office.

He had, apparently, no autograph copies, at least of many of them, but was driven to apply to his friends, and especially to Sir Henry Goodere, the Warwickshire friend to whom the larger number of his letters are addressed. "This made me ask to borrow that old book of you." The edition in question never appeared, but when, in 1633, the first collection was issued posthumously, the source was very probably this same "old book" (though Goodere had died before Donne), for, along with the poems, were printed eight letters addressed to Goodere and one to the common friend of Goodere and Donne, the countess of Bedford. In this edition, the poems were arranged in a rather chaotic sequence of groups.

The volume opened with *The Progresse of the Soule* and closed with the paraphrased *Lamentations of Jeremy* and the *Satyres*, the latter edited with a good many cautious dashes. There are obvious errors in the printing, but the text of such poems as this edition contains is more correct than in any subsequent one.

In 1635, a second edition was issued, in which many fresh

poems were added, and the grouping of the poems was carried out more systematically, the arrangement being adopted which has been generally adhered to since, and is useful for reference—*Songs and Sonets, Epigrams, Elegies, Epithalamiums, Satyres, Letters to Severall Personages, Funerall Elegies, The Progresse of the Soule, Divine Poems.*

The editions which followed that of 1635 added individual poems from various sources, sometimes rightly, sometimes wrongly; and made alterations from time to time in the text, conjecturally, or with the help of MS. copies, which are sometimes emendations, more often further corruptions. Modern editors have followed in their wake, printing more carefully, correcting many errors, but creating not a few fresh ones. The canon of Donne's poems is far from being settled. Modern editions contain poems which are demonstrably not his, while there are genuine poems still unpublished. The text of many of his finest poems is disfigured by errors and misprints.

The order of the groups in the edition of 1635 corresponds, roughly, to the order of composition. Donne's earliest works were love songs or sonnets (using the word in the wider, freer sense of the Elizabethans) and elegies (after the manner of the Latin poets), through many of which runs a vein of pungent and personal satire, and regular verse satires. Of these last the editions since 1669 contain seven. We have, however, the explicit testimony of Sir William Drummond that Donne wrote only five. It is clear, from MSS. such as Harleian 5110 and others which have survived in whole or in part, that the first five, or some of them, were copied and circulated by themselves. These alone were included in the edition of 1633.

The so-called sixth, which was added in 1635, if it be Donne's, is much more in the manner of the satirical elegies than of the regular satires; while the seventh, addressed *To Sir Nicholas Smith,* which was first inserted in the edition of 1669, an edition the text of which abounds in conjectural emendations, differs radically in style and tone from all the others, and there can be little doubt that it is the work of Sir John Roe, to whom it is assigned in more than one MS.

Chapter 23

His Satires

Donne's satires have features in common with the other imitations of Juvenal, Persius and Horace which were produced in the last decade of the sixteenth century, notably a heightened emphasis of style and a corresponding vehemence and harshness of versification. But, in verse and style and thought, Donne's satires are superior to either Hall's "dashing, smirking, fluent imitations of the ancients" or Marston's tedious and tumid absurdities. The verse of these poets is much less irregular than Donne's. It approximates more closely to the balanced couplet movement of Drayton's *Heroicall Epistles*.

Hall's couplets are neat and pointed, Marston's more irregular and *enjambed*. But Donne's satiric verse shows something like a consistent effort to eschew a couplet structure, and to give to his verse the freedom and swiftness of movement to which, when he wrote, even dramatic blank verse had hardly yet attained. He uses all the devices—the main pause in the middle of the line, weak and light endings (he even divides one word between two lines)—by which Shakespeare secured the abrupt, rapid effects of the verse of *Macbeth* and the later plays:

Gracchus loves all [*i.e.* religions] as one, and thinks that so

As women do in divers countries go
So doth, so is Religion; and this blind-
Ness too much light breeds; but unmoved thou
Of force must one, and forc'd but one allow;
And the right? ask thy father which is she,

Let him ask his; though truth and falsehood be
Near twins yet truth a little elder is;
Be busy to seek her. Believe me this,
He 's not of none, nor worst, that seeks the best.

Such verse is certainly not smooth or melodious. Yet the effect is studied and is not inappropriate to the theme and spirit of the poem. Donne's verse resembles Jonson's much more closely than either Hall's or Marston's. He had certainly classical models in view—Martial and Persius and Horace.

But imitation alone will not account for Donne's peculiarities. Of the minor [char] of verse, he is always a little careless; but if there is one thing more distinctive than another of Donne's best work it is the closeness with which the verse echoes the sense and soul of the poem. And so it is in the satires. Their abrupt, harsh verse reflects the spirit in which they are written. Horace, quite as much as Persius, is Donne's teacher in satire; and it is Horace he believes himself to be following in adopting a verse in harmony with the unpoetic temper of his work:

And this unpolish'd rugged verse I chose,
As fittest for discourse and nearest prose.

The urbane spirit of Horace was not caught at once by those who, like Donne and Jonson, believed themselves to be following in his footsteps.

The style of Donne's satires has neither the intentional obscurity of Hall's more ambitious imitations of Juvenal, nor the vague bluster of Marston's onslaughts upon vice. If we allow for corruptions of the text, one might say that Donne is never obscure. His wit is a succession of disconcerting surprises; his thought original and often profound; his expression, though condensed and harsh, is always perfectly precise. His out-of-the-way learning, too, which supplies puzzles for modern readers, is used with a pedantic precision, even when fantastically applied, to which his editors have not always done justice.

In substance, Donne's satires are not only wittier than those of his contemporaries, but weightier in their serious criticism of life, and happier in their portrayal of manners and types. In this respect, some of them are an interesting pendant to Jonson's comedies. The first describes a walk through London with a giddy ape of fashion, who is limned with a lightness and vivacity wanting to Jonson's more laboured studies of Fastidous Brisk and his fellows.

The second, opening with a skit on the lawyer turned poet, passes into a trenchant onslaught—obscured by some corruptions of the text—upon the greedy and unprincipled exacter of fines from recusant Catholics, and "purchasour" of men's lands:

Shortly (as the sea) he 'll compass all the land;
From Scots to Wight; from Mount to Dover strand.

He is the lineal descendant of Chaucer's Man of Law, to whom all was fee-simple in effect, drawn in more angry colours. The third stands by itself, being a grave and eloquent plea for the serious pursuit of religious truth, as opposed to capricious or indolent acquiescence, on the one hand, and contemptuous indifference on the other. The lines which are quoted above in illustration of Donne's verse, and, indeed, the whole poem, were probably in Dryden's mind when he wrote his first plea for the careful quest of religious truth, and concluded that,

't is the safest way
To learn what unsuspected ancients say.

These three satires are ascribed in a note on one manuscript collection to the year 1593. Whether this be strictly correct or not, they seem to reflect what we may take to have been the mind of Donne during his early years in London, at the inns of court, when he was familiar with the life of the town, but not yet an *habitué* of the court, and in a state of intellectual detachment as regards religion, with a lingering prejudice in favour of the faith of his fathers.

The last two satires were written in 1597, or the years immediately following, when Donne was in the service of the lord keeper, and they bear the mark of the budding statesman. The first is a long and somewhat over-elaborated satire on the fashions and follies of court-life at the end of queen Elizabeth's reign. The picture of the bore was doubtless suggested by

Horace's *Ibam forte via sacra,* but, like all Donne's types, is drawn from the life, and with the same amplification of detail and satiric point which are to be found in Pope's renderings from Horace. The last of Donne's genuine satires is a descant on the familiar theme of Spenser's laments, the miseries of suitors.

Donne's satires were very popular, and, to judge from the extant copies or fragments of copies as well as from contemporary allusions, appear to have circulated more freely than the songs and elegies, which were doubtless confined so far as possible, like the *Paradoxes* and *BIA[char]ANATO[char],* to the circle of the poet's private friends. A Roman Catholic controversialist, replying to *Pseudo-Martyr,* expresses his regret that Donne has "passed beyond his old occupation of making Satires, wherein he hath some talent and may play the fool without controll."

Such a writer, had he known them, could hardly have failed to make polemical use of the more daring and outrageous *Elegies* and those songs which strike a similar note. But, though less widely known, the *Songs and Sonets* and the *Elegies* contain the most intimate and vivid record of his inner soul in these ardent years, as the religious sonnets and hymns do of his later life. And the influence of these on English poetry was deeper, and, despite the temporary eclipse of metaphysical poetry, more enduring, than that of his pungent satires, or of his witty but often laboured and extravagant eulogies in verse letter and funeral elegy.

Chapter 24

Donne's Relation to Petrarch

From the time of Wyatt, Surrey and their contemporaries of the court of Henry VIII, English lyrical and amatory poetry flowed continuously in the Petrarchian channel. The tradition which these "novices newly crept out of the schools of Dante, Ariosto and Petrarch" brought from Italy, after languishing for some years, was revived and reinvigorated by the influence of Ronsard and Desportes.

Spenser in *The Shepheards Calender,* Watson with his pedantic *EKATOMIIA[char]IA* and Sidney with the gallant and passionate sonnets to Stella, led the way; and thereafter, till the publication of Davison's *Poetical Rapsody,* in 1602, and, subsequently, in the work of such continuers of an older tradition as Drummond, the poets, in sonnet sequence or pastoral eclogue and lyric, told the same tale, set to the same tune. Of the joy of love,

The deep contentment of mutual passion, they have little to say (except in some of the finest of Shakespeare's sonnets to his unknown friend), but much of its pains and sorrows—the sorrow of absence, the pain of rejection, the incomparable beauty of the lady and her unwavering cruelty. And they say it in a series of constantly recurring images: of rain and wind, of fire and ice, of storm and warfare; comparisons

With sun and moon, and earth and sea's rich gems,
With April's first born flowers and all things rare,
That heaven's air in this huge rondure hems;

allusions to Venus and Cupid, Cynthia and Apollo, Diana and Actaeon; Alexander weeping that he had no more worlds to conquer, Caesar shedding tears over the head of Pompey;

abstractions, such as Love and Fortune, Beauty and Disdain; monsters, like the Phoenix and the Basilisk. Here and there lingers a trace of the metaphysical strain which, taking its rise in the poetry of the troubadours, had been most fully elaborated by Guinicelli and Dante and Cavalcanti, the analysis of love in relation to, and its effect on, the heart of man and its capacity for virtue:

The sovereign beauty which I do admire,
Witness the world how worthy to be praised!
The light whereof hath kindled heavenly fire
In my frail spirit by her from baseness raised.

But the most prevalent reflective note derives not from Petrarch and Dante, but, through Ronsard and his fellow-poets of *La Pléiade,* from Catullus and the Latin lyrists: the pagan lament for the fleetingness of beauty and love—Ronsard's

Ah, love me love! we may be happy yet,
And gather roses while 't is called to-day,
Shakespeare's
Since brass, nor stone, nor earth, nor boundless sea,
But sad mortality o'er-sways their power,
How with this rage shall beauty hold a plea,
Whose action is no stronger than a flower?

The poet who challenged and broke the supremacy of the Petrarchian tradition was John Donne. Occasionally, when writing a purely complimentary lyric to Mrs. Herbert or lady Bedford, Donne can adopt the Petrarchian pose; but the tone and temper, the imagery and rhythm, the texture and colour, of the bulk of his love songs and love elegies are altogether different from those of the fashionable love poetry of the sixteenth century, from Wyatt and Surrey to Shakespeare and Drummond.

With Donne, begins a new era in the history of the English love lyric, the full importance of which is not exhausted when one recognises in Donne the source of the "metaphysical" lyric as it flourished from Carew to Rochester. Nor was this Donne's only contribution to the history of English poetry. The spirit of his best love poetry passed into the most interesting of his elegies and his religious verses, the influence of which was not less, in the earlier seventeenth century perhaps even greater, than that of his songs.

Of our regular, classically inspired satirists, he is, whether actually the first in time or not, the first who deserves attention, the first whose work is in the line of later development, the only one of the sixteenth century satirists whose influence is still traceable in Dryden and Pope. *Religio Laici* is indebted for some of its most characteristic arguments to Donne's "Kind pity checks my spleen"; and Pope found in Donne a satirist whose style and temper were closer in essential respects to his own than those of the suave and urbane Horace.

For evil and for good, Donne is the most shaping and determining influence that meets us in passing from the sixteenth to the seventeenth century. In certain aspects of mind and training the most medieval, in temper the most modern, of his contemporaries, he is, with the radically more pedantic and neo-classical Jonson, at once the chief inspirer of his younger contemporaries and successors, and the most potent herald and pioneer of the school of poetic argument and eloquence.

SERMONS

But Donne's fame as a prose writer rests not on these occasional and paradoxical pieces, but on his sermons. His reputation as a preacher was, probably, wider than as a poet, and both contributed to his most distinctive and generally admitted title to fame as the greatest wit of his age, in the fullest sense of the word.

Of the many sermons he preached, at Whitehall, at St. Paul's as prebend and as dean, at Linocln's inn, at St. Dunstan's church, at noblemen's houses, on embassies and other special occasions, some five were issued in his lifetime; and, after his death, three large folios were published by his son containing eighty (1640), fifty (1649) and twenty-five (1669) sermons respectively. Some are still in manuscript.

In Donne's sermons, all the qualities of his poems are present in a different medium; the swift and subtle reasoning, the powerful yet often quaint imagery; the intense feeling; and, lastly, the wonderful music of the style, which is inseparable from the music of the thought. The general character of the sermon in the seventeenth century was such as to evoke all Donne's strength, and to intensify some of his weaknesses. The minute analysis of the text with a view to educing from it what the preacher believed to be the doctrine it taught or the practical lessons it inculcated, by legitimate inference, by far-fetched analogy, or by quaint metaphor, was a task for which Donne's intellect, imagination and wide range of multifarious learning were well adapted.

The fathers, the schoolmen and "our great protestant divines" (notably Calvin, to whom, in subtlety of exposition, he reckons even Augustine second) are his guides in the interpretation and application of his text; and, for purposes of illustration, his range is much wider—classical poets, history sacred and secular, saints' legendaries, popular Spanish devotional writers,

Jesuit controversialists and casuists, natural science, the discoveries of voyagers and, of course, the whole range of Scripture, canonical and apocryphal. It is strange to find, at times, a conceit or allusion which had done service in the love poems reappearing in the texture of a pious and exalted meditation. In the sermons, as in the poems (where it has led to occasional corruptions of the text), he uses words that, if not obsolete, were growing rare—"bezar," "defaulk," "triacle," "lation"—but, more often, he coins or adopts already coined "inkhorn" terms—"omnisufficiency," "nullifidians," "longanimity," "exinanition."

Breadth and unity of treatment in seventeenth century oratory are apt to be sacrificed to the minute elaboration of each head, and their ingenious, rather than luminous and convincing, interconnection. But Donne's ingenuity is inexhaustible, and, through every subtlety and bizarre interpretation, the hearer was (and, even to-day, the reader is) carried forward by the weight and force of the preacher's fervid reasoning.

Much of the Scriptural exegesis is fanciful or out of date. The controversial exposure of what were held to be Roman corruptions and separatist heresies has an interest mainly for the historian. In Donne's scholastic, ultra-logical treatment, the rigid skeleton of seventeenth century theology is, at times, presented in all its sternness and unattractiveness.

From the extremest deductions, he is saved by the moderation which was the key-note of his church, and by his own good sense and deep sympathy with human nature. But Donne is most eloquent when, escaping from dogmatic minutiae and controversial "points," he appeals directly to the heart and conscience.

A reader may care little for the details of seventeenth century theology and yet enjoy without qualification Donne's fervid and original thinking, and the figurative richness and splendid harmonies of his prose in passages of argument, of exhortation and of exalted meditation. It is Donne the poet who transcends every disadvantage of theme and method, and an outworn fashion in wit and learning.

There are sentences in the sermons which, in beauty of imagery and cadence, are not surpassed by anything he wrote in verse, or by any prose of the century from Hooker's to Sir Thomas Browne's:

The soul that is accustomed to direct herself to God upon every occasion; that, as a flower at sun-rising, conceives a sense of God in every beam of his, and spreads and dilates itself towards him in a thankfulness in every small blessing that he sheds upon her; that soul that as a flower at the sun's declining contracts, and gathers in and shuts up herself, as though she had received a blow,

Whensoever she hears her Saviour wounded by an oath, or blasphemy, or execration; that soul who, whatsoever string be strucken in her, base or treble, her high or her low estate, is ever tun'd towards God, that soul prays sometimes when it does not know that it prays.

The passage on occasional mercies (LXXX. 2); the peroration of the sermon on "a better resurrection" (LXXX. 22); the meditations on death, as the leveller of earthly distinctions, or the portal to a better life; the description of the death "of rapture and ecstasy" (LXXX. 27) are other passages which illustrate the unique quality, the weight, fervour and wealth, of Donne's eloquence.

HIS LIFE

The life of Donne—especially that part of it which concerns the student of his poetry—as well as the canon and text of his poems presents problems which are only in process of solution: some of them probably never will be solved. A full but concise statement of all that we know regarding his *Lehr-* and *Wander-jahre* is necessary both for the sake of what it contains, and because of the clearness with which it defines the questions that await further investigation.

John Donne (the name was pronounced so as to rime with "done" and was frequently spelt "Dun" or "Dunne") was the eldest son of a London ironmonger—probably of Welsh extraction—and of Elizabeth, the third (not, as hitherto believed, the only) daughter of John Heywood, the famous dramatist of queen Mary's reign, by his wife Elizabeth Rastell.

This Elizabeth was herself the daughter of John Rastell and Elizabeth the sister of Sir Thomas More. Donne thus, on his mother's side at any rate, came of a line of distinguished and devoted adherents of the old faith. He himself was bred in that faith, and, despite his conversion and later polemical writing and preaching, his most intimate religious poems indicate very clearly that he never ceased to feel the influence of his Catholic upbringing.

According to Walton and Anthony à Wood, Donne proceeded to Oxford in 1584 at the early age of eleven. Here, he formed a friendship with Henry Wotton, a friendship which counted for something in Donne's later life. From Oxford, he passed to Cambridge, where, Walton tells us, he studied diligently till the age of seventeen, but, neither here nor at Oxford, endeavoured after a degree on account of the "averseness of his friends to some parts of the oath that is always tendered at those times." Nevertheless, in 1610 he was entered in the Oxford registers as already an M.A. of Cambridge. Of these college years, no contemporary documentary evidence is extant.

Our first scrap of such evidence dates from 1592, the year of the first unmistakable reference to Shakespeare as a London actor and playwright.

On the 6th of May in that year, Donne was entered at Lincoln's inn, having been already, the document testifies, admitted at Thavies's inn. Of his life between that year and his marriage in 1601, we have very few particulars, but these appear to indicate a life spent in England; a life similar to that led by many young members of the inns of court as Donne describes them,

Of study and play made strange hermaphrodites;

a life, too, of gradually broadening activity, which led him to the doorway of a public and political career.

In Donne's case, both the study and the play of these years were more than ordinarily intense. The record of the latter is his songs and elegies and earliest satires, the greater number of which were written, Donne told Jonson, before his twenty-fifth year.

That he did not neglect law entirely for poetry, we know from his own statement, and this is corroborated by the poems themselves, in which legal metaphors abound. But the years 1593 and 1594 were also given to a serious and careful survey "of the body of divinity as it was then controverted betwixt the Reformed and the Roman Church." "About his twentieth year," Walton says, that is, apparently, in his twenty-first, he showed, to the then dean of Gloucester, all the works of Bellarmine, "marked with many weighty observations under his own hand."

Bellarmine's *Disputationes,* indeed, were not published until 1593, and Rudde, who is the dean in question, ceased to hold that office in 1594, which gives but a short time for the study of such an important issue. But it is quite possible that Bellarmine's work, in which Donne found the best defence of the Roman cause, may have fallen into his hands at the end, not (as Walton implies) at the beginning, of a course of theological and controversial reading.

To a mind that worked with the rapidity of Donne's, the analysis and digestion of an elaborate argument would not prove a lengthy task. Nor was his active adherence to the Anglican church precipitate. All that we can say with confidence is that when he entered the service of Sir Thomas Egerton, in 1597, he cannot have been a professed Romanist, and, in 1601, he disclaimed indignantly "love of a corrupt religion."

Donne's first approach to a public career was made by service as a volunteer in two combined military and naval expeditions. In 1595, Henry Wotton returned from a prolonged residence in Germany and Italy, to become at once an adherent of Essex, whom he had already served by his correspondence while abroad.

The letters in verse and prose which passed between Donne and Wotton during the next few years (some of them yet unpublished) show that the intimacy begun at Oxford was renewed with ardour; and it is a fair conjecture, though only a conjecture, that it was Wotton's influence which brought Donne into contact with Essex, and induced him to join his friend as a volunteer in the expedition to Cadiz in 1596, and to the Azores in 1597.

One of the letters referred to was written from Plymouth when the fleet, on the second of these expeditions, was driven back by press of weather; and Donne's verse epistles to Christopher Brooke, a Cambridge friend, *The Storm* and *The Calm,* describe, with extraordinary vividness and characteristic extravagance of "wit," the experiences of his voyage. They were the first of his poems, apparently, to attract attention outside the circle of his friends. Another verse epistle, dated 20 July, 1598, to Wotton, refers to their common adventure:

Here's no more newes than vertue,
he cries, writing "At Court,"
I may as well
Tell you Cales or St. Michaels tales for newes, as tell
That vice doth heere habitually dwell.

On the second of these expeditions, Donne and Wotton were accompanied by another young volunteer, Thomas, eldest son of Sir Thomas Egerton, lord keeper of the great seal. By this young man, who was among those knighted for gallantry after the expedition, Donne was recommended to the lord keeper towards the close of 1597, and for four years was secretary to that influential statesman. The door which was thus opened to Donne leading to preferment, it might be even to wealth and station, was abruptly closed by his own rash action, a runaway marriage with Anne More, daughter of Sir George More of Losely and niece of the lord keeper's second wife.

It may be that, in Donne's complex nature, love was blended with ambitious hopes of securing his position and strengthening his claims on Sir Thomas Egerton. If so, he was grievously disappointed. At the instance of Sir George More, he and his friends Christopher and Samuel Brooke, who assisted at the marriage, were thrown into prison; and, although Donne was soon released, and his father-in-law by degrees and perforce reconciled to the marriage, the poet's hopes of preferment were blasted by his dismissal from the service of the lord keeper.

This sketch of Donne's earlier years would be incomplete without a reference to the problem of his residence abroad, a residence the effect of which on his work is palpable. Through Walton, we have Donne's own authority for the statement that he visited Italy with the intention of proceeding to the east to view the Holy Sepulchre; that, prevented from doing so, he passed over into Spain; that he "made many useful observations of those countries, their laws and manners of government, and returned perfect in their languages."

Walton assigns this episode to the years following the "Islands expedition"; but this is manifestly erroneous, for, during these years, Donne was actively employed as Egerton's secretary.

It is almost equally difficult to find a place for it in the years from 1592 to 1596, when he was studying law, theology and life in London. It is noteworthy that the earliest portrait of Donne, dated 1591, shows him in military dress and bears a Spanish motto. Again, in one of the three earlier satires, which Harleian MS. 5110 assigns to 1593, Donne describes his library as already lined with

Giddie fantastique poets of each land, and, long afterwards, he declared that it contained more Spanish authors than of any other nation, "and that in any profession from the mistress of my youth, Poetry, to the wife of mine age, Divinity."

The books in a man's library would not, to-day, be a safe index to his travels, but, in the sixteenth and seventeenth centuries, it was not usual for a young man to have a considerable collection of foreign books unless, like Drummond and Milton, he had himself brought them home.

It is difficult to avoid the conclusion that the time which Donne spent abroad must have been in the last years of his earlier education, when he was still a Catholic and under Catholic direction. If this were so, it would explain his silence about the exact circumstances of a voyage probably undertaken without the permission of the government, and, possibly, with the intention on the part of his guardians that he should enter a seminary, despite the law of 1585, or take service under a foreign ruler.

With more light on this point, we might be able to see in the singularly emancipated moral tone of Donne's mind and its complete openness on religious questions during the early years in London something of a reaction in his nature against a bent which others would have imposed upon it. Lastly, an early date fits best the evidence in the poems of foreign influence, which is not to be found specially in Donne's "wit," but in the spirit of Italian literature and life reflected in the frank sensuality of some, the virulent satire of others, of his elegies and songs.

The spirit of the renascence in Latin countries, and a wide acquaintance with Spanish casuists and other religious writers, are the most palpable indications of foreign influence in Donne's work. His direct indebtedness to any particular poet, Italian or Spanish, has not been established. Of all Elizabethan poets, he is, for good or evil, the most independent.

From 1601 to 1615, Donne's life was one of dependence on, and humiliating adulation of, actual or possible patrons. He lived at Pyrford on the charity of his wife's cousin Francis

Wooley; at Mitcham or in the Strand, on his wife's allowance from her father; at the town house of Sir Robert Drury, whose patronage he had gained by writing on the death of Elizabeth Drury, a girl of sixteen whom he had never seen, the most elaborate and exalted of his *Funerall Elegies.* He twice went abroad, on the second occasion accompanying Sir Robert Drury to France and Spa.

He assisted Thomas Morton, afterwards dean of Gloucester and bishop of Durham, in his controversies with Roman Catholics, for, though by no means yet a devoted adherent of the Anglican church, he heartily detested the Jesuits.

He wrote courtly letters in verse and prose to the countess of Bedford and other great ladies, or elegies on the death of their friends and relatives. He found one patron in the person of lord Hay, later earl of Doncaster, and he courted another in the king's favourite, Robert Carr, earl of Somerset, for whose marriage with the divorced countess of Essex he wrote a splendid epithalamium.

Of his writings of this period, some are in the brilliant, but often coarse, satiric vein of his earlier satires and satiric elegies; one, *BIA[char]ANATO[char],* is an erudite, subtle and strangely mooded excursus into the field of casuistry; and one, *Pseudo-Martyr,* published in 1610, is a more restrained and official contribution to the controversies of the day, a defence of the oath of allegiance,

Donne's first public appearance on the Anglican side, in which, however, he does not wander far from the single point at issue, and writes, not to convert Catholics, but to persuade them that they may take the oath.

Such were Donne's "steps to the altar." As early as 1607, Morton, on being appointed dean of Gloucester, had urged upon his collaborator the advisability of taking orders. But Donne did not feel that the author of the popular and widely circulated *Satyres* and *Elegies,* the *Paradoxes* and *Problems* and *The Progresse of the Soule,* could become a "priest to the temple" without some scandal to the friends and admirers of the brilliant and irregular "Jack Donne," not yet quite buried in the sage and serious husband and father, the controversialist and the courtly friend of Mrs. Herbert and lady Bedford. *Ignatius his Conclave* was written about this very year, the witty verses prefixed to *Coryats Crudities* in 1611, and he was yet to write the *Epithalamium* for Somerset. It is easier to respect, than to wonder at, such a decision, whether in 1607 or 1610. Moreover, it is doubtful, as Gosse has insisted, if, in his heart of hearts, Donne, by 1607 or 1610, was a convinced Anglican. As late as 1617, when he had been nearly three years in orders, he could write:

Show me, dear Christ, Thy Spouse so bright and clear.
What? Is it she who on the other shore
Goes richly painted? or who robb'd and tore
Laments and mourns in Germany and here?
Sleeps she a thousand, then peeps up one year?

This is not the language of one who is walking in the *Via Media* with the intellectually untroubled confidence of Herbert.

When Donne at length became a priest in Anglican orders, it was as one convinced that, for him, every other path to preferment was closed, not to be opened even by the influence of Somerset. The king had resolved that Donne should enter the church, and, on 25 January, 1615, he was ordained by bishop King of London. The period of privation and suitorship was over.

In 1616, he became divinity reader at Lincoln's inn, where many of his sermons were preached. In 1619 and 1620, he was in Germany as chaplain to his friend the earl of Doncaster, and preached before the unfortunate queen of Bohemia one of the noblest and most illuminating of his sermons.

In 1621, king James appointed him dean of St. Paul's, where his fame as a preacher attracted large audiences and rose to its height about the beginning of Charles's reign. For a moment he fell under suspicion with the pedantic and imperious Laud. But the cloud soon passed and, had Donne lived, he would have been made a bishop. But, often ailing, he was stricken down at his daughter's house in the late summer of 1630.

The strange and characteristic monument which stands

in St. Paul's was prepared by his own directions while he lay ill. Some of the most intense and striking of his hymns were written at the same time. Once, he rose from his bed to preach the sermon entitled *Death's Duel*. Six weeks later, on 31 March, 1631, he died.

However blended the motives may have been which carried Donne into holy orders, he gave to the ministry a single-hearted and strenuous devotion. Whatever doubts may, at times, have agitated his secret thoughts, or found expression in an unpublished sonnet, they left no reflection in his sermons. He adopted and defended the doctrines of the church of England, and the policy in church and state of her rulers, in their entirety and without demur.

His was a nature in which the will commanded, but was always able to enlist in the service of its final choice a swift and subtle intellect, an intense and vivid imagination and a vast store of varied erudition.

And, while he made amends for his Catholic upbringing, and for a middle period of mental detachment, by the orthodoxy of his Anglicanism, the memory of the licence of his earlier life and wit was forgotten in his later asceticism and in the spiritual exaltation of the *Sermons*, the *Devotions* and the *Divine Poems*.

Chapter 25

The Secret History of Voluptuous Rationalism

A secret history is by definition a coterie history, just as Donne is by definition a coterie poet who writes for a select circle of initiates. Yet because such circles are never hermetically sealed—because their work circulates in manuscripts that can be copied, miscopied, or otherwise circulated among the uninitiated—poetry of this kind often bears an inner seal that blocks or conceals its hidden sense from outside readers.

As Sears Jayne points out in his introduction to Marsilio Ficino's Commentary on Plato's Symposium, esoteric writing of this kind especially flourishes during periods when old hierarchies of birth begin to be replaced by new hierarchies of merit, and when old orthodoxies begin to give way to new and potentially heretical doctrines. In the most extreme cases, esoteric ideas (particularly those bordering upon, if not actually crossing, the frontier of heresy) will appear to the exoteric reader as versified ravings or nonsense rhymes rather than as riddles to be unraveled by discovering the hidden key to their inner sense.

In less extreme cases, the presence of a meaningful paradox or riddle will be obvious, but the quest for a solution will appear either impossible or unsuitable; the former when the poem must be taken seriously but its key is irretrievably lost, and the latter when it can simply be passed off as a jest. Donne's erotology typically combines the former with the latter kinds of obscurity, which, as this essay will argue, helps to explain the long controversy not only over major love lyrics such as "The Extasie," but also over what would later be known as the metaphysical style.

From this perspective, Samuel Johnson's insight that metaphysical poetry violently "yoked together" disparate ideas or images is at once nearly right and entirely wrong. Even the most disharmonious imagery (like for instance that found in such poems as Shakespeare's "The Phoenix and the Turtle") may lack true metaphysical violence if its paradoxes are not "contaminated" with a riddling logic that produces metaphysical doubt.

So long as their allegorical mystery remains safely insoluble or transcendental, such poems produce complacent wonder instead of violent controversies over their missing or nonexistent keys.

In contrast, Donne's Songs and Sonets provoke such controversies by playing with glaring inconsistencies—verbal, musical, or intellectual—that challenge both the speaking voice and his readers to critique or explain his practice. These resulting tensions have long prevented the libertine "Jack Donne" from being fully separated from the devoutly or despairingly questioning "Dr. Donne" who first emerges in the early Satyres and never completely disappears in either the Holy Sonnets or the sermons.

For all these works "contaminate" spiritual and rational arguments with sensual analogies that continue to perplex, astonish, or even outrage their readers. Yet Donne himself is openly unapologetic about the metaphysical obscurity into which this technique so often plunges his meaning and intentions. As in the prefatory epistle to Metempsycosis, which demands "no such Readers as I can teach," he consistently appeals to an audience as excessive in seeking out secrets as he is.

He has not always found that audience; recent readers have been as ready as Johnson was to dismiss his metaphysics (particularly in "seduction" poems such as "The Extasie") as violently elitist, egoistic, insincere, neurotic, or all of the above. At least in part, this dismissal seems linked to his obvious learning, for while no one denies his intimate acquaintance with the new philosophy that called all in doubt, few seem to recall the perplexities involved in trying to synthesize it with the semiheretical "pagan mysteries" of his beloved "old philosophy."

While as in Metempsycosis Donne sometimes sports with these mysteries, he just as often plays with obscure doctrines in which he almost certainly believed. Yet however serious the doctrine, most modern critics seem to agree that such "play" is not free, that his Neo-Platonic erotology is typically or even universally put to cynically seductive purposes. But this consensus is both newer and more tenuous than it seems; only a generation ago, literary critics regularly followed Herbert J. C. Grierson and Helen Gardner in regarding the major love lyrics as sincere if also riddling defenses of incarnational Neo-Platonism.

This view first faded under the influence of Pierre Legouis, whose rereading of "The Extasie" as a seduction poem proved broadly influential among second-generation New Critics, for whom the ironic mode was fast becoming the insincere mode later canonized in Stephen Greenblatt's Renaissance Self-Fashioning.

Yet one of the standard objections to this new orthodoxy—that it turns all forms of inwardness, including religious meditation, into mere social constructions—is especially applicable to Donne's erotic meditations.

More than any other poet of the period, Donne represents his inner search for religious and erotic authenticity in such essentially continuous terms that even New Historicists find themselves forced to admit that the "sexual adverturism of [his] cynical young manhood" and "his adult religiosity" represent cognate "forms of passion radiat[ing] from Donne's frantic quest for personal immortality." Quoting Kathryn R. Kremen, Robert N.

Watson argues that the failure of this quest for transcendence leads not just to the misogynistic scapegoating or seduction of the women in the libertine lyrics, but also to the devout love lyrics' fantasy of making the "'sexual union of man and woman on earth... the temporal and secular image which prefigures... the hypostatical union in body and soul of man and the Godhead in heaven.'"

Although Watson treats this fantasy with considerable skepticism (he is, after all, mainly concerned with psychoanalyzing the poet's wish fulfillments), such skepticism must be lessened in relation to the "devoutly" sexual dimension of the religious lyrics.

Donne most notoriously exploits this dimension in Holy Sonnet 14, "Batter My Heart," where he fervently hopes to gain the beatific "rapture" of salvation by inviting the violent "ravishment" of divine rape.

Although, like Watson, most critics associate this violence with an unconsciously despairing attitude toward divine grace, a fuller awareness of the secret history behind Donne's sacred and profane erotology would indicate precisely the reverse. (12) By adopting Ficino's strategy of self-consciously merging the "antithetical meaning of primal words" (as Sigmund Freud would call it),

"Batter My Heart" punningly points to the underlying continuity between the superficially opposed senses of raptus—in its Latin root, both rapture and rape. Ficino's similarly suspicious but also serious reunion of two antithetical primal words, voluntas (will or restraint) and voluptas (pleasure or release), uses the same technique to establish the anti-Stoic position that the will is properly fulfilled in, not prohibited from, pleasurable release.

By expanding upon this theme, Donne's erotic lyrics delve ever deeper into both the active and passive aspects of desire that subterraneanly link the sacred and profane "dying" into love, or what both Ficino and Freud would refer to as eros and thanatos.

Thus psychoanalytic critics such as Watson are ironically right to insist that the unconscious desires analyzed by Freud were first explored by the poets, even though these same critics too often wrongly indulge in a post-Platonic amnesis or "forgetting" of the fact that long before Freud, the poets and Platonists consciously unmasked the hidden links between the higher and the lower Venuses. While critics such as Watson often generate stunning psychological insights, they thus fall short of fulfilling their goal of historicizing the philosophical content of Donne's sexual poetics.

Peter De Sa Wiggins takes an important step toward historicizing the secret history of this content by resolving a notorious crux in "Aire and Angels." For as he shows, the crux disappears once the reader drops the "guilty," misogynistic assumption that the speaker must be insincere to claim that "just as the Incarnation spiritualized and revalued matter," so "perfect human love obliterates sharp distinctions between the purity of lovers."

Once that assumption is dropped, a new answer can emerge to the old question of whose love, man's or woman's, is said to be the most pure; that is, whose love is likened to the angel's enveloping "sphere" in the poem, and whose to its pure inner essence? Unlike the "male coterie" answer to this question,

De Sa Wiggins's solution assumes that the speaker's effectiveness in arguing that his love should be given physical expression demands that his initial description of the lady as his angel remain consistent. Less sympathetic critics who accuse the speaker of changing his argument midstream are thus themselves inconsistent in failing to see how his complimentary purposes require the referent of the word "love" in line 11 to be transferred from his passion to hers, its only proper object.

Here Donne argues that just as an invisible angel—first equated with the woman and then with the love she inspires—can only appear to humans by taking a body of less perfectly pure "aire," "so thy love may be my loves spheare" (lines 23-5). But rather than reading "thy love" as you who must become my outer sphere, a "plain paraphrase of the lines should read, 'So I may [then] be your [airy] sphere,'" the "translated" body of your angelic essence.

This solution not only seems true to Donne's witty incarnational logic and his frank exploitation of the "grosser" aspects of male desire, but also to his "excessive" attraction to "rythmique" riddles and reversals of all kinds. It also fulfills both of these agendas by implying that in the familiar schema of five elements (earth, air, water, fire, and a fifth angelic "quintessence"), woman now belongs not below but above man, who had traditionally been associated with the "higher" elements of air and fire.

No longer linked to the "lower" elements of earth and water but to the mysterious chora or "womb" of elements sublimed in angelic quintessence, she will now "redemptively guide him in her embrace as an angel guides the sphere of its domination." Of course, De Sa Wiggins does not deny the "glint in the eye of this lover," but adds that any suggestion of cynical self-interestedness would undermine both his high-minded compliment and the courtship it serves.

Although this reading implies a radical reversal not just of conventional gender roles but of conventional erotology, Louis Bredvold long ago agreed that Donne's erotology was serious but questioned how far he would actually take this new "code of ethics." While clearly this code was no mere "literary trick" but rather a redemptive twist on earlier forms of "libertine Naturalism,"

Donne's devotion to the "Aphrodite Pandemos," who in this tradition banishes the harsher "Stoic Nature," clearly gave Bredvold some pause. But Bredvold's doubts again indicate a general lack of familiarity with the semisecret tradition of "voluptuous rationalism" descending from the Italian Neo-Platonists, to whom a long line of critics from Helen Gardner through Edgar Wind have traced what Rosalie Colie calls Donne's "spiritual cult of the senses."

From Colie's perspective, even Donne's most overtly libertine lyrics employ Ciceronian paradoxes for the potentially serious purpose of countering "public opinion in their ultimate affirmation of the official—and ignored—Stoic morality." Critiquing "accepted manners and... accepted hypocrisy," even their un-Stoic sensualism affirms "a simpler, truer morality than was possible in sophisticated... society."

The current problem with accepting this older view is not that anyone doubts Donne's endorsement of the earlier humanists' more naturalistic morality. One recent editor finds him quoting Ficino alongside scripture in "Aire and Angels," and his admiration for both Pico della Mirandola and Pico's biographer, Donne's own ancestor Sir Thomas More, is clear from Donne's comment that Pico was "happier in no one thing in this life than in the author [More] which writ it to us."

A letter to his friend Henry Goodyer even more plainly admits that his early years had been consumed by "the worst voluptuousness, which is an Hydroptique immoderate desire of humane learning and languages," a "thirst" that in historical context can refer only to his love of secular Latin, neo-Latin, and French literature.

This literature almost certainly included the high-minded erotology inspired by Ficino's Commentary on Plato's Symposium, the fountainhead not only for the Neo-Platonists' spiritualization of an originally homoerotic tradition, but also for that tradition's later conversion to heterosexual ideals of love.

The real problem in agreeing with Colie et al. is then that these typically extramarital erotic ideals had by Donne's day degenerated into fairly cynical courtly conventions, making it extremely difficult to determine whether his love lyrics belong to the more decadent tradition or to the secret countermovement that continued to maintain voluptuous rationalism as a serious, sage, and innocent—but also increasingly incarnational—ideal.

The earlier origins of this countermovement can be traced not only in the Epicureanism of More's Utopians but also in the earthly paradisum voluptatis (Gen. 2:15) of Desiderius Erasmus's Convivia. In the latter, Dennis Costa finds Erasmus exploring the limits of Neo-Platonic idealism, which Erasmus found too dependent upon mathesis or abstraction and too little concerned with pathesis or the power of being moved by real things.

While maintaining a conventional distinction between matter and spirit, he thus rejected the standard Platonic spirit/matter dualism as too radical, since he regarded even fallen nature as potentially sacramental. For Erasmus, gardens such as the one framing "The Extasie" thus become a historical mediation "between a perfect Eden irrevocably lost and a perfect Heaven yet to come."

More fully joins his friend in pursuing the original spirit of Ficinian humanism and portraying unfallen voluptas as the key to both the beginning and the end of the divine plan, a project broadly rooted in the Neo-Epicurean thought of Nicholas of Cusa, Cristoforo Landino, and Giorgio Valla. These humanists were attracted both by Epicurus's unceasing war on superstition and imposture and by his reconciliation of knowledge and virtue with pleasure.

By showing that virtue had no real meaning apart from pleasure, they broke down the strict Stoic distinction between voluptas (which for thinkers such as Cicero carried only the negative "connotation of gratification of the body or the senses") and true joy (laetitia) or gladness (gaudium). According to Edward Surtz, More reunifies these joys by identifying the object of Utopian life with "pleasure so defined and so described that it rises from physical gratification in excretion and copulation and from intellectual enjoyment in this life to eager delight in the presence of God in the next."

As a result, both More and Erasmus vigorously defend Ficino's view that since "Pleasure [voluptas]... has been given both for the sake of preserving life and for the sake of propagating the species," social conventions (including property rights) that violate these natural purposes are arbitrary or irrational.

Although virtuous pleasure still "must not be sought for its own sake," it can remain innocent so long as it is reintegrated into the spiritual realm that provides its final fruition and "home." These fuller materializations of Ficino's original spiritualization of beauty as a necessary intermediary between earthly and heavenly love had a well-known appeal to English poets, who as Robert Ellrodt reminds us, were keenly aware "that the love did not always tend upward, nor would it always 'contemplate' but, in Donnean phrase, would sometimes 'do.'"

This emphasis set them apart from the "high" Neo-

Platonists of Italy and France, who carefully distinguished "between the heavenly and the earthly Venus founded on the Plotinian emanation theory and hierarchy of principles: between the One (or the Platonic Good), the First Intellect or Angelic Mind, and the World-Soul," only the latter of which did the work of procreation.

Ficino himself offers conflicting views on this subject—on the one hand limiting love to mental, visual, or aural pleasure and decrying lust, yet on the other asserting, as Ellrodt explains, that "Physical union between the lovers is free from all blame when inspired by a recognition of beauty in the beloved and a desire to propagate it."

Thus, later interpretations of this doctrine produced a wide variety of opinions among Renaissance Neo-Platonists. Initially, they tended to distinguish heterosexual love from divine or platonic love and to limit the former to bounds prescribed by natural and civil law, and thus to the marital bond itself.

While these doctrines hardly invited romantic idealizations of heterosexual passion, once Protestant and courtly love poets looked at them through a "soft haze of idealism and mysticism the earlier exaltation of love and the Neo-Platonic philosophy of love could melt into each another, as the poetry of the age often shows."

Ellrodt particularly identifies this typically English fusion of Platonic abstraction (or love through Christ) and the Petrarchan ideal of incarnate love (or love in Christ) with Edmund Spenser, who grounds the physical fruition of heterosexuality in active virtue, not in "mere" beauty of mind or body. Hence Ellrodt finds Spenser's erotology closer to the original spirit of Ficino and Pico than to their more austere Italian followers.

For unlike Bembo in The Courtier, Ficino willingly admitted that while the soul might be satisfied with the idea of the beloved, "the eye and spirit require the presence of the body, and the soul, which is usually dominated by them, is forced to desire the same thing."

Like Spenser, the Sidney circle generally followed a

version of Ficinian erotology that refused to identify the cause of love with beauty alone and instead traced it to being born under the same planet.

Through this sidereal influence, the true lover is able to abstract the image of the beloved, conform it to the "idea" formed in his own soul, and then to admire the synthesis as a reflection of the ideal. The synthetic image is thus fairer than the actual beloved but not fairer than the "idea" of her soul. While here, as among the later followers of Ficino and especially Pico, the emphasis remains primarily on spiritual love, sensual love inside or outside of matrimony was often accepted or at least tolerated.

Spenser himself is relatively conservative in this regard, but like Louis Le Roy in France, he converts Platonism from the mere worldly game and pretense played by the trattatisti and courtiers by turning "[w]hat had only been a 'step'... a self-contained, self-complete experience," into a form of "[r]omantic love, [which,] contrary to Platonic love, does not transcend itself."

Restoring the original sincerity of Ficino's creed by once again making it a living inspiration. Spenser justifies his erotology by means of a Christian schema not very different from Donne's: since "[l]ove is of heavenly nature, but its consummation is earthly," then "Christ's redeeming love has not only justified sinners; it justifies human love." This schema represents a radical departure from the original spirit not only of late-classical Platonism but also of Christian asceticism, both of which had characteristically sought "to divest all love of earthliness." As the seventeenth century approaches, this earthliness becomes even franker as it absorbs the materialist tendencies of Hermeticism, natural magic, and Paracelsan iatrochemistry.

Yet, as noted above, by Donne's day a conservative reaction to these descendants of radical humanism was already setting in, which in part explains why he adopts a much more defensive argumentative strategy than Spenser. Since the elder poet had the advantage of simply taking the physical consummation of love between man and woman for granted without any "dialectical justification" offered or required, as Ellrodt notes, the "uniformly Platonic atmosphere" of his poetry makes it unnecessary to "introduce Aristotelian considerations on the union of matter and form, or body and soul" such as we find in Donne's serious love lyrics.

Yet by the same token, Donne's adoption of the casuistic mode of argumentation in these lyrics does not prove that he defends these positions sophistically. In fact, he most often seems to be "secretly" merging the procreative natura of the lower Venus with the more ethical, nonlibertine nature defended in Biathanatos and his youthful Paradoxes and Problems.

In the latter, he echoes Erasmus's Praise of Folly by paradoxically praising feminine "weakness" as a virtue, and at the same time reaf-firms the Paracelsans' rejection of traditional Galenic or allopathic remedies for the defects of fallen nature.

Instead endorsing the homeopathic therapy of "curing like by like," the Paradoxes and Problems answers the question of whether "Virginity is a Virtue" in the negative. By also alluding to Michel de Montaigne's intentional misreading of Tertullian on the interdependence of continence and incontinence, Donne then takes the giant leap of denying the perfect coexistence of virginity and motherhood in the divine Virgin herself.

Donne realistically and non-casuistically grounds his basic position on virginity's status as a natural condition subject to organic growth, maturation, and cessation. From this perspective, "true" virginity consists in true maturity, which in turn consists in the sempiternal procreation of life in the womb, where the seed of Eve transmitted to each fetus successively gives the head or death wound to the seed of Satan.

Thus "female Virgins by a discreet mariage should swallow down into their Virginity another Virginity, and devour such a life and spirit into their womb, that it might make them, as it were, immortal here on earth, besides their perfect immortality in heaven: And that Vertue which otherwise would putrifie and corrupt, shall then be complete; and shall be recorded in Heaven, and enrolled here on Earth; and the name of Virgin shal be exchanged for a farre more honorable name, A Wife."

As in his serious love lyrics, the difference between this "voluptuous" paradox and the more conventional libertine carpe diem argument is that Donne does not take a serious-sounding proposition and, through a clever dialectic of rhetorical inflation and deflation, use it to parody conventional mores. Instead, he begins with an outrageous Paracelsan analogy that he systematically justifies in ever more orthodox terms.

The final phase of his argument is thus based on the ultraorthodox analogy of Christ's marriage to his Bride, the holy church, which like its human counterpart in Canticles, must finally be granted that most holy and "honorable name, A Wife." Thus like both Pico's Oration and Lord Herbert's contemporaneous "Ode on a Question," the argument of Donne's "The Extasie" continues the revaluation of the body and of physical beauty begun by Ficino's Commentary on Plato's Symposium.

Like Pico's, Donne's central point is that since love provides the one true path from the finite to the infinite, the natural/divine course of the will or appetite (voluntas) is to expand into voluptas, or pleasure.

This doctrine in turn follows directly from Ficino's simultaneous appropriation and inversion of Plotinus, the locus classicus of both ascetic Neo-Platonism and negative theology. Yet as Wind shows, Ficino ironically bases his belief that ecstatic union could be attained "not only after the present life but also while we are living" on the ascetic Plotinus's own admission that he "had experienced these extreme states occasionally, and without detriment to his sober vision, and he did not hesitate to speak of them as reflected or copied in more familiar states of love."

In fact, "the frequent allusions to the passions of lovers, by which Plotinus paraphrased the mystical ecstasy, encouraged Ficino in his belief that voluptas should be reclassified as a noble passion... [in] agreement... with the Christian creed, [into which] he tried to infuse... a kind of neopagan joy, for which the passio amatoria served as a model."

While these doctrines were obviously susceptible to both libertine and ethically serious interpretations, George Williamson argues that Donne's friend and literary disciple, Lord Herbert, closely follows him in "nobly" defending the serious, vitalist-materialist end of the spectrum. In terms consistent with the rationalist premises of his De Veritate, Herbert's "Ode on a Question" shows that heaven's laws cannot logically exclude either love or sense if bodies rise again. He also overgoes Spenser and the Sidney circle in arguing that through love, human immortality ascends from earth to heaven rather than vice versa:

"Were not our souls immortal made, / Our equal loves can make them such." This position allows Herbert to take a frankly Donnean turn "toward propagation as a final answer to the question moved": just as "one wing can make no way," but

Two joyned can themselves dilate,
So can two persons propagate,
When singly either would decay.

For Williamson, this incarnational turn counters libertine "dislocation[s] of the Platonic mode" by exploring an erotic realm no longer automatically idealized and abstracted as it had been in mainline Neo-Platonism and Petrarchanism.

Later, as Robert Hinman has shown, Abraham Cowley continues this voluptuous rationalist tradition by producing his own incarnational "Answer to the Platonicks." As in Cowley's "Platonick Love," here "sex, though secondary, is the vitally important modus operandi of human love," not only in its own terms but also in gaining "an awareness of their relationship to God." Yet "The Extasie" admittedly overgoes all of these parallels in performing such a daring, dialectical exposition of its own secret history that it inevitably calls both that history and its own motives and assumptions into question.

It does so in part by "seeking the very secrets" that Donne's "Litanie" excuses him for seeking: the mystery that "made of two / one law, and did unite, but not confound" (lines 66-7) the letter of the old law with the spirit of the new.

Donne states that the prophets foresaw this divine unity but that its mysteries have not yet been exhausted. Who then has further explicated them? One most probable candidate is Nicholas of Cusa, whose Docta Ignorantia or "Learned Ignorance" anticipates Renaissance skepticism by overturning the classic Thomistic synthesis of faith and reason and seeking a new reintegration.

Montaigne brings this tradition to a head by pushing natural reason and law to the breaking point where the need for an entirely new revelation becomes manifest. Yet as Williamson notes, this higher unity is already implicit in Thomas Aquinas's insistence that the "natural light is both stronger and darker, while supernatural light is smaller, more remote, and yet more powerful."

This Thomistic paradox grows more attractive to Donne as his religious feeling grows "more passionate, more anxious," but like Montaigne, he never wholly abandons the lower light of nature. For like Ficino, he needs this "lower light" to locate the "subtle knot" uniting flesh and spirit, the missing link "'element[ing]' the ecstasy of the flesh or the exaltation of the spirit."

Cusa enables these explorations by locating microcosmic man's perfection in his "middle" capacity to understand universal or macrocosmic being through dialectical human reason. According to Gordon Worth O'Brien, he accomplishes this by exploiting Aquinas's elevation of "two-fold" human reason above the unitary intuition of the angels.

Although Aquinas still orthodoxly conceives divine perfection as a mysterious Oneness and the discursive human mind as a lesser light than the intuitive angelic mind, he makes man's need to exercise free will (which angels conventionally lack) a closer reflection of the divine image than the angelic mind. Cusa's main addition to this line of thought derives from his principal axiom, that "if a thing is not purely its own essence it suffers limitation." This innovation becomes especially radical in rebutting the orthodox view that all created things differ from God as the finite from the infinite, the active from the static, or the embodied from the ineffable. Since the essence of Cusa's deity is action, not passive contemplation, his material creation now mirrors him not through its static immortal soul but through "motion, or the spirit of connection... the 'third something' between body and soul, power and act, matter and manner."

As the spirit of motion, the human imago dei thus acquires an active godlike dimension even though its passive matter remains conventionally subordinate to its spirit. This new identification of man's essence with his "animate" freedom from restraint then prepares the way for the Italian Neo-Platonists' celebration of mankind's dialectical capacity to ascend toward an "uninhibited and limitless power" not possessed by the angels themselves.

While the fullness of this capacity is still conventionally reserved for the incarnate Christ, as his bride and image, the elect become the true counterparts of this man-god. Yet while O'Brien traces the influence of Cusa's revolutionary thought to "Pico, Ficino, Lord Herbert, and Milton," he fails to place Donne in this lineage, perhaps because Donne's Anniversaries seems to renounce the "Faustian" or alchemical dream of abstracting the "'knot and band' of all phenomena, both material and spiritual," so that either base matter or microcosmic man can take on "whatever nature he might will it to assume."

For O'Brien, this aspiration is the materialist culmination of Cusa's dynamic philosophy of motion as the essence of godlikeness, which in turn proceeds from his revitalization of the formerly static doctrine of correspondences. Although devout Neo-Platonists such as Ficino will continue to conceive of spiritual ascent as a process of purging the passive, enlightened soul and replacing its gross material "knot with divine essences," his increasingly radical heirs begin to conceive of liberated matter as the philosophical soul's conduit to light.

Yet Cusa's schema is only superficially inconsistent with that of Donne's Anniversaries, which while lamenting the degenerative influence of the Copernican and Baconian "new philosophy," also reaffirms the heritage of Paracelsan iatrochemistry. By practicing a kind of poetic alchemy upon the "glimmering light" of Elizabeth Drury's soul (First Anniversarie, line 70), the poet "abstracts" her essence,

Which, from the carcasse of the old world, free,
Creates a new world; and new creatures be
Produc'd: The matter and the stuffe of this,
Her vertue, and the forme our practice is.
(lines 75-8)

This new alchemical "concoction" (lines 453-7) will not only elementally unite "the matter and stuffe" of her virtue with his poetic "forme," but also, as in "Aire and Angels," it will create a host of "new creatures," new reunions of body and soul and a new synthesis of feminine and masculine elements. "The Extasie" prepares for this "practice" by meditating upon the Cusan/Ficinian theme that man is higher than angels not through his intellect but through his active, "voluptuous," or pleasurable will.

It is also more Cusan than "Aire and Angels" in arguing that not the angelic female but both lovers must suffer an incongruous form of limitation if they are not allowed to expand into the "matter" of heterosexual enactment, the final "revelation" of their spiritual love.

This logic is obviously seductive, but it is no more necessarily cynical, illegitimate, or libertine than Cusa's or Ficino's contention that active, material virtus is "intrinsic to the essentia or nature of a given substance." For Ficino, this virtus or "knot" at once passively and actively unites intelligence and will, mediates between "its internal or self-returning" and its "external or out-going" natures, and creates a dynamic interchange intrinsic to vita or life. As in "The Extasie," the "eternal knot and link" in this process is love.

The difference is that Donne's poem now makes this dialectic a heterosexual "symposium" in which masculine and feminine elements gradually merge into a higher "dialogue of one" (line 74). Since these two elements are initially in conflict not so much with each other as with themselves, at first, both lovers accept the more orthodox or Stoic limitation of angelic love to the spiritual realm. They then go on to overturn this conventional view with the "learned ignorance" acquired as they are Neo-Platonically and alchemically refined and fitted for their ecstatic union.

As the dialogue opens, both lovers clearly associate "sexe" with the gross matter of original sin that must be purged from their motionless, disembodied encounter. In Petrarchan fashion they declare that

it was not sexe
Wee see, we saw not what did move:
But as all severall soules containe
Mixture of things, they know not what,
Love, these mixt soules, doth mixe againe,
And makes both one, each this and that.
(lines 31-6)

In the process, they begin to approach Ficino's strict criteria for holy lovers, who do not "desire this or that body but the splendour of the divine presence... [which] is why lovers are ignorant of what they desire." However, passing this test permits their further spiritual progress in voluptuous rationalism, so that they can accept passionate desire to the extent that its own inexhaustibleness "proves" that it is not for tangible, finite bodies, but for the infinite souls actively linked both to God and to each other.

Since the splendor of the soul's celestial image now shines through the body, the true lover at once fears and worships the sight of the beloved, spurning riches and honors for his or her sake and preferring to become godlike through love. But "The Extasie" then clearly goes beyond Ficino, who, as we have seen, regards beauty as a mediator between goodness and justice but restricts love's realization in pleasure by requiring it to return to its transcendent source—the infinite beauty, goodness, and justice of God.

This emphasis upon beauty as an abstract mirror of goodness is neither fully incarnational nor fully compatible with Donne's erotology, which rejects this restrictive lineage by pointedly excluding any description of the woman's beauty or physical appearance from his love lyrics.

In doing so, Donne avoids not only the "angelic mysticism" and "erotic formalism" of the later Italian tradition, but also what John Freccero calls the neo-Petrarchan "dehumanization of love." Nevertheless, as Donne also sinks deeper into Ficino's roots, he is also able to revitalize not just Cusa but also the original "incarnational" Platonism of dialogues such as the Phaedrus, the Symposium, and the Timaeus.

"The Extasie" initally signals its adherence to this revitalized voluptuous rationalism by frankly situating the evolving transmutation of its "mixt soules" upon a "Pregnant banke" or swelling "bed" (lines 1-2). This natural "couch" shows that this is not a site of seduction but of spiritual exploration for lovers who would alchemically distill a mysterious third "something," "they know not what," from their symposium.

By freely employing the procreative imagery generally absent from libertine lyrics, they look forward to a potentially redemptive paradisum voluptatis. For like the human progeny and the divine marriage their union anticipates, the lovers' transubstantiation can only occur through a new fusion of body and blood, in Donne's period, the physical vehicle of the immortal soul.

But this final fusion is first alchemically/sacramentally "sealed" and "firmely cimented / With a fast balme, which thence did spring, /... So to 'entergraft our hands'" (lines 5-6, 9). As a 1607 letter to Goodyer reveals, Donne typically thinks of "balme" in a positive Paracelsan sense—as a natural preservative (in this case of stead-fast or "chaste" lovers)—not as a negative sign of lust as the Stoic tradition would have it.

Hence his lovers' ritual preparation for their hieros gamos naturally demands that this chaste "chemistry" is as yet "all the meanes to make us one," exactly mirroring the doubled "pictures in our eyes" which is as yet "all our propagation" (lines 10-2). This "double vision" is produced by twinned "eye-beames" that twist and "thred / Our eyes, upon one double string" (lines 7-8), which again is not double in the tainted sense of "duplicitous," but innocent in the sense of intertwined.

Ascending from the primary or physical level of Paracelsus's ascending/descending orders, they are materially "redoubled" like violets at the first level of his chain of being, and then reach the secondary or angelic level of Paracelsan existence once they have visually "growen all minde" (line 23) or mental image.

Attaining this level prepares them for the third and highest level, that of the Paracelsan Sapientia brutalis or instinctive will, the sphere of motion or incarnation. But rather than simply consummating their perceptually refined and perfected union, the lovers must first "stand aside" (as ek-stasis literally means) and revisualize its "fruits" by means of what appears to be their new "sidereal body," the Paracelsan term for the reflection of the material soul/body as "in a mirror." At this point, their union becomes such a purely reflected image that only "some lover, such as wee" (line 73) can chastely see it.

This poetic progress implies that the grosser elements of these lovers' "several" souls may sacredly "marry" as soon as their higher elements have been distilled into a new prima materia, which for postscholastic English Protestants composes the substance of angelic bodies. At this point, the higher "Atomies" of which their "new soule" is "compos'd, and made" (lines 45-7) can alchemically form whatever new nature they might will it to assume.

Isolating the common "bond" or quintessence of their newly purified "atomies" also prohibits any ultimate distinction between the physical and the spiritual elements of their new single/double soul, for love, the true philosopher's stone, has made the lovers' material substance infinitely protean. Conventionally, of course, the soul lacks any physical components whatsoever, but Donne once again seems to draw upon Ficino's description of the soul and spirit as having a "diffusely corporeal" existence:

"The soul and the body, which are by nature very different from each other, are joined by means of the spirit, which is a certain very thin and clear vapour produced by the heat of the heart from the thinnest part of the blood. Spread there through all parts of the body, the spirit receives the powers of the soul and transmits them to the body."

Donne's distinction between the body's "dross" and its "allay" (line 56) suggests that he similarly conceives of its physical elements as existing on a progressively refined continuum, so that much as Milton's "atomies" will later be "by gradual scale sublim'd" until they "[t]o vital spirits aspire," Donne's vaporous

blood labours to beget
Spirits, as like soules as it can,
Because such fingers need to knit
That subtile knot, which makes us man.
(lines 61-4)

These spirits are of course dominated by the intellectual soul that "interanimates" the whole (line 42), but in this context it also justifies its hypostatic descent "T'affections, and to faculties,z / Which sense may reach and apprehend, / Else a great Prince in prison lies".

Both the sudden appearance of this intellectual soul as a "Prince" and his paradoxical descent/ascent have generated a great deal of controversy that can be usefully resolved by the context outlined above.

For regardless of whether Donne is thinking of earthly princes or celestial ones (the angels or daemons who direct the course of the planets), both act as animating "intelligences" of their spheres only by not being confined to their centers, that is, by refusing the limitation from which both the incarnate god/man and the alchemical adept have been liberated—a freedom to which angels might also aspire once the old chain of being has imploded.

As for Cusa, for Donne perfect "mirroring" naturally begets perfect motion. Ficino too seems to accept the newly decentered chain of being, since he explicitly denies that the heavenly daemons (or rulers of the spheres) are or ought to be confined to those spheres. Nevertheless, this analogy does not wholly exonerate either the motives of the philosophic lovers or those of the lyric voice, whose argument that the two souls have been joined in one "abler soule" (line 43) scarcely seems disinterested. For he now argues that this new union licenses them to enjoy "love reveal'd" in the "body [which] is his booke" (lines 70, 72) by means of a dubious analogy that treats the body as the scriptural "letter" of the spirit of love, a conceit which in Elegy 19 ("To His Mistress Going to Bed") conveys a frankly libertine sense.

The dubiousness of the analogy is hardly lessened by the boastful invitation that immediately follows, the challenge to another lover "such as wee" to witness the "small change" (lines 74, 76) they will undergo in consummating their love. Yet this challenge is also properly self-questioning as well as liberating.

The statically negotiating souls, who "like sepulchrall statues lay" (line 18) all day now spontaneously speak, move, and have their being in a new incarnational Oneness that then summons a proper "witness" (God, a pure lover, or their own consciences).

This witness is authorized by Ficino, who in considering vision as a kind of human/divine "fire" that alchemically refines and purifies physical love, suggests that this fire is a "trial" through which only true lovers can pass. Once they have passed through it, they stand in a divine light where, since they "never lack a witness, they abstain from sin."

Yet as its critics rightly note, the poem's speakers do not seem soberly to invoke a higher Ficinian "witness" but almost defiantly to challenge a voyeuristic or libertine audience to "see" the consummation of their love. But this defiance is actually a natural concommitant of their decision to bring voluptuous rationalism to its logical conclusion and at the same time to overturn its patriarchal foundations.

This rebellion may even reflect Donne's real historical situation if, as many literary historians suspect, his marriage to Ann More was consummated in advance to prevent her father's likely attempt at annulling it. Moreover, while his speaking voice opens itself to skeptical criticism and doubt much as it does in serious poems such as the Holy Sonnets, this strategy is predictably absent in overtly libertine poems such as Elegy 19, where no questioning interlocutor is ever summoned.

Hence, unlike the Elegy but like "Aire and Angels," "The Extasie" seems seriously to propose that the material "key" to the mystic "book"—the revealed female invisibilia—is not the "spirit" of male desire but vice versa: the masculine "letter" or lover finds his natural "sphere" and perfect "orbit" in the feminine spirit of angelic freedom. That this is no mere trick (i.e., a sleight-of-hand whereby the "spirit" of consummation is gleefully turned into the "letter" of conquest) becomes even more apparent in Donne's carefully Platonic handling of the lovers' entwined hands and eye beams.

For while apparently conventional, the idea that their only "propagation" lies in the "pictures" reflected in the spiritual mirrors of their eyes, the windows of their souls, also triumphantly overcomes an older and more inhibiting tradition. In this tradition, the lovers' eyes could only perform a purely symbolic "union between object and reflected image."

In the context of "the expression of courtship and affection," this mirroring was often referred to as "'looking babies in [their] eyes,'" which was generally considered innocent only so long as the eyes conveyed merely a passive, empty, or (for Augustine) even a "'dead' and incomprehensible quantity or entity whereas only the internal image in the soul could bring about true perception."

Historically, Augustine's emphasis on the ideal passivity of the pure soul can be understood as an attempt to save soulful contemplation—the Empedoclean idea that the beloved's eye is truthful insofar as it remains a passive mirror—from the competing or Euclidean conception of the lover's eye as an active and dangerous "dart" capable of piercing, inflaming, and ultimately captivating the heart.

Again, Donne's originality—and difficulty—can be traced to his "hydroptique thirst" for returning to root sources, in this case apparently to Plato's original, dynamic synthesis of the two theories of vision in his Timaeus. Like most of the ancients, Plato associates light with fire and vision with the passive coalescence of internal and external fire "into one homogenous body which can transmit the motions from object to eye."

Yet according to the Timaeus, "in the special case of reflections or mirrors, there is a second condition" that actively allows the "visual ray which has coalesced with the daylight [to] encounter... a stream of fire from the object, and the two now form 'a single fire.'"

This "crossing" of passive with active vision produces a significant change in perception, most notably an inversion "from right to left," so that the double rays do not merely coalesce but twist or reverse as if refracted in a mirror [see diagram in the appendix].

In this more dynamic version of correspondence theory later "tamed" by Augustine, "the analogy between the bodily eye and the eye of the soul... [like that] between sunlight and [invisible] truth," is the basis of two closely related but distinct forms of true knowledge, both of which play a part analogous to the mirror holding the reflections of actual things.

Like the cosmic structure of the Timaeus, this schema is fundamentally tripartite. Normally, the inner and outer fires "interanimate" one another in the same naturalistic manner that human knowledge communicates with divine wisdom, which as Plato says, "invented and gave us vision in order that we might observe the circuits of intelligence in the heaven and profit by them for the revolutions of our own thought, which are akin to them, though ours be troubled and they are unperturbed."

However, the highest or "tertiary" form of Platonic vision actively and prophetically mediates between the static divine forms responsible for the actual "fire" of the sun and the spheres, and the passive images received by the light of physical perception—the reflected shadows in his famous myth of the cave.

In "The Extasie," the "eye-beams" that actively twist and thread the lovers' eyes "upon one double string" (line 8) thus allude to this protodivine synthesis of passive and active vision, which ultimately licenses their frankly carnal "propagation" as a form of spiritual knowledge.

Although this optical argument may seem suspect, in Donne's day Platonic optics remained the most authoritative explanation for the otherwise wholly mysterious phenomenon of sight, which like his contemporaries,

Donne privileges as the primary physical imprint or mark of the imago dei. His direct reliance on the Timaeus is also rendered more probable by the fact that the lovers of "The Extasie" only complete the dialectical circle of vision through a form of struggle that Plato associates with active or prophetic dream vision.

Although more Euclidean or violent, this form of vision is also more worthy or "true" in proportion to its ability to produce visual pleasure. For while "no violence at all is involved in the separation and reunion of the [ordinary] visual ray... bodies formed of larger particles yield to the agent only with a struggle, and then they import their motions to the whole and cause pleasure and pain—pain when alienated from their natural conditions, and pleasure when restored to them."

Donne represents the struggle involved in determining whether the "difficult" perceptions associated with sleeping or waking dreams will produce visual alienation (limitation or pain) or visual reunion (expansion or ecstasy) through the conventional metaphor of military contest:

As 'twixt two equall Armies, Fate
Suspends uncertain victorie,
Our soules, (which to advance their state,
Were gone out,) hung 'twixt her, and mee.
(lines 13-6)

As in Plato, the vehicle of this quasi-alchemical battle between the male and female principles of Mercury and Venus is fundamentally spiritual. The outcome of their struggle alone "prophesies" whether the "knot" of limitation or expansion will prevail—whether they will pleasurably expand into the "farre purer" "new concoction" of the "abler soule, which thence doth flow" (lines 27-8, 43), or relapse into alienation and pain. Donne's direct reliance on the Timaeus—in the Renaissance, still Plato's most highly regarded work—is additionally suggested by the fact that his lovers are frankly represented as needing to overcome the skepticism foregrounded in the opening passages of its famous dialogue. Following Plato's example, Donne chooses to dramatize rather than sidestep the speculative daring of his enterprise, in this case by issuing the challenge to other lovers noted above.

As in other major love lyrics such as "The Canonization" and "Twicknam Garden," the simultaneously physical and mental "testing" of the lovers' purity is classically Platonic as well as neo-Epicurean in at once accepting and transcending the limits of ignorance and folly.

Via Erasmus and St. Paul, it can also be taken as a Pauline affirmation (1 Cor. 1:30, 25, 27) of the serious mysteries whose untranslatable essence we "know" even though we can now only "see" through a glass darkly. For Paul, that meant looking through his epoch's gross metallic mirrors, which at the Last Day will be replaced by the blinding vision of light accompanying the body's resurrection (1 Cor. 13:12).

For Donne, it meant looking through the grossly physical bodies of mortal humans to see the blinding miracle of the incarnation and resurrection experienced here below in the anticipatory ecstasy of fully requited love. The poem's incarnational culmination is therefore genuinely governed by a learnedly ignorant in-sight: that pure lovers will discover ironically "small change" in this first of the many future incarnations they will undergo before reentering the prophesied paradisum voluptatis.

The insight is doubly learned because it rehearses the experience outlined in the Phaedrus, where the lovers pass "from a plurality of perceptions to a unity," where they at once look down upon passing things and gaze "up to that which truly is."

Yet to those outside their secret society the transcendent vision appears simply ignorant, since whoever "approaches to the full vision of the perfect mysteries... is rebuked by the multitude as being out of his wits." Yet to true lovers, the process is as simple and unmysterious as the transformation of the single or "scant" violet, which when "transplanted" not only partakes of the same unity in plurality, but also redemptively "redoubles still and multiplies" (lines 37, 40). For those so "transplanted," rapture is no rupture, but a divine ravishment that can only hint at the miracle experienced once "we are to bodies gone" (lines 75-6)—once the tiny seed sown in corruption is ecstatically redeemed in the reborn flesh, flower, and fruit of love.

Works: "Pseudo-Martyr." 1610; "Conclave Ignatii," 1610 [?] (only two copies known); an English version of preceding, "Ignatius his Conclave" (anon.), 1611, "An Anatomy of the World" (anon.), 1611, "The Progress of the Soule" (anon.), 1621, "A Sermon" [on Judges xx. 15], 1622; "A Sermon" [on Acts i. 8], 1622; "Encaenia," 1623; "Devotions upon Urgent Occasions," 1624 (2nd edn. same year),

"The first Sermon preached to King Charles," 1625, "A Sermon preached to the King's M[ajes]tie" 1626; "Four Sermons," 1625; "A Sermon of Commemoration of the Lady Da[n]vers," 1627; "Death's Duell," 1630; Posthumous: "Poems by J. D.," 1633; "Juvenilia," 1633, "Six Sermons," 1634; "LXXX Sermons," 1640; "*Biathanatos*,"1644; "Poems,"1649; "Fifty Sermons," 1649; "Essays in Divinity," 1651; "Letters to Several Persons of Honour, " 1651;

"Paradoxes, Problemes, Essayes, etc.," 1652; "Fasciculus Poematum" (mostly spurious), 1652; "Six and twenty Sermons," 1660; "A Collection of Letters," 1660; "Donne's Satyr," 1662. *Collected Works*: "Poetical Works," ed. by Izaak Walton (3 vols.), 1779;(?) "Poems," ed. by Hannah, 1843; "Unpublished Poems," ed. by Sir John Simeon, [1856]; "Poems," ed. by Sir John Simeon, 1858; "Works," ed. by Alford, 1839, "Poems," ed. by Grosart (2 vols.), 1872-73. *Life*: by Walton, ed. by Causton, 1855. — SHARP, R. FARQUHARSON, 1897, *A Dictionary of English Authors*, p. 84.

To have lived eminent, in a degree
Beyond our lofti'st flights, that is, like Thee
Or t' have had too much merit, is not safe;
For such excesses find no Epitaph.

At common graves we have Poetic eyes
Can melt themselves in easy Elegies.
But at Thine, Poem, or Inscription
(Rich soul of wit, and language) we have none.
Indeed, a silence does that tomb befit,
Where is no Herald left to blazon it.

— *KING, HENRY, 1631? To the Memory of My Ever desired Friend Doctor Donne.*

He was of stature moderately tall; of a straight and equally-proportioned body, to which all his words and actions gave an unexpressible addition of comeliness. The melancholy and pleasant humour were in him so contempered, that each gave advantage to the other, and made his company one of the delights of mankind. His fancy was unimitably high, equalled only by his great wit; both being made useful by a commanding judgment.

His aspect was cheerful, and such as gave a silent testimony of a clear knowing soul and of a conscience at peace with itself. His melting eye showed that he had a soft heart, full of noble compassion, of too brave a soul to offer injuries, and too much a Christian not to pardon them in others.... He was by nature highly, passionate, but more apt to reluct at the excesses of it. A great lover of the offices of humanity, and of so merciful a spirit, that he never beheld the miseries of mankind without pity and relief. — WALTON, IZAAK, 1639, *The Life of Dr. John Donne.*

Mr. John Dunne, who leaving Oxford lived at the Innes of Court, not dissolute but very neat; a great Visitor of Ladies, a great frequenter of Playes, a great writer of conceited Verses; until such times as King James taking notice of the pregnancy of his Wit, was a means that he betook him to the study of Divinity, and thereupon proceeding Doctor, was made Dean of Pauls; and became so rare a Preacher, that he was not only commended but even admired by all who heard him. — BAKER, SIR RICHARD, 1641, *A Chronicle of the Kings of England.*

This is that Dr. Donne born in London (but extracted from Wales,) by his mother's side, great great-grandchild to Sir

Thomas More, whom he much resembled in his endowments; a great traveller; first, secretary to the lord Egerton, and after, by the persuasion of king James and encouragement of bishop Morton, entered into Orders, made doctor of divinity, (of Trinity College in Cambridge,) and dean of St. Paul's. — FULLER, THOMAS, 1655, *The Church History of Britain*, vol. III, bk. x, par. 17, p. 324.

Dr. Donne,... a laureate wit, neither was it impossible that a vulgar soul should dwell in such promising features. — HACKET, JOHN, 1693, Life of Archbishop Williams, 74.

The life of Donne is more interesting than his poetry. — CAMPBELL, THOMAS, 1819, *Specimens of the British Poets*.

Dr. Donne, once so celebrated as a writer, now so neglected, is more interesting for his matrimonial history, and for one little poem addressed to his wife, than for all his learned, metaphysical, and theological productions. — JAMESON, ANNA BROWNELL, 1829, *The Loves of the Poets*, vol. II, p. 94.

The knowledge of Donne's immense learning, the subtlety and capacity of his intellect, the intense depth and wide scope of his thought, the charm of his conversation, the sadness of his life, gave a vivid meaning and interest to his poems... circulated among his acquaintances, which at this distance of time we cannot reach without a certain effort of imagination.... Dr. Donne is one of the most interesting personalities among our men of letters.

The superficial facts of his life are so incongruous as to be an irresistible provocation to inquiry. What are we to make of the fact that the founder of a licentious school of erotic poetry, a man acknowledged to be the greatest wit in a licentious Court, with an early bias in matters of religion towards Roman Catholicism, entered the Church of England when he was past middle age and is now numbered among its greatest divines?

Was he a convert like St. Augustine, or an indifferent worlding like Talleyrand? Superficial appearances are rather in favour of the latter supposition. — MINTO, WILLIAM, 1880, *John Donne, The Nineteenth Century*, vol. 7, p. 849.

Against the wall of the south choir aisle in the Cathedral

of St. Paul is a monument which very few of the thousands who visit the church daily observe, or have an opportunity of observing, but which, once seen, is not easily forgotten. It is the long, gaunt, upright figure of a man, wrapped close in a shroud, which is knotted at the head and feet, and leaves only the face exposed a face wan, worn, almost ghastly, with eyes closed as in death.

This figure is executed in white marble, and stands on an urn of the same, as if it had just arisen therefrom. The whole is placed in a black niche, which, by its contrast, enhances the death-like paleness of the shrouded figure. Above the canopy is an inscription recording that the man whose effigy stands beneath though his ashes are mingled with western dust, looks towards Him whose name is the Orient....

It was not such a memorial as Donne's surviving friends might think suitable to commemorate the deceased, but it was the very monument which Donne himself designed as a true emblem of his past life and his future hopes. — LIGHTFOOT, J. B., 1895, *Historical Essays*, pp. 221, 223.

His graceful person, vivacity of conversation, and many accomplishments secured for him the entree at the houses of the nobility and a recognized position among the celebrities of Queen Elizabeth's court. He was conspicuous as a young man of fortune who spent his money freely, and mixed on equal terms with the courtiers and probably had the character of being richer than he was.... The young man, among his other gifts, had the great advantage of being able to do with very little sleep.

He could read all night and be gay and wakeful and alert all day. He threw himself into the amusements and frivolities of the court with all the glee of youth, but never so as to interfere with his duties. The favourite of fortune, he was too the favourite of the fortunate the envy of some, he was the darling of more.

Those of his contemporaries who knew him intimately speak of him at all times as if there was none like him; the charm of his person and manners were irresistible. He must have had much love to give, or he could never had so much bestowed upon him. — JESSOPP, AUGUSTUS, 1897, John Donne, Sometime Dean of St. Paul's, pp. 13, 18.

History presents us with no instance of a man of letters more obviously led up to by the experience and character of his ancestors than was John Donne. As we have him revealed to us, he is what a genealogist might wish him to be. Every salient feature in his mind and temperament is foreshadowed by the general trend of his family, or by the idiosyncrasy of some individual member of it....

The greatest preacher of his age.... No one, in the history of English literature, as it seems to me, is so difficult to realize, so impossible to measure, in the vast curves of his extraordinary and contradictory features. Of his life, of his experiences, of his opinions, we know more now than it has been vouchsafed to us to know of any other of the great Elizabethan and Jacobean galaxy of writers and yet how little we fathom his contradictions, how little we can account for his impulses and his limitations.

Even those of us who have for years made his least adventures the subject of close and eager investigation must admit at last that he eludes us. He was not the crystal-hearted saint that Walton adored and exalted. He was not the crafty and redoubtable courtier whom the recusants suspected. He was not the prophet of the intricacies of fleshly feeling whom the young poets looked up to and worshipped.

He was none of these, or all of these, or more. What was he? It is impossible to say, for, with all his superficial expansion, his secret died with him. We are tempted to declare that of all great men he is the one of whom least is essentially known. Is not this, perhaps, the secret of his perennial fascination? — GOSSE, EDMUND, 1899, *The Life and Letters of John Donne,* vol. I, pp. 3, 11, vol. II, p. 290.

A preacher in earnest; weeping sometimes for his auditory, sometimes with them; always preaching to himself, like an angel from a cloud, but in none; carrying some, as St. Paul was, to heaven in holy raptures; and enticing others by a sacred art and courtship to amend. their lives: here picturing a Vice so as to make it ugly to those that practised it; and a

Virtue so as to make it beloved, even by those who loved it not; and all this with a most particular grace and an unexpressible addition of comeliness. — WALTON, IZAAK, 1639, *The Life of Dr. John Donne.*

The sermons of Donne have sometimes been praised in late times. They are undoubtedly the productions of a very ingenious and a very learned man; and two folio volumes by such a person may be expected to supply favorable specimens. In their general character, they will not appear, I think, much worthy of being rescued from oblivion.

The subtility of Donne, and his fondness for such inconclusive reasoning as a subtle disputant is apt to fall into, runs through all of these sermons at which I have looked. His learning he seems to have perverted in order to cull every impertinence of the fathers and schoolmen, their remote analogies, their strained allegories, their technical distinctions; and to these he has added much of a similar kind from his own fanciful understanding. — HALLAM, HENRY, 1837-39, *Introduction to the Literature of Europe,* pt. iii, ch. ii, par. 70.

Donne's published sermons are in form nearly as grotesque as his poems, though they are characterized by profounder qualities of heart and mind. It was his misfortune to know thoroughly the works of fourteen hundred writers, most of them necessarily worthless; and he could not help displaying his erudition in his discourses. Of what is now called taste he was absolutely destitute.

His sermons are a curious mosaic of quaintness, quotation, wisdom, puerility, subtilty, and ecstasy. The pedant and the seer possess him by turns, and in reading no other divine are our transitions from yawning to rapture so swift and unexpected.

He has passages of transcendent merit, passages which evince a spiritual vision so piercing, and a feeling of divine things so intense, that for the time we seem to be communing with a religious genius of the most exalted and exalting order; but soon he involves us in a maze of quotations and references, and our minds are hustled by what Hallam calls "the rabble of bad authors" that this saint and sage has always at his skirts, even when be ascends to the highest heaven of contemplation. — WHIPPLE, EDWIN P., 1859-68, *The Literature of the Age of Elizabeth,* p. 237.

The sermons of Donne, while they are superior in style, are sometimes fantastic, like his poetry, but they are never coarse, and they derive a touching interest from his history. — BOTTA, ANNE C. LYNCH, 1860, *Hand-Book of Universal Literature,* p. 476.

In Donne's sermons, an intellectual epicure not too fastidious to read sermons will find a delicious feast. Whether these sermons can be taken as patterns by the modern preacher is another affair.

It will not be contended that any congregation is equal to the effort of following his subtleties. In short, as exercises in abstract subtlety, fanciful ingenuity, and scholarship, the sermons are admirable. Judged by the first rule of popular exposition, the style is bad — a bewildering maze to the ordinary reader, much more to the ordinary hearer. — MINTO, WILLIAM, 1872-80, *Manual of English Prose Literature,* p. 253.

During this year, 1622, Donne's first printed sermon appeared. It was delivered at Paul's Cross on 15 Sept. to an enormous congregation, in obedience to the king's commands, who had just issued his "Directions to Preachers," and had made choice of the dean of St. Paul's to explain his reasons for issuing the injunctions.

The sermon was at once printed; copies of the original edition are rarely met with. Two months later Donne preached his glorious sermon before the Virginian Company.... Donne's Sermon struck a note in full sympathy with the larger views and nobler aims of the minority.

His sermon may be truly described as the first missionary sermon printed in the English language. The original edition was at once absorbed. The same is true of every other sermon printed during Donne's lifetime; in their original shape they are extremely scarce. The truth is that as a preacher at this time Donne stood almost alone.

Andrewes's preaching days were over (he died in September 1626), Hall never carried with him the conviction of being much more than a consummate gladiator, and was rarely heard in London, of the rest there was hardly one who was not either ponderously learned like Sanderson, or a mere performer like the rank and file of rhetoricians who came up to London to air their eloquences at Paul's Cross.

The result was that Donne's popularity was always on the increase, he rose to every occasion and surprised his friends, as Walton tells us, by the growth of his genius and earnestness even to the end — JESSOPP, AUGUSTUS, 1888, *Dictionary of National Biography*, vol. xv, p. 229.

One thing more I must tell you; but so softly, that I am loth to hear myself: and so softly, that if that good lady were in the room, with you and this letter, she might not hear. It is, that I am brought to a necessity of printing my poems, and addressing them to my Lord Chamberlain. This I mean to do forthwith: not for much public view, but at mine own cost, a few copies.

I apprehend some incongruities in the resolution; and I know what I shall suffer from many interpretations, but I am at an end, of much considering that; and if I were as startling in that kind as fever was, yet in this particular, I am under an unescapable necessity, as I shall let you perceive when I see you. By this occasion I am made a rhapsodist of mine own rags, and that cost me more diligence to seek them, than it did to make them.

This made me ask to borrow that old book of you, which it will be too late to see, for that use, when I see you; for I must do this as a valediction to the world, before I take orders. But this is it, I am to ask you: whether you ever made any such use of the letter in verse, *a nostre comtesse chez vous,* as that I may not put it in, amongst the rest to persons of that rank, for I desire it very much, that something should bear her name in the book, and I would be just to my written words to my Lord Harrington to write nothing after that.

I pray tell me as soon as you can, if I be at liberty to insert that: for if you have by any occasion applied any pieces to it, I see not, that it will be discerned, when it appears in the whole piece. Though this be a little matter, I would be sorry not to have an account of it, within as little after New Year's-tide, as you could. — DONNE, JOHN, 1614, Letter to Sir Henry Goodyere, Dec. 20, Alford, vol. VI, p. 367.

Donne, the delight of Phoebus and each Muse
Who, to thy one, all other brains refuse;
Whose every work of thy most early wit
Came forth example, and remains so yet;
Longer a-knowing than most wits do live
And which no affection praise enough can give!
To it, thy language, letters, arts, best life,
Which might with half mankind maintain strife;
All which I meant to praise, and yet I would;
But leave, because I cannot as I should!
— JONSON, BEN, 1616, To John Donne.

That Done's Anniversarie was profane and full of blasphemies: that he told Mr. Done, if it had been written of the Virgin Marie it had been something; to which he answered, that he described the Idea of a Woman, and not as she was. That Done, for not keeping of accent, deserved hanging....

He esteemeth John Done the first poet in the world in some things: his verses of the "Lost Chaine" he hath by heart; and that passage of the "Calme," *That dust and feathers doe not stirs, all was so quiet.* Affirmeth Done to have written all his best pieces ere he was 25 years old. — DRUMMOND, WILLIAM, 1619, *Notes on Ben Jonson's Conversations.*

The Muses' garden, with pedantic weeds
O'erspread, was purg'd by thee, the lazier seeds
Of servile imitation throwne away,
And fresh invention planted; thou didst pay
The debts of our penurious banquerout age:
... whatsoever wrong
By ours was done the Greek or Latin tongue,
Thou hast redeem'd, and opened as a mine
Of rich and pregnant fancie...
... to the awe of thy imperious wit
Our troublesome language bends, made only
With her tough thick-rib'd hoopes, to gird about
Thy gyant fancy.

— CAREW, THOMAS, 1631? An Elegie upon the Death of Doctor Done, Works, ed. Hazlitt, pp. 93, 94.

... all the softnesses,
The Shadow, Light, the Air, and Life, of Love;
The Sharpness of all Wit; ev'n bitterness
Makes Satire Sweet; all wit did God improve,
'Twas flamed in him, 'Twas but warm upon
His Embers; He was more; and it is Donne.
— DANIEL, GEORGE, 1647, A Vindication of Poesy.

Would not Donne's satires, which abound with so much wit, appear more charming if he had taken care of his words, and of his numbers? But he followed Horace so very close, that of necessity he must fall with him; and I may safely say it of this present age, that if we are not so great wits as Donne, yet, certainly, we are better poets. — DRYDEN, JOHN, 1692, *Essay on Satire, Works,* ed. Scott and Saintsbury, vol. XIII, p. 109.

If it be true that the purport of poetry should be to please, no author has written with such utter neglect of the rule. It is scarce possible for a human ear to endure the dissonance and discord of his couplets and even when his thoughts are clothed in the melody of Pope, they appear to me hardly worth the decoration. — DRAKE, NATHAN 1798, *Literary Hours,* No. xxviii.

Donne had not music enough to render his broken rhyming couplets sufferable, and neither his wit, nor his pointed satire were sufficient to rescue him from that neglect which his uncouth and rugged versification speedily superinduced. — WHITE, HENRY KIRKE, 1806, *Melancholy Hours, Remains,* ed. Southey, vol. II, p. 286.

Since Dryden, the metre of our poets leads to the sense: in our elder and more genuine bards, the sense, including the passion, leads to the metre. Read even Donne's satires as he meant them to be read, and as the sense and passion demand, and you will find in the lines a manly harmony. — COLERIDGE, SAMUEL TAYLOR, 1818, *Notes on Beaumont and Fletcher,* ed. Ashe, p. 427.

Nothing could have made Donne a poet, unless as great

a change had been worked in the internal structure of his ears, as was wrought in elongating those of Midas. — SOUTHEY, ROBERT, 1807, *Specimens of the Later English Poets*, vol. I, p. xxiv.

Donne was the "best good-natured man, with the worst natured Muse." A romantic and uxorious lover, he addresses the object of his real tenderness with ideas that outrage decorum. He begins his own epithalamium with most indelicate invocation to his bride.

His ruggedness and whim are almost proverbially known. Yet there is a beauty of thought which at intervals rises from his chaotic imagination, like the form of Venus smiling on the waters. — CAMPBELL, THOMAS, 1819, *An Essay on English Poetry*.

Donne is the most inharmonious of our versifiers, if he can be said to have deserved such a name by lines too rugged to seem metre. Of his earlier poems, many are very licentious, the later are chiefly devout. Few are good for much; the conceits have not even the merit of being intelligible: it would perhaps be difficult to select three passages that we should care to read again. HALLAM, HENRY, 1837-39, *Introduction to the Literature of Europe*, pt. iii, ch. v, par. 39.

Having a dumb angel, and knowing more noble poetry than he articulates. — Browning, Elizabeth Barrett, 1842-63, *The Book of the Poets*, vol. II, p. 50.

With verses gnarl'd and knotted, hobbled on. — LANDOR, WALTER SAVAGE, 1846, Satirists.

Of stubborn thoughts a garland thought twine;
To his fair Maid brought cabalistic posies,
And sung quaint ditties of metempsychosis;
"Twists iron pokers into true love-knots,"
Coining hard words, not found in polyglots,
— COLERIDGE, HARTLEY, 1849, Donne, Sketches of English Poets, Poems, vol. II, p. 295.

With vast learning, with subtile and penetrating intellect, with a fancy singularly fruitful and ingenious, he still contrived to disconnect, more or less, his learning from what was worth learning, his intellect from what was reasonable, his fancy from what was beautiful. His poems, or rather his metrical problems, are obscure in thought, rugged in versification, and full of conceits which are intended to surprise rather than to please but they still exhibit a power of intellect, both analytical and analogical, competent at once to separate the minutest and connect the remotest ideas.

This power, while it might not have given his poems grace, sweetness, freshness, and melody would still, if properly directed, have made them valuable for their thoughts; but in the case of Donne it is perverted to the production of what is *bizarre* or unnatural, and his muse is thus as hostile to use as to beauty. The intention is, not to idealize what is true, but to display the writer's skill and wit in giving a show of reason to what is false. The effect of this on the moral character of Donne was pernicious.

A subtile intellectual scepticism, which weakened will, divorced thought from action and literature from life, and made existence a puzzle and a dream, resulted from this perversion of his intellect.

He found that he could wittily justify what was vicious as well as what was unnatural; and his amatory poems, accordingly, are characterized by a cold, hard, labored, intellectualized sensuality, worse than the worst impurity of his contemporaries because it has no excuse of passion for its violations of decency. — WHIPPLE, EDWIN P., 1859-68, *The Literature of the Age of Elizabeth,* p. 231.

Donne, altogether gives us the impression of a great genius ruined by a false system. He is a charioteer run away with by his own pampered steeds. He begins generally well, but long ere the close, quibbles, conceits, and the temptation of strewing off recondite learning, prove too strong for him, and he who commenced following a serene star, ends pursuing a will-o'-wisp into a bottomless morass.

Compare for instance, the ingenious nonsense which abounds in the middle and the close of his "Progress of the Soul" with the dark, but magnificent stanzas which are the first in the poem. In no writings in the language is there more spilt treasure a more lavish loss of beautiful, original, and striking things than in the poems of Donne. — GILFILLAN, GEORGE, 1860, *Specimens with Memoirs of the Less-Known British Poets*, vol. I, p. 203.

On a superficial inspection, Donne's verses look like so many riddles. They seem to be written upon the principle of making the meaning as difficult to be found out as possible, — of using all the resources of language, not to express thought, but to conceal it.

Nothing is said in a direct, natural manner; conceit follows conceit without intermission; the most remote analogies, the most far- fetched images, the most unexpected turns, one after another, surprise and often puzzle the understanding; while things of the most opposite kinds — the harsh and the harmonious, the graceful and the grotesque, the grave and the gay, the pious and the profane — meet and mingle in the strangest of dances.

But running through all this bewilderment, a deeper insight detects not only a vein of the most exuberant wit, but often the sunniest and most delicate fancy, and the truest tenderness and depth of feeling. — CRAIK, GEORGE L., 1861, *A Compendious History of English Literature and of the English Language*, vol. I, p. 579.

There is indeed much in Donne, in the unfolding of his moral and spiritual life which often reminds us of St. Augustine. I do not mean that noteworthy as on many accounts he was, and in the lan- guage of Carew, one of his contemporaries

"A king who ruled as he thought fit
The universal monarchy of wit."

he at all approached in intellectual or spiritual stature to the great Doctor of the Western Church. But still there was in Donne the same tumultuous youth, the same final deliverance from them, and then the same passionate and personal grasp of the central truths of Christianity, linking itself as this did with all that he had suffered, and all that he had sinned, and all through which by God's grace he had victoriously struggled. — TRENCH, RICHARD CHENEVIX, 1868, *A Household Book of English Poetry*, p. 403.

The central thought of Dr. Dònne is nearly sure to be just: the subordinate thoughts by means of which he unfolds it are often grotesque, and so wildly associated as to remind one of the lawlessness of a dream, wherein mere suggestion without choice or fitness rules the sequence.

As some of the writers of whom I have last spoken would play with words, Dr. Donne would sport with ideas, and with the visual images or embodiments of them. Certainly in his case much knowledge reveals itself in the association of his ideas, and great facility in the management and utterance of them.

True likewise, he says nothing unrelated to the main idea of the poem, but not the less certainly does the whole resemble the speech of a child of active imagination, to whom judgment as to the character of his suggestions is impossible, his taste being equally gratified with a lovely image and a brilliant absurdity: a butterfly and a shining potherd are to him similarly desirable. Whatever wild thing starts from the thicket of thought, all is worthy game to the hunting intellect of Dr. Donne, and is allowed without question of tone, keeping, or harmony.

In his play with words Sir Philip Sidney kept good heed that even that should serve the end in view; in his play with ideas, Dr. John Donne, so far from serving the end, sometimes obscures it almost hopelessly: the hart escapes while he follows the squirrels and weasels and bats. It is not surprising that, their author being so inartistic with regard to their object, his verses themselves should be harsh and unmusical beyond the worse that one would imagine fit to be called verse.

He enjoys the unenviable distinction of having no rival in ruggedness of metric movement and associated sounds. This is clearly the result of indifference; an indifference, however, which grows very strange to us when we find that he can write a lovely verse and even an exquisite stanza. — MACDONALD, GEORGE, 1868, *England's Antiphon*, p. 114.

A pungent satirist, of terrible crudeness, a powerful poet, of a precise and intense imagination, who still preserves something of the energy and thrill of the original inspiration.

But he deliberately abuses all these gifts, and succeeds with great difficulty in concocting a piece of nonsense.... Twenty times while reading him we rub our brow, and ask with astonishment, how a man could so have tormented and contorted himself, strained his style, refined on his refinement, hit upon such absurd comparisons? — Taine, H. A., 1871, *History of English Literature*, tr. Van Laun, vol. I, bk. ii, ch. i, pp. 203, 204.

His reputation as a poet, great in his own day, low during the latter part of the seventeenth and the whole of the eighteenth centuries, has latterly revived. In its days of abasement, critics spoke of his harsh and rugged versification, and his leaving nature for conceit.

It seems to be now acknowledged that, amidst much bad taste, there is much real poetry, and that of a high order, in Donne. — Chambers, Robert, 1876, *Cyclopcedia of English Literature*, ed. Carruthers.

Better and truer verse none ever wrote...
Than thou, revered and magisterial Donne!
— Browning, Robert, 1878, The Two Poets of Groisic.

Donne's contemporary reputation as a poet, and still more as a preacher, was immense; and a glance at his works would suffice to show that he did not deserve the contempt with which he was subsequently treated. But yet his chief interest is that he was the principal founder of a school which especially expressed and represented a certain bad taste of his day. Of his genius there can be no question; but it was perversely directed.

One may almost invert Jonson's famous panegyric on Shakespeare, and say that Donne was not for all time but for an age. His natural gifts were certainly great. He possesses a real energy and fervour. He loved, and he suffered much, and he writes with a passion which is perceptible through all his artificialities. — Hales, John W., 1880, *English Poets*, ed. Ward, vol. i, pp. 558, 560.

We find little to admire, and nothing to love. We see that farfetched similes, extravagant metaphors, are not here occasional blemishes, but the substance. He should have given us simple images, simply expressed; for he loved and suffered much: but fashion was stronger than nature. — WELSH, Alfred, 1882, *Development of English Literature and Language,* vol. I, p. 413.

Donne's poems were first collected in 1633: they cover an extraordinary range in subject, and are throughout marked with a strange originality almost equally fascinating and repellent. It is possible that his familiarity with Italian and Spanish literatures, both at that time deeply coloured by fantastic and far-fetched thought, may have in some degree influenced him in that direction.

His poems were probably written mainly during youth. There is a strange solemn passionate earnestness about them, a quality which underlies the fanciful "conceits" of all his work. — Palgrave, Francis T., 1889, *The Treasury of Sacred Song,* note, p. 333.

In him the Jacobean spirit, as opposed to the Elizabethan, is paramount. His were the first poems which protested, in their form alike and their tendency, against the pastoral sweetness of the Spenserians. Something new in English literature begins in Donne, something which proceeded, under his potent influence, to colour poetry for nearly a hundred years.

The exact mode in which that influence was immediately distributed is unknown to us, or very dimly perceived. To know more about it is one of the great desiderata of literary history. The imitation of Donne's style begins so early, and becomes so general, that several critics have taken for granted that there must have been editions of his writings which have disappeared....

The style of Donne, like a very odd perfume, was found to cling to every one who touched it, and we observe the remarkable phenomenon of poems which had not passed through a printer's hands exercising the influence of a body of accepted classical work.

In estimating the poetry of the Jacobean age, therefore, there is no writer who demands more careful study than this enigmatical and subterranean master, this veiled Isis whose utterances outweigh the oracles of all the visible gods. — GOSSE, EDMUND, 1894, *The Jacobean Poets*, pp. 47, 48.

After he had taken holy orders Donne seldom threw his passions into verse; even his "Divine Poems" are, with few exceptions, of early date; the poet in Donne did not cease to exist, but his ardour, his imagination, his delight in what is strange and wonderful, his tenderness, his tears, his smiles, his erudition, his intellectual ingenuities, were all placed at the service of one whose desire was that he might die in the pulpit, or if not die, that he might take his death in the pulpit, a desire which was in fact fulfilled....

Donne as a poet is certainly difficult of access. He sometimes wrote best, or thought he wrote best, when his themes were wholly of the imagination. Still it is evident that Donne, the student, the recluse, the speculator on recondite problems, was also a man who adventured in pursuit of violent delights which had violent ends....

In whatever sunny garden, and at whatever banquet Donne sits, he discerns in air the dark Scythesman of that great picture attributed to Orcagna. An entire section of his poetry is assigned to death. — Dowden, Edward, 1896, *New Studies in Literature*, pp. 90, 91, 107, 117.

As in the case of the pastoral fashion there were other currents of lyrical production, less directed by the conventionalities of the moment. Spenser aside, whose elaborated state does not lend itself readily to the shorter lyric and whose singing robes are stiff with tissue of gold, wrought work, and gems inlaid, and Shakespeare, also, whose non-dramatic Muse is dedicated to thoughtful sonnet and mournful threnody, as well as to the sprightlier melodies of love, wine, and merriment, the most important poetical influence of this decade is that of that grave and marvelous man, Dr. John Donne.

I would respectfully invite the attention of those who still persist with Dr. Johnson in regarding this great poet as the founder of a certain "Metaphysical School of Poetry," a man all but contemporary with Cowley, and a writer harsh, obscure, and incomprehensible in his diction, first to an examination of facts which are within the reach of all, and, secondly, to an honest study of his works. Just as Shakespeare touched life and man at all points, and, absorbing the light of his time, gave it forth a hundredfold, so Donne, withdrawn almost wholly from the influences affecting his contemporaries, shone and glowed with a strange light all his own....

It seems to me that no one, excepting Shakespeare, with Sidney, Greville, and Jonson in lesser measure, has done so much to develop intellectualized emotion in the Elizabethan lyric as John Donne. — Schelling, Felix E., 1895, *A Book of Elizabethan Lyrics*, pp. xxi, xxii, xxiii.

There is hardly any, perhaps indeed there is not any, English author on whom it is so hard to keep the just mixture of personal appreciation and critical measure as it is on John Donne. It is almost necessary that those who do not like him should not like him at all, should be scarcely able to see how any decent and intelligent human creature can like him.

It is almost as necessary that those who do like him should either like him so much as to speak unadvisedly with their lips, or else curb and restrain the expression of their love for fear that it should seem on that side idolatry. But these are not the only dangers. Donne is eminently of that kind which lends itself to sham liking to coterie worship, to a false enthusiasm; and here is another weapon in the hands of the infidels, and another stumbling-block for the feet of the true believers....

In Donne's case the yea-nay fashion of censorship which is necessary and desirable in the case of others is quite superfluous. His faults are so gross, so open, so palpable, that they hardly require the usual amount of critical comment and condemnation. But this very peculiarity of theirs constantly obscures his beauties even to not unfit readers.

They open him; they are shocked, or bored, or irritated, or puzzled by his occasional nastiness (for he is now and then simply and inexcusably nasty), his frequent involution and eccentricity, his not quite rare indulgence in extravagances which go near to silliness and so they lose the extraordinary beauties which lie beyond or among these faults.... For those who have experienced or who at least understand, the ups-and- downs,the ins-and-outs of human temperament, the alternations not merely of passion and satiety, but of passion and laughter, of passion and melancholy reflection, of passion earthly enough and spiritual rapture almost heavenly, there is no poet and hardly any writer like Donne. — SAINTSBURY, GEORGE, 1896, *Poems of John Donne,* Introduction, vol. I, pp. xi, xxxi, xxxii.

"The Will of John Donne" is probably the wittiest and the bitterest lyric in our language. Donne's love passages and their record in verse were over before the author was of age. His wit then turned into metaphysical sermon-writing and theological polemics, and his bitterness into a despairing austerity. — Crawfurd, Oswald, 1896, *Lyrical Verse from Elizabeth to Victoria,* p. 426.

Donne is a thoroughly original spirit and a great innovator; he is thoughtful, indirect, and strange; he nurses his fancies, lives with them, and broods over them so much that they are still modern in all their distinction and ardour, in spite of the strangeness of their apparel — a strangeness no greater perhaps than that of some modern poets, like Browning, as the apparel of their verse will appear two hundred years hence. Ingenuity, allusiveness, the evocation of remote images and of analogies that startle the mind into a more than half acquiescence, phantoms of deep thoughts, and emotions half-sophisticated and wholly intense: these things mark the poetry of Donne. His Iyric is original and taking, but it lacks simplest thoughts; it does not sing.

It is ascetic and sometimes austere; the sense of sin, the staple of contemporary tragedy, enters the lyric with Donne. He is all for terseness and meaning, and his versification accords with his thought and is equally elliptical. — Carpenter, Frederic Ives, 1897, *English Lyric Poetry, 1500-1700,* Introduction, p. lviii. One of the most enigmatical and debated, alternately one of the most attractive and most repellent, figures in English literature. — HANNAY, DAVID, 1898, *The Later Renaissance,* p. 220.

In one way he has partly become obsolete because he belonged so completely to the dying epoch. The scholasticism in which his mind was steeped was to become hateful and then contemptible to the rising philosophy, the literature which he had assimilated went to the dust-heaps, preachers condescended to drop their doctorial robes,

Downright common-sense came in with Tillotson and South in the next generation, and not only the learning but the congenial habit of thought became unintelligible. Donne's poetical creed went the same way, and if Pope and Parnell perceived that there was some genuine ore in his verses and tried to beat it into the coinage of their own day, they only spoilt it in trying to polish it.

But on the other side, Donne's depth of feeling, whether tortured into short lyric or expanding into voluble rhetoric, has a charm which perhaps gains a new charm from modern sentimentalists. His morbid or "neurotic" constitution has a real affinity for latter-day pessimists. If they talk philosophy where he had to be content with scholastic theology the substance is pretty much the same.

He has the characteristic love for getting pungency at any price; for dwelling upon the horrible till we cannot say whether it attracts or repels him; and can love the "intense" and supersublimated as much as if he were skilled in all the latest Esthetic canons. — Stephen, Leslie, 1899, *John Donne, The National Review,* vol. 34, p. 613.

[His] was the mind of the dialectician, of the intellectual adventurer, he is a poet almost by accident, or at least for reasons with which art in the abstract has but little to do. He writes verse, first of all, because he has observed keenly, and because it pleases the pride of his intellect to satirise the pretensions of humanity. Then it is the flesh which speaks in his verse the curiosity of woman, which he has explored in the same spirit of adventure; then passion, making a slave of him for love's sake, and turning at last to the slave's hatred; finally, religion, taken up with the same intellectual interest, the same subtle indifference, and, in its turn, passing also into passionate reality.

A few poems are inspired in him by what he has seen in remote countries; some are marriage songs and funeral elegies, written for friendship or for money. But he writes nothing "out of his own head," as we say; nothing lightly, or, it would seem, easily; nothing for the song's sake.

He speaks, in a letter, of "descending to print anything in verse" and it is certain that he was never completely absorbed by his own poetry, or at all careful to measure his achievements against those of others.

He took his own poems very seriously, he worked upon them with the whole force of his intellect; but to himself, even before he became a divine, he was something more than a poet. Poetry was but one means of expressing the many-sided activity of his mind and temperament. Prose was another, preaching another; travel and contact with great events and persons scarcley less important to him, in the building up of himself. — Symons, Arthur, 1899, *John Donne, Fortnightly Review*, ns., vol. 66, p. 735.

John Donne is of interest to the student of literature chiefly because of the influence which he exerted on the poetry of the age. His verse teems with forced comparisons and analogies between things remarkable for their dissimilarity. An obscure likeness and a worthless conceit were as important to him as was the problem of existence to Hamlet.

Chapter 26

Religious Poetry and Prose of John Donne

It has been twenty years since I picked up a volume of John Donne's works. I expected that the writings of this seventeenth-century Christian pastor would be quaintly distant, linked in my mind with the Book of Common Prayer and the King James Bible. I recalled some of his famous lines, made more famous by later writers' repetition of them: "Death be not proud..."

"No man is an island..." "never send to know for whom the bell tolls; it tolls for you...." I thought I would find Donne's religious writings frequently familiar, mildly inspirational and safely archaic. With that mindset, I found "The "Prayers" were mostly what I had expected. The language is formal, ritualized, and distanced by the baritone public voice of a preacher. In contrast to the prayers, the excerpts from the sermons speak more directly of practical matters.

In a voice more like that of Brother Lawrence than Jeremy Taylor, the preacher describes to his congregation how "a piece of straw beneath his knee distracts his prayer. Using intimate, almost conversational language, Donne speaks plainly to the listeners/readers of his sermons. John Donne's poetry is a different matter altogether. Throughout his poetry, Donne has the mystic's passionate desire to be overwhelmed by God; the poet seeks images to give us a glimpse of that moment when the self is absorbed into the whole, when the individual becomes an indistinguishable part of all time and creation. He wants to be burned, battered, drowned in blood, flooded, ravished. Some of these images are grotesque; some are of sexual union, even rape; certainly the imagery goes beyond the bounds of good taste. Contemporary critic Stanley Fish goes so far as to say that "Donne is sick and his poetry is sick...". I disagree with Fish; to take Donne literally as a sick proponent for rape or sadism is to seriously misread him. He is using shocking imagery to convey a mystic's passionate desire to be alive in a faith that is indelicate, forceful, and consuming. In Donne's poetry, it is in the paradox, the space between opposites, where his God is most likely to be found. For example, when he describes the Trinity as "the unnumbered three" it brings to mind the mystery of that which is one and yet many. It is, however, when Donne combines sexual and religious imagery that his work is most shocking, as when he imagines God as a rapist or describes the Holy Church as a wife made more holy by her sexual availability to all men. Here we see Donne's God as the taut energy holding together paradox, the unthinkable union of good and evil.

Like a rubber band stretched almost to the breaking, Donne's God is in the vibration, the hum of the tension, the second before the rubber band snaps. Much of what I read in Mousley's casebook did not seem relevant to my experience of reading Donne's religious works. Several of the essays focused on work of Donne's secular period, which are not included in the Carrigan collection. Some essays assumed specialist's detailed critical knowledge and background.

I did find Fish's article, "Masculine Persuasive Force: Donne and Verbal Power," thought-provoking; he raises issues and questions that are perhaps necessarily addressed before contemporary first-time readers can appreciate Donne's work. I also found William Kerrigan's "The Fearful Accommodations of John Donne" to be helpful as a positive counterpoint to Fish. It is good to be startled again by religious writing. Donne reminds us that our faith is not always a comfort and he boldly acknowledges that true spiritual discipleship requires not only acknowledging the contradictions in our understanding of God, but also a willingness to be consumed by that divine entity whom we can never fully comprehend.

Bibliography

John Carey, *John Donne: Life, Mind and Art,* (London 1981)

A. L. Clements (ed.) *John Donne's Poetry* (New York and London, 1966)

Stevie Davies, *John Donne* (Northcote House, Plymouth, 1994)

T. S. Eliot, *"The Metaphysical Poets", Selected Essays,* (London 1969)

G. Hammond (ed.) The Metaphysical Poets: A Casebook, (London 1986)

Sir Geoffrey Keynes, *Bibliography of Donne,* (Cambridge, 1958)

George Klawitter, *The Enigmatic Narrator: The Voicing of Same-Sex Love in the Poetry of John Donne* (Peter Lang, 1994)

Arthur F. Marotti, *John Donne, Coterie Poet,* (Madison: University of Wisconsin Press, 1986)

H. L. Meakin, *John Donne's Articulations of the Feminine,* (Oxford, 1999)

Joe Nutt, *John Donne: The Poems,* (New York and London 1999)

E.M. Simpson, *A Study of the Prose Works of John Donne,* (Oxford, 1962)

C. L. Summers and T. L. Pebworth (eds.) *The Eagle and the Dove: Reassessing John Donne* (Columbia: University of Missouri Press, 1986)

John Stachniewski, *The Persecutory Imagination,* (Oxford, 1991)

Ceri Sullivan, *The Rhetoric of the Conscience in Donne, Herbert, and Vaughan* (Oxford 2008)

James Winny, *A Preface to Donne* (New York, 1981)

Astington, John H. "*Disvalu'd in Levity*': *Measure for Measure* at Stratford, Ontario, 1975-76." *English Studies in Canada* 3 (1977): 231-40.

Baines, Barbara J. "*Assaying the Power of Chastity in Measure for Measure.*" *Studies in English Literature* 30 (1990): 283-301.

Black, James. "*The Unfolding of Measure for Measure.*" *Shakespeare Survey* 26 (1973): 119-28.

Bock, Judith. Rev. of *Measure for Measure. Theatre Journal* 44 (1992): 118-19.

"*Directing Problem Plays: John Barton Talks to Gareth Lloyd Evans.*" *Shakespeare Survey* 25 (1972): 63-71.

Fly, Richard. *Shakespeare's Mediated World*. Amherst: U of Massachusetts P, 1976.

Jones, D.A.N. "*Hard Cases, Bad Law.*" *Listener* 9 April 1970: 493.

Lyons, Charles R. "*Silent Women and Shrews: Eroticism and Convention in Epicoene* and *Measure for Measure.*" *Comparative Drama* 23 (1989): 123-40.

McGee, C.E. "*Shakespeare in Canada: The Stratford Season, 1992.*" *Shakespeare Quarterly* 44 (1993): 477-83.

Riefer, Marcia. "'*Instruments of Some More Mightier Member': The Constriction of Female Power in Measure for Measure.*" *Shakespeare Quarterly* 35 (1984): 157-69.

Shakespeare, William. *The Complete Works of Shakespeare*. Ed. David Bevington. 4th ed. New York: Harper Collins, 1992.

Measure for Measure. The Arden Shakespeare. Ed. J.W. Lever. London: Routledge, 1965.

Sinfield, Alan. *Faultlines: Cultural Materialism and the Politics of Dissident Reading*. Berkeley: U of California P, 1992.

Sundelson, David. "*Misogyny and Rule in Measure for Measure.*" *Women's Studies* 9 (1981): 83-91.

Weil, Herbert S., Jr. "*Stratford Festival Canada.*" *Shakespeare Quarterly* 37 (1986): 245-50.

Williamson, Marilyn L. *The Patriarchy of Shakespeare's Comedies*. Detroit: Wayne State UP, 1986.

AN.P.